T0272484

DEANNE STILLMAN

AMERICAN CONFIDENTIAL

UNCOVERING THE BIZARRE STORY OF LEE HARVEY OSWALD AND HIS MOTHER

MELVILLE HOUSE BROOKLYN · LONDON

AMERICAN CONFIDENTIAL
UNCOVERING THE BIZARRE STORY OF
LEE HARVEY OSWALD AND HIS MOTHER

First published in 2023 by Melville House
Copyright © 2023 by Deanne Stillman
All rights reserved
First Melville House Printing: September 2023

Melville House Publishing
46 John Street
Brooklyn, NY 11201

and

Melville House UK
Suite 2000
16/18 Woodford Road
London E7 0HA

mhpbooks.com
@melvillehouse

The Exodus Song (This Land Is Mine)
Written by Charles E. Boone, Ernest Gold
Courtesy of Spoone Music Corp (ASCAP) Adm by Sweet On Top /
Peer Music; Chappell Music LTD (PRS) Adm by Warner Chappell Music.

EVERY MAN A KING
By Huey Long and Castro Carazo
© Copyright 1935 Bourne Co. (Renewed)
All Rights Reserved; International Copyright Secured
ASCAP

ISBN: 978-1-68589-068-1
ISBN: 978-1-68589-069-8 (eBook)

Library of Congress Control Number: 2023942594

Designed by Beste M. Doğan

Printed in the United States of America
10 9 8 7 6 5 4 3 2 1

A catalog record for this book is available from the Library of Congress

"The essential American soul is hard, isolate, stoic, and a killer." **—D.H. LAWRENCE**

"But officer. How come the other guy didn't get a ticket?" **—OFT-ASKED QUESTION IN AMERICA, WITH MANY VARIATIONS**

"My son is innocent." **—MARGUERITE OSWALD**

TABLE OF CONTENTS

INTRODUCTION	ix
PART ONE: EVERY MAN A KING	3
PART TWO: ROAD TRIP	29
PART THREE: BACK IN THE USA, OR, THE SON MAKES HIS MARK	145
PART FOUR: AFTERMATH OF AN EXECUTION	175
ACKNOWLEDGMENTS	211
AUTHOR'S NOTE	217
BIBLIOGRAPHY & CREDITS	227

INTRODUCTION

With every one of my books, there always comes a moment when the subject matter is completely overwhelming and sometimes unbearably sad. I have to step away, sometimes for months, and then something inevitably pulls me back in. Actually, it's more than that; some sort of miracle unfolds, and I take such occurrences as a sign to stay the course, and not to ignore my original instinct. So, just when I was feeling utterly morose and bereft while working on this book, there did come one of those universal indicators. My computer had crashed weeks earlier and I had to switch servers for whatever reason, and therefore a number of links had vanished.

I love looking into the backstories of my characters, especially because I always find things that others have overlooked, and with these two, Marguerite and Lee Harvey Oswald, I had discovered many things that were crucial to my story and to puzzling them out regarding temperament and how they moved through their worlds and the world at large. To a great degree, I had already laid a serious foundation for this book. With the vanishing of my server, it was all gone, and that only added to my discouragement. While I had remembered what some of the links were, there were literally dozens. The disappearance had been a total nightmare.

Then one day, while I was in the middle of my funk, my original server opened of its own accord—really! I hadn't even clicked on it, and there they were: what seemed like miles of links, and I could immediately retrieve what I needed. These included a trove of links having to do with Lee and his mother, pathways I had been saving for months.

On the day they reappeared, it was as if my road map, or at least a "this way" arrow, was once again directing my journey. When the links manifested themselves, I realized I just hadn't been ready to continue this journey until that moment, no matter how much I had thought about it over the years. So just when I needed it most, there was the skeleton key (and, in the end, in the sense that Lee Harvey Oswald haunts this country, he is very much a ghost), a miraculous visitation from the digital ethers.

As I began scrolling through the links, one jumped out. This was the link to an exhibit at the Bronx Zoo that debuted on April 26, 1963, seven months before John Fitzgerald Kennedy was assassinated. The exhibit was called the *Most Dangerous Animal in the World*. It was a mirror. In other words, you would look into it and see yourself. The installation recalled the matter at hand, and not just in a general sense. Lee Harvey Oswald lived and played in the Bronx when he was a teen-ager, during 1952 and 1953, often hanging out at the zoo after he and his mother moved to an apartment that was within striking distance of it, seeking communion with the wild animals behind bars and in cages. It was at the Bronx Zoo that he was busted for truancy—the truant officer, it's been said, laughed at his hayseed getup, his jeans, and his corresponding Texas accent (though it's not really discernible as such on subsequent recordings)—and thus, as we shall see, a marker in his life was reached.

There followed hearings and juvenile lockup and probation and warnings, and shortly after his troubles in the Bronx his mother ignored a note from his probation officer asking for another meeting, and the pair moved back to New Orleans, hometown to both mother and son. That time in the Bronx was a crossroad—or one of them—that sent Lee en route to Dallas ten years later—the moment that changed history and allowed him to enter into it.

Lee liked animals, his mother later told everyone (but so what? a lot of killers like animals; John Wilkes Booth loved flowers and butterflies and once said that fireflies were "the bearers of sacred torches," and then he shot Abraham Lincoln in the head). Yet clearly, for Oswald, there was something going on at the zoo that was a draw. I've long wondered which animal Lee most identified with. Was it the great apes? Not likely. Reptiles? Probably not. He did have dogs as a young boy and once even gave a puppy to a neighbor, probably as a way of seeking something else (friendship, refuge, gratitude?). He also gave his mother a bird in a cage years later. But then again, he used to shoot squirrels—a not-uncommon thing in rural areas across America and in Texas, where he once lived with his brothers. Yet one of them, his older brother Robert Oswald, remarked after the assassination of JFK that Lee's killing of rabbits, one in particular, when they were hunting was of a nature that was cruel and unnecessary. So was it lions and tigers at the zoo that he went to visit? I would venture a yes. They are powerful and majestic predators who would catch the fancy of any teenage boy. (And it was ten years after Lee lived in the Bronx that Ford unveiled the Cougar—like the Mustang, a muscle car that tapped into the ethers of the time. The lions and tigers were probably pacing when Lee visited, for that's what caged animals did at zoos of that era; their habitats were not like those of today). We can imagine teenage Lee gazing at one and trying to make eye contact, perhaps doing so, and returning to visit that one, engaging in a conversation with it (as many of us would in those situations). "I know . . . you want out," he might have said out loud or thought to himself. "Who

doesn't?" Maybe he even apologized for the lockup, and then when
the truant officer busted him, asking why he wasn't in school, maybe
he shrugged and said, "See ya later, alligator" to his animal friend,
a typical teenage wise guy. And it could have been later that day or
around that time that he pulled a small knife on his brother's wife or
shot a BB gun at elderly folks in his building—the BB gun a perennial
gift from parents to sons—and, as always, his mother made excuses.

Later, back in his hometown of New Orleans, Lee frequented
Audubon Gardens, known for its walkways of live oaks and its famous Tree of Life, an enormous oak with boughs that reach the
ground, and then, much later, when he returned from Russia with his
wife Marina, he would take her there for visits. It's not something we
picture the assassin doing, for such information has been glossed over
or not even ascertained, and it took me a while to imagine Lee taking
a woman he loved (or had some sort of relationship with, clearly a
complicated one) to what is traditionally a romantic location. Did he
see his reflection in the lagoon, a foretelling of the Bronx Zoo installation? Did he linger under the Tree of Life or venture next door to the
adjacent zoo, expressing excitement about the prospect of visiting the
animals? It was literally a walk on the wild side, the name of Nelson
Algren's famous dark novel set in New Orleans which featured the
legendary drifter Dove Linkhorn and other outcasts of the Big Easy.
Later, Hunter S. Thompson would say that the Hell's Angels were
manifestations of these characters, the offspring of Linkhorn and his
associates on the streets. Was Lee Harvey Oswald a rebel without a
cause? While he certainly allied himself with various causes, and he
may have convinced himself that one or the other of these was an
identity for him at one time or another, the only cause he really had
was himself—a distinctly American condition that in his case, and
in the case of many who have followed the killing path, could have
revealed itself in only one way.

Like many of my generation, I first learned of the assassination in junior high school. I was sitting in my eighth-grade classroom, and there sounded the melodic notes of a xylophone on the public-address system, signaling an important announcement. "Boys and girls," said the principal. "This is Mrs. Lang." Her voice quavered and she cleared her throat and went on. "I have some terrible news. The President has been shot." She could barely continue, and there were gasps across the room. "At 12:30 today, he died." We could hear her crying then, and she said some other things that I don't remember and then the signing-off tone was sounded and there was sheer silence. There followed expressions of disbelief and gasps; there was weeping and the shuffling of papers. A body blow had struck our schoolroom just as surely as if we were in Dallas at the moment JFK was taken down while riding through Dealey Plaza in his motorcade. Very soon after the announcement, class was dismissed and we all returned to our homes, joining citizens across the land as we all turned on the television set and watched. There it was, over and over again, the news reports and the limo with the President careening away from the site of the assassination and sobbing reporters and onlookers everywhere, each person, one and all, struck by the shot heard round the world. We had all become eyewitnesses to the crime of the century, compounded by the fact that we soon watched another murder: two days after Lee Harvey Oswald had killed the President, he himself was killed before our eyes in an act that heightened the nightmare. We were to spend the rest of our lives trying to understand what happened.

At the time of the JFK assassination, my parents had recently gotten a divorce. It was an unexpected act that ruptured my family, shattering our snow globe in a way that still reverberates decades later. Fortunately for me, my father had taught me how to write, and I don't just mean write down the alphabet and compose sentences, but write stories and plays and scenes and all sorts of literary concoctions.

Together we would invent characters and watch the news and wonder why and how things led to other things, and we would marvel at all the strange things people did. "You can't make this stuff up," my father always said, and over the years I have come to realize that you certainly can't. When my mother and sister and I ended up on the "wrong" side of town following the dissolution of my parents' marriage, I picked up pen and pad, and I haven't stopped writing. It was a way out of turmoil and into a universe of endless possibility and attempts to heal the world. Looking back at things that I wrote then, I see that my concerns had to do with a wish for people to stop fighting, written as only a little girl can. I discovered pieces such as "They Got Divorced at the End of a Decade" and something called "Security Council," a story about how the UN kept us all together in spite of wars that were raging everywhere. I've come to realize that the pieces I wrote long ago prepared the way for all of my books; they were expressions of a desire for reconciliation, mostly about internal family rifts and a disconnect from surroundings. My subsequent explorations of our shadowlands have taken me right into the dark heart of the American dream. Perhaps it was inevitable that I now turn to the act from which the country has yet to recover.

We are in an era of great flux, involving mass extinction of wildlife and severe weather changes, and when it comes to atmospheric upheaval, the situation on the ground in the United States is moving on a parallel track, rife with all manner of violence, often involving guns. Discussion of men who commit violent acts is front and center, with terms such as "toxic masculinity" and "dysfunctional families" swirling through the ether. There are countless social media forums dedicated to ongoing gun violence in America, and those who commit violent acts often record them via "selfies," knowing that records of their acts will fly from forum to forum and in those quarters they will gain attention by becoming idolized or scorned. The country is so obsessed with true crime and how and why the crimes have happened that it can't stop listening to podcasts about said criminal acts, featuring blood-soaked recreations and graphic interviews with those involved, including cops, victims, and perpetrators.

With the sixtieth anniversary of the assassination of JFK upon us, it's time to revisit the man in whom such afflictions took root and exploded onto the national scene, before these afflictions had names that were part of daily vernacular. And it is also the time to cast a new light on his mother, the progenitor, after all (his father died before he was born), and learn what we can about her hopes and desires, her involvement with the promise and failure of the American dream, how she passed on such information to her benighted son—and, ultimately, how he chose to respond to this knowledge.

In 1965, the writer John Clellon Holmes penned a piece for *Playboy* called "The Silence of Oswald." Many of our citizens, he wrote, possess "cocked rifles [and are] walking anonymously through the streets, with little or nothing in our society, offering any sure way by which these rifles can be disarmed. At least not until they have gone off, and it is too late." While the conventional wisdom suggests that making access to certain guns more difficult will solve this problem (and indeed, it is a necessary Band-Aid), what goes on in America does not go on anywhere else in the world, and easy access to guns alone does not take us to the heart of the problem. As we shall see in *American Confidential*, the credo of the Wild West—"It's a free country and I can do what I want"—takes us right to the center of our love affair with violent self-expression. When coupled with a disconnect that runs through many families, with personal pathologies shaped by those families, there is nothing that can stop this violence—other than meeting the shadow that haunts America and many of our young men.

"It is believed that more words have been written about the

assassination [of John Fitzgerald Kennedy] than any other single, one day event in world history," Vincent Bugliosi wrote in *Reclaiming History*, his sweeping study of that subject. This includes over one thousand books and countless articles, essays, and songs. Most of the books (with several exceptions that explore Oswald family dynamics) present conspiracy theories, and I've read a number of them. "Things have been reduced to this mind-numbing debate about forensics and ballistics that really misses the whole point," the great novelist Robert Stone has written. In fact, his own book, *A Hall of Mirrors*, written three years after the assassination, sounds the depths of that moment and portrays an Oswald-like character who is a creature of the corrosive atmosphere of New Orleans, Lee's birthplace.

To broaden the conversation about this thing that plagues us, in this book, I reverse the conventional narrative about Lee Harvey Oswald and suggest that it's of little consequence if he was a patsy, a spy, a double agent, or any of the myriad other roles he is said to have played in the assassination of America's thirty-fifth President. I suggest that whether or not he had accomplices or was used, whether or not he acted alone, as a solitary figure, a nobody, the act of destroying America's most powerful and adored figure, a somebody, was his only route to immortality, the only way for a man with his temperament and legacy to pass a different one on. As we shall see, Oswald's act was class warfare writ large—America's dirty little secret front and center, in full bloody dimension on our television screens, if only it had been recognized as such at the time. In the end, for all the questioning and riddling over his motives in the assassination of President John Fitzgerald Kennedy, Lee Harvey Oswald was simply fulfilling his mother's lifelong dream—to matter. In the end, they were a conspiracy of one.

On November 22, 1963, JFK was shot in the head, but America was shot in the heart. To this day we have yet to recover. The young

boy who liked to gaze at stars and aim his toy guns at strangers became the living embodiment of the installation at the Bronx Zoo, the
Most Dangerous Animal in the World. By enacting the wildest thing
possible for a man of his making, taking down the President of the
United States, he had broken out of his cage at the age of twenty-
four and entered the stream of history. "That fellow Oswald uncorked
something in this country," JFK's brother Robert said following the
assassination of Martin Luther King, Jr., in 1968—and then he himself was assassinated shortly thereafter. His remark couldn't have been
more accurate. What Lee Harvey Oswald tapped into and made his
own has taken the country into years of violence. There are dangerous
animals everywhere, and the shots fired that day in Dallas are ricocheting in the malls and schools of today.

AMERICAN CONFIDENTIAL

PART ONE

EVERY MAN A KING

"They told me to take a streetcar named Desire, and transfer to one called Cemeteries, and ride six blocks and get off at—Elysian Fields!"
—Blanche DuBois in *A Streetcar Named Desire*, Tennessee Williams

"I'm for the poor man—all poor men, black and white, they all gotta have a chance. They gotta have a home, a job, and a decent education for their children. 'Every man a king'—that's my slogan."
—Louisiana governor and US senator Huey P. Long

"All means of inquiry have to be available when one is steering one's way through a cloud."
—Norman Mailer, *Oswald's Tale*

In the 1940s, Tennessee Williams was living at 632 ½ St. Peter Street in the French Quarter of New Orleans, and there he wrote *A Streetcar Named Desire*. It portrayed a side of life in the Crescent City that was startling to those who would see it for the first time at its Broadway premiere in 1947, and it had the same effect on the audiences who first saw the movie version in 1950 and it would continue to resound deeply, and it still does, with its portrayal of brutality, madness, and want amid a squalid tenement where people no longer dreamed or desired except for those who did and then they were crushed or rescued by the kindness of strangers.

Like other street and place names in New Orleans, "desire" is poetic and conjures so many things. Where is the streetcar going? Is there really a destination called Desire? Isn't that a condition of longing to which we all belong? In his small railroad flat, Tennessee would listen to the clanging of the trolley nearby—and yes, there really was a destination called Desire—and along with Stanley Kowalski and his wife Stella, the unforgettable characters he created, he placed Blanche DuBois on that train, or rather fate did, and then it proceeded on its designated route through that landscape we all inhabit: the human condition, American style.

THE TIME HAS COME TO speak of New Orleans as not only the birthplace of jazz, a font of fine dining in fancy restaurants and dives, and the land of Mardi Gras and its joyful witness to life everlasting, but as the place where Lee Harvey Oswald was born and the place that informed his early years and intermittently, the rest of his brief life. Strangely, given what has become chapter and verse about this confounding figure, it's as if he came from nowhere, a man apart from latitude and longitude and all manner of other triangulation. This is true in some ways; he certainly was no fun-loving free spirit who would close down bars New Orleans–style or march in a second line just for the heck of it as a hired band played "When the Saints Go Marching In" at one of the funerals that regularly plied the byways of New Orleans.

And the city itself can be very disorienting, surrounded as it is on all sides by water. To the north is Lake Pontchartrain, and to all other directions is the river, which meanders everywhere. "Cardinal directions are of little use," Rebecca Snedeker tells Rebecca Solnit in *Unfathomable City: A New Orleans Atlas*, and the city is so low that when you look down the street, ships going by on the Mississippi appear to be above you, while the river itself, behind levees, is invisible.

And so, it is easy to lose your moorings in New Orleans, especially if you are already untethered.

And yet, as we shall see, Lee Harvey Oswald was, in a most fundamental way, a child of the Crescent City, which after all is the Deep South. This connection is readily apparent and yet rarely discussed, and when it is, it is only in a most cursory manner. Yet it tells us much about a man believed to be a cipher, and is one of the keys to his final act. Let us note that in 1963, near the end of a journey that would take him from the wharves of the Mississippi Delta and across the ocean to the faraway land of Russia and finally to Dallas, Texas, he returned once again to New Orleans, his place of origin, the motherland after all. It was in September, a time when "Louisiana was like an obscene phone call from nature," wrote Tom Robbins in his novel *Jitterbug Perfume*. "The air—moist, sultry, secretive, and far from fresh—felt as if it were exhaled into one's face . . . It was aphrodisiac and repressive, soft and violent at the same time." Sense memory is everything, actors often say, and they are right. Perhaps this essence grounded the restless Oswald, rooted and exhilarated him at the same time; perhaps this visit to New Orleans was designed to give it—and himself—one more chance. Would the city of dancing in the streets and all the oysters you can eat for a dollar reveal a way out of things and into something new and promising? If so, this particular move was an especially American act. *I can always start over*, he may have thought. *Lee-boy*—for that was a family nickname—*everything will be fine. Fine and dandy in fact. Just you wait.*

LIKE MANY AN AMERICAN TALE, Lee Harvey Oswald's family story was a quest for a lifeline. On his mother's paternal side, his ancestors were fleeing kings and monarchies in France, and so they hit the high seas, joining those who were forced to do so by way of debt and criminal acts, heading for a place that assured a clean start, untold treasures, and yes, unlimited supplies of nourishment. For there was a food shortage in France and elsewhere, and scant promise that the situation would ever change, especially for those on the low end of things.

In New Orleans you could scent and see the bounty, the coffee and bananas coming in from the Caribbean, the animal skins taken from American forests piled up and heading for fashion-minded populations abroad, for it was a port city, downriver from other settlements on the Mississippi, opening the way towards the equator and points beyond, and it facilitated the shipment of goods from the New World back to the Old and the shipment of same from points south to itself, and thus did a lively transoceanic exchange begin.

Unlike some other newly flourishing American cities, coastal New Orleans conveyed an instantly palpable sense of connection with the faraway. It was quite visibly a place to which many could escape, and did, in frequent ocean crossings and debarkations at its busy wharves, carrying elements of their varying points of origin. "It's not an easy thing to describe one's first impressions of New Orleans," the writer Lafcadio Hearn said in a well-known 1877 essay called "At the Gate of the Tropics," which he penned after finding refuge there from Cincinnati, a lesser port city along the Ohio River which flows through several states and finally empties into the Mississippi. "For while it resembles no other city upon the face of the earth, it recalls vague memories of a hundred other cities. It owns suggestions of towns in Italy, and in Spain, cities in England and in Germany, of seaports in the Mediterranean, and of seaports in the tropics." Today, its *cri de couer*—*laissez les bon temps rouler*—could be viewed as a mash-up of all of the above but with music, especially when we factor Creole, Cajun, African, Seminole, and Caribe culture into the mix and throw in a corresponding buffet.

It was under the auspices of the crown that the Frenchman Jean-Baptiste Le Moyne, Sieur d'Iberville, founded La Nouvelle Orleans.

Accompanying him on his voyage and present on subsequent journeys led by other explorers from France were the first settlers in the area: convicts, slaves, and prostitutes who joined the local indigenous population on the shores of the Mississippi where it emptied into the Gulf of Mexico, linking the region to the Caribbean and all that lay south of a burgeoning America in a time of unchecked enterprise. In its early years, there were so many ne'er-do-wells, pirates, blackguards, and all-around rebellious types in New Orleans that nuns were dispatched from France to save those who dwelled in what became known as the Devil's Empire. It was a swamp, after all, a vast lagoon, with strange creatures lurking in the waters that breathed decay and rot, brightly colored birds that flew in and out of the mangroves, and they had feathers so desirable that they dared men to kill them and place the plumes in hats that decorated the heads of millionaires. Later, such things as voodoo and its legendary practitioner Marie Laveau added to the region's reputation as an alluring vortex of black magic and the dark arts. Others followed the call, offering readings and guidance in a similar vein, and purveying curses and spells in bottles and dolls and beads, plying devotees with relics and intercessions guaranteed to fend off or cause evil to visit the unlucky, catering to all manner of the lost, the ailing, the seeking, a spiritual state that was mirrored, is still mirrored, all over town when the carillon bells at the Cathedral-Basilica of Saint Louis, King of France, sounded on the hour and quarter hour from Jackson Square. "Flores. Flores para los muertes," calls the blind woman in *A Streetcar Named Desire*—a request for a passing funeral and a haunting reminder of what lies beyond the apartment door behind which Blanche seeks a home and where Stanley is regularly brutalizing her sister, his wife Stella, just like Lee Harvey Oswald would later beat his wife Marina and hardly anyone, after witnessing the black eyes, would say a word.

It was against this backdrop that one New Orleans family headed towards infamy, and when they were stopped in their tracks because of one son's act, there was no mourning procession or someone singing about saints like Louis Armstrong, but Lee Harvey Oswald's mother Marguerite did claim that Lee was martyred and compared herself to Mary, mother of Jesus. *"And one more thing, mister, are you listening? The Oswalds have a coat of arms, see, I have a copy right here, and it was certified by Burke's Peerage and my son's ancestor as you can see right here was a man of import in service to a king."* Marguerite Oswald nee Claverie was not making this up. If you go back far enough in the history of any American family that emigrated from England, Wales, Scotland, or France, you will likely find such a thing, which is to say you will find a person who was accorded rank, he or she counted, they mattered in the scheme of things, and in that regard, Lee Harvey Oswald, according to Marguerite, had a lot in common with John Fitzgerald Kennedy and should have been buried like JFK at Arlington National Cemetery. In fact, he was a national hero.

HOW TO EXPLAIN THE STRANGE, overbearing, beleaguered, self-obsessed, hardworking woman who gave birth to one of the twentieth century's most wayward sons? Well, for starters, you could say that she was vexed and culturally hexed, perhaps for real, considering that she was born and raised in New Orleans, land of the orchestrated whammy. You could also say that she was paranoid and overflowing with grievances. And about this, too, you'd be right. She had her reasons, after all, and she'd be happy to explain them to you. But then again, you might be a spy or just someone who was out to get her, so what's the point? On the other hand, do you happen to have $1,000? Yes, long before access journalism and paying your sources, Marguerite had been on the cutting edge of cash for information. And why not? A single mother with limited income has to earn a living, and if her son, assassinated just like the President, was finally earning his keep, so to speak, then what's the problem?

Indeed, so elusive and evasive was Marguerite as I "spoke" to her in the beyond and read and listened to many interviews that during the course of my investigations, I found it helpful to turn to film noir and fiction for insight into this hard-boiled and dark figure. In such works, we find people who have no regrets and tell it like it is. They are hyper aware of their "station in life," and it is through that prism that they engage with the rest of the world. As this story unfolds, perhaps you'll see as I did that Marguerite had certain things in common with such characters as Mildred Pierce in the acclaimed James M. Cain novel of the same name, a woman who was immortalized by Joan Crawford in the eponymous movie and later memorably played once more by Kate Winslet in the remake; the unforgettable Amanda Wingfield in *The Glass Menagerie*—another play written by Tennessee Williams, who often wrote his plays with specific actresses in mind and frequently spoke of "the sad outcasts from Dixie," surely a description that fits Marguerite—featuring great actresses such as Katherine Hepburn and Joanne Woodward in two of the various film adaptations; and Lilly Dillon in *The Grifters*, portrayed by Anjelica Huston in the gripping adaptation of the Jim Thompson novel, with John Cusack as her tormented son Roy, both fine actors delivering a presentation of mother and son that in many ways (and not intentionally) evokes the strange and harrowing dynamic between Marguerite and Lee Harvey Oswald.

Marguerite Frances was born in New Orleans in 1907 to John Claverie and Dorothea Eva Stucke (known as Dora), the fifth of their six children. John's family was of French descent, from the Pyrenees, and French was the language that his parents and siblings spoke in their homes, as did many other residents of New Orleans. He was born in New Orleans around 1870, and his own father, Lee's great-grandfather, Jean Martial Claverie, appears in the 1871 city directory, living at 54 Orleans Street and working as a butcher. Dora's family was Dutch by way of Germany, and like her husband John was a New Orleans native, born in 1876. John and Dora lived on Phillips Street, in a poor neighborhood where most families were just getting by. John was one of the first streetcar conductors in the city, earning ninety dollars per month. The family paid fourteen dollars per month for rent, and every day John would give his children a small sum for groceries. They purchased beans, rice, spinach, and bananas for meals, and their other household expenses were minimal. They didn't have a gas stove, for example, but they did have a furnace. There were no electric lights. If anything was left from the one-dollar allotment, the children kept the change and could spend it as they pleased. Pearl Claverie, for instance, would buy fabric and make a dress for herself. The family made do with what they had, and although poor, they did not want for material goods.

As it happened, John Claverie may well have worked on the street-car line called Desire. It was launched in 1920, and ran in proximity to the Claverie household, all the way to the cemeteries at the outskirts of town, and one can imagine the word "Desire" popping up as a des-tination in the streetcar window as it clanged through the fog and humidity of the burgeoning city that was below sea level. Although there are no records of which men were conductors on which exact line, it is likely that John was engaged as such on that particular one. There were few trolley lines at that time, and there is mention in vari-ous accounts of Marguerite's early life of a certain streetcar line that was in the vicinity of her family's flat. That would probably have been the Desire line. Most likely, Marguerite and her siblings—Charles, Lillian, John, and Pearl—would hear the clang of that trolley, perhaps thinking of their father as he went about his day ferrying citizens of New Orleans to and from work.

We do not know if John liked his job, or what if anything he might have said about it to his wife or children. But he was celebrated in an article in the *New Orleans Times Picayune* when he retired after forty years of service. While he would be dead by the time Lee was born, we can imagine that Lee's love of subways, which emerged years later when he was living with his mother in the Bronx, was possibly a way of connecting with his grandfather, having heard stories of the man conducting streetcars through the byways of New Orleans from his mother. Or perhaps it was just by way of an old map, or a mention. Lee had a fondness for maps and in New York especially would carry one in his pocket, navigating his way through the underground of the crowded metropolis, from the Grand Concourse to the Staten Island Ferry, possibly attuned to the conductor announcing each station stop en route to who knows where and back again. Such are the ways that flickers of a life are passed on, and it was in the Manhattan subway system where Lee seems to have found some solace, riding it to and fro for hours on end, partly because it was an entertainment that once you were on board the ride required no more cost and his family was always strapped for spare change. Perhaps, more significantly, another reason was that—as studies have shown—the vibrations of the fast-moving subway have an effect on the nervous system, or the body's system in general, acting as a kind of tuning fork, like an old-time train, calming and adjusting physiological quirks and functioning as a kind of antidepressant or mood transformer for those who might need such a thing. And it was in New York that Lee began seeing psychiatrists after getting into trouble, and one of them said he was schizophrenic, or used terms that today would serve as indicators of a bipolar personality or someone afflicted with other disorders. In any case, riding the rails was in the family's blood, and it was there that the soon-to-be Presidential assassin spent hours, following in the tradition of his grandfather.

"My father was a very good man," Lee's aunt—Marguerite's sister—Lillian Murret recalled years later during investigations of Lee Harvey

Oswald when she and other family members were called to testify before the Warren Commission, the government body formed at the request of Lyndon B. Johnson when he assumed the Presidency after John Fitzgerald Kennedy was killed. "We did pretty well," she continued. "We were a happy family. We were singing all the time, and I often say that we were much happier than children are today, even though we were very poor."

This was in spite of the fact that their mother, although five years younger than her husband, had died when Marguerite was four. The children pitched in on housekeeping tasks, along with neighbors and other helpers, except for two of her brothers who were gone, serving in World War I. Upon their return both of them succumbed to a tuberculosis epidemic that was sweeping through New Orleans, following the yellow fever plague of the 1870s that cut down the city's population like a harrow. Dozens of burial grounds were set aside, leading Mark Twain to note in 1875 that "there is no architecture in New Orleans, except in the cemeteries." During that era, New Orleans became known as the "city of the dead," a pejorative so widely known that it was cited in an official guide published in 1938 by the Federal Writers' Project of Louisiana, a wide-ranging account of the city's history and heritage.

But even that ominous description didn't tell the full story. Burying people in New Orleans was not a simple matter of digging a grave in the ground and covering the plot with dirt and marking it with a tombstone. "In most parts of New Orleans," as Nathaniel Rich wrote much later in *Unfathomable City*, "if you plunge your arm into the ground to the depth of your elbows, your fingertips will touch water. Your fingertips might even touch other fingertips. It took more than a century for the city's early settlers to realize that the ground beneath New Orleans is too low, and the water is too high, to allow traditional Christian burial . . . for more than a hundred years after

New Orleans was founded, every time it rained, bodies popped out of the ground." This prompted the transfer of coffins and bodies to other locations, and over time, it became clear that the city required a different kind of placement for the dead. Thus began the enterprise of mausoleums—known locally as "ovens" because the white stone chambers sometimes bake the corpses in the Louisiana sun. "And yet even the mausoleums were not entirely foolproof," Rich wrote. "During a flood," as the nation witnessed during Hurricane Katrina, "coffins would slide out of their cubbyholes and float down the avenues like canoes."

Shortly before he left New Orleans for Dallas in 1963, Lee Harvey Oswald wanted to visit his father, Robert E. Lee Oswald. Robert had died in 1939, two months before Lee was born, and it is said by many, including his own late brother, that having never met his father and having grown up without an adequate substitute is one of the elements that formed the future assassin. (I have found in my own writings that the same can be said of many of today's lost souls who turn their attention to the dark side; the operative question is "Where's Dad?")It is noteworthy that in his final search for his father, Lee visited a relative and asked for a picture of him, which suggests that his mother did not have one or he did not want to ask her because he preferred having no contact—something that characterized his relationship with her throughout his life, as we shall see. This distant relation gave the picture to Lee and it has never been found. He then went to his father's grave at the Cypress Grove Cemetery, adjacent to the Greenwood Cemetery, established in the 1830s to accommodate victims of the yellow fever epidemic.

Oswald's visit to his father's final resting place was, as far as is publicly known, his first and only one. Most likely, he took the Cemeteries streetcar line to the end of Canal Street and then headed through the Egyptian-style ceremonial gates to site number 439. Along with many volunteer firefighters (the cemetery was originally built to honor their service and that of their families), two nineteenth-century mayors of the city in their elaborate mausoleums, and other esteemed fellows—such as the man who brought gaslight to New Orleans and became known as the "Father of Light" and the first man in the country to market Tabasco sauce—there lies Robert E. Lee Oswald, under a slab and marked by a tombstone that bears his name and identifies him as a sergeant in World War I.

With this visit to his father, we do not know if Lee was saying hello, goodbye, or both; John Fitzgerald Kennedy's route through Dallas had not yet been announced, and Lee himself was not yet employed at the Texas Book Depository from whose sixth-floor perch he would kill the President. So while he may not have had that specific moment in mind, you could say that in a general sense, he always had it in mind, which is to say that in the scheme of things he knew he counted for nothing, and he wanted to be famous, had an urge to kill a famous person, a figure of gravitas, in order to attain fame; we know that he tried to do so earlier in an attempt on a controversial general, and of course failed. In other words, there would have been no reason for Lee to have had a graveside conversation with his father about, specifically, the President. In any case, when one visits the final resting place of a parent, the motive is to tap into certain family currents; Oswald clearly wanted to connect with his male forebear and maybe talked about nothing, but later that day or shortly afterwards, he told his wife about his visit to Cypress Grove Cemetery, site number 439. And there were other indications, momentary though they had been, that he wanted to continue the family line via a son (as opposed to or in addition to the daughters he already had), telling Marina about this desire several times during the immediate years preceding his death, and at least once expressing a serious aspect of the American dream: that one day, his son could grow up to become president.

At what point does a family go off the rails? Or is that even what happens when, down the line, one of its own brings dishonor and worse to all involved? In the early years of the Claveries, Lee's mother's side, there is nothing that stands out as a barometer of what was coming. John Claverie had bought a piano for five dollars, and Marguerite had learned to play it by ear. She also taught herself to play the ukulele. It was said that she had an outstanding voice, and at one time wanted to become a professional singer. Later, after Lillian had her own family, she took on a pivotal role, making sure that Marguerite and her siblings found joy in their lives by clearing her living room for family dance and song sessions. At their aunt's home, the kids would revel, and Marguerite liked to join in on music that was played at neighborhood house parties—the essence of New Orleans. In fact, according to her own accounts of that period in her life, along with those of her sister, she appeared to embody the Crescent City code of *laissez les bons temps rouler*, an aspect of her personality that manifested periodically over the years though seems to have been diminished by time and circumstances. "We had a lot of fun," Lillian recounted, recalling Marguerite's lovely voice, and Marguerite would say that she had "a very happy childhood and a very full childhood." Something that she often recalled was wearing a pink dress to her elementary school graduation—a moment that years later takes on a certain poignance when she is locked out of the lives of her grandchildren, for reasons that go beyond this particular image, able to see them only by peering through a barbed-wire fence outside their school playground.

At her grade school graduation, Marguerite sang a song called "A Little Pink Rose," with the lyrics "Oh little pink rose of your mother's heart / Have you faded and gone away? / Has the garden gathered my little pink rose / for his loveliest garden today?" This could have been a plea for her departed mother; perhaps it was a song that her mother sang to her and she was recalling it, for it was a popular tune of the day. Marguerite dropped out of high school in her freshman year and went to work as a receptionist at a local law firm. It certainly was not unusual for the children of the working poor to leave school to supplement family income—though it became one of the grievances that Marguerite cited on an ever-growing list of things that shouldn't have happened to her.

IN 1964, WHEN THE ACCOMPLISHED writer Jean Stafford visited Marguerite following the assassination of JFK and Lee's murder, she spent several days with her for an article for *McCall's* magazine which then became a book called *A Mother in History*. Like many prominent writers of her era, Stafford was of a mindset that mostly did not really understand residents of the working class. This is a curious matter, for her own life in some ways paralleled Marguerite's, which is to say that Stafford was no stranger to troubled relationships with problematic men; both women experienced emotional abuse and, in Stafford's case, there was physical mistreatment as well. Stafford was raised in the citrus boomtown of Covina, a Los Angeles suburb. Her father was an alcoholic who fancied himself an unrecognized literary talent and her long-suffering mother often supported the family. Stafford had always wanted to be a writer and to escape her family's turmoil, she headed to college in Colorado and then continued the eastward flight to New York, where she became part of the literary scene. In 1940 she married the poet Robert Lowell, who became unhappy when she became a success before he did, and began hitting her and expected her to take on menial jobs so that he could pursue his literary genius. Throughout her life, in spite of her own accomplishments and fame, she never had enough money, and she was constantly juggling routine matters. In this regard, which is to say being able to support oneself without constant fear and anxiety, she too was not unlike Marguerite, though Mrs. Oswald's choices were certainly much more limited than Stafford's, as we'll see.

Stafford's book about Marguerite Oswald, published in 1966, was deservedly heralded for taking readers behind the curtain of Oswald family life in a way that had not yet been done. Yet for all its revelations, the book lacked something fundamental. "We met some interesting poor people" was the undertone, "and they talk funny." Much of the coverage of Marguerite was in this vein, often referring to her frequent changes of address (true), boorish behavior (true), and lack of even the most rudimentary social skills (also seems to have been true). Yet there is no context for any of this. The fact is that she was a working mother of three who earned a living as a visiting nurse, babysitter, occasional employee of department stores, and self-employed peddler of notions and small gifts. This latter occupation brings to mind the wrenching phone call of Amanda Wingfield in *The Glass Menagerie*, set in 1937 amid the Depression—the same time that Marguerite was raising two sons. In this unforgettable Tennessee Williams play, a single mother of two grown-ups, a disabled daughter and a son at the end of his rope, desperately tries to sell subscriptions to *The Homemaker's Companion* over the phone:

> Ida Scott? This is Amanda Wingfield!
> We *missed* you at the D.A.R. last Monday!
>
> . . .
>
> How is that sinus condition?
> Horrors! Heaven have mercy!—You're a Christian martyr,
> yes, that's what you are, a Christian martyr! Well, I just have
> happened to notice that your subscription to the *Companion*'s
> about to expire! Yes, it expires with the next issue, honey!—
> just when that wonderful new serial by Bessie Mae Hopper is
> getting off to such an exciting start. Oh, honey, it's something
> that you can't miss! You remember how *Gone With the Wind*
> took everybody by storm? You simply couldn't go out if you

hadn't read it. All everybody talked was Scarlet O'Hara. Well,
this is a book that critics already compare to *Gone With the
Wind*. It's the *Gone With the Wind* of the post-World War
generation!—What?—Burning?—Oh, honey, don't let them
burn, go take a look in the oven and I'll hold the wire! Heavens
—I think she's hung up!

And then she turns to her beleaguered son and starts hectoring
him about his life. In today's era, Tom might go out and shoot up
the Continental Shoemakers warehouse where he works. "I think to
myself how lucky dead people are," he tells his mother, and then heads
to the movies, wresting away from Amanda as she tries to grab him
at the door.

Like Marguerite Oswald, Amanda Wingfield is divorced—aban-
doned, actually; the last she heard from her husband was a postcard
from Mexico sometime after he left her sixteen years ago. Marguerite
herself does Amanda one better: she was on the cutting edge of divorce, having been severed from two husbands in an era that used
the derogatory label "divorcee" to describe women of that condition.
There was no escape from this path, short of hitting the lottery, bilking
someone for their life savings, finding a kindhearted donor, or mar-
rying out of it, which she did for a time. There were millions who led
similar lives, all with different temperaments, yet all locked out of the
promise of the American dream.

When the Depression hit in 1929 with the devastating collapse
of financial markets, desperation swept through the land, affecting
bankers and shopgirls, millionaires and drifters, captains of industry
and people who mopped the floors at bus stations. Hotshots on Wall
Street were flinging themselves out of windows and many of the lesser
heeled were out on the streets singing, "Brother, can you spare a dime?"

Amid this upheaval and desperation arose a flamboyant and

bombastic son of Louisiana named Huey Long. A charismatic and smart con man who said he came from a poor family but didn't, he tapped into a deep well of grievance and hurt in the country. It had to do with the fact that the dice are loaded and the dealer works for the house; the man was out to get you—and did. Just look around. There's a Depression going on, in case you haven't heard. "There were cotton farmers and fur trappers and plowmen and tree cutters all around him who worked in medieval conditions and never got ahead," Garry Boulard wrote in *Huey Long Invades New Orleans*. "There were men and women who never went to school . . . Common laborers did not know how to write or read, had no friends who were lawyers or politicians, knew absolutely no one who would help them . . . . They were an old story whose roots reached back to the Bible and told an eternal tale of masters and slaves, of power and bondage."

In New Orleans, the Depression kicked off with a streetcar conductor strike in 1929. It was supported by many who rode the trolleys, but to no avail: the drivers lost and were ordered back to work. It is noteworthy that John Claverie died a year later at the age of sixty-one, and although he had retired shortly before the strike, perhaps the plight of his fellows was difficult to bear. In the early years of the 1930s, New Orleans was hit hard. Manufacturing in the Crescent City had declined by 50 percent since the stock market crash. "The docks were haunted by hollow-eyed men looking for work and angry union men caught in labor disputes," historian Joe Jackson later noted. A prominent businessman lost $300,000 when the market disintegrated and then, Boulard reported, shot himself in the mouth at the park where his baseball team played—a startling act at the grounds that came alive in the springtime, symbolizing new beginnings with its first call of "batter up."

"Two months later," Boulard continued, "a small riot broke out in the French Quarter when 400 men responded to a classified ad for a

single job opening." Huey Long—a man of instinct and impulse—
knew that there was a vast constituency of the discontented across the
land and someone could lead them to the heights of power.

In many ways, he prefigured Trump, though he was much smarter,
a Democrat running for office on a platform that was to the left of
President Franklin Delano Roosevelt. Quite simply, FDR and his New
Deal were not radical enough, failing to address what was really ailing
the country. "Every man a king" became his slogan as he embarked
on his quest, and it was picked up everywhere as he toured the country and held countless rallies, galvanizing the discontent and fueling
a resentment of those now referred to as "the elite." The slogan soon
became the name of his autobiography and battle cry of his "Share
Our Wealth" plan, which proposed capping fortunes at $100 million
as just one part of a general redistribution of monies, free college for
everyone, and monthlong vacations for workers, among other daring
ideas for a restoration of common men and women to their rightful
place in America. His "man of the people" presentation and affect led
to landslide victories in the race for state governor, a position he held
from 1928 to 1932, and for US senator, a position he held from 1932
to 1935, when he was assassinated at the height of his national acclaim
and notoriety, just shy of a bid for the White House, as was made
clear in what became known as his second autobiography, published
posthumously, called *My First Days in the White House.*

Long's center of gravity was New Orleans, which in the 1930s,
Boulard wrote, was "a city of intrigue and imagination, of things
showy and seductive, giving to the nation much of its richest and most
enduring music and literature." There was Louis Prima at the Shim
Sham Club and gambling wherever you could find it; and then there
was Storeyville, the red-light district, and writers such as William
Faulkner and Sherwood Anderson would drop in from time to time,
drawn by the city's allure; and other literary luminaries accorded Long

respect and admiration, impressed by his ability to connect with the people, not unlike reporters who extolled the virtues of Trump after dowsing the political and cultural ethers surrounding patrons of Midwestern diners.

Amid the tumult of the city, Huey Long held court at the Roosevelt Hotel, running his campaign for governor out of a suite that he maintained for several years and playing political impresario to all who sought favor. Although many found him fascinating and worthy of support, he had growing legions of detractors and those who felt compelled to warn about his unchecked rise and desire for power, including prominent locals who knew him well and feared for New Orleans, the entire state of Louisiana, and the country. Long's mania for control did not go unnoticed by writers such as Sinclair Lewis, whose seminal work *It Can't Happen Here* told the story of the rise of a Hitler-like dictator based on Huey Long. Later Robert Penn Warren would write *All the King's Men*, the definitive, Pulitzer Prize–winning novel about another Huey Long–like figure, and it too was a bell tolling for America.

We do not know if Marguerite Oswald attended any of Long's many rallies in New Orleans. But during the 1930s, when she was a young woman who was either out and about or getting married or between marriages, what Long was talking about was in the air, and if you lived in the Crescent City, the man himself, and whether or not you supported his policies, could not be avoided as a topic of conversation. For someone like Marguerite, a woman whose life was very much informed by class and want, his views must have been an echo of her own inner monologue.

After dropping out of hgh school, Marguerite got a job as a receptionist at a local law firm just before her seventeenth birthday. She had claimed on her job application that she was a high school graduate. Later, her son Lee would follow her lead, dropping out of high school at seventeen and joining the Marines. While working at the law firm, she met Edward John Pic, Jr., a stevedore clerk. On August 1, 1929, just as the Depression was about to sweep the land, Marguerite married Pic. Both were twenty-two years old. Relatives and friends recalled that she was a pretty girl; there are no public images of Edward, but we do know that when he was a boy, he lost sight in one eye because of a mishap during a basketball game. The young couple married and rented a house just off Canal Street. Marguerite quit her job, her husband would later say. Soon the marriage ran into turbulence, and a year later, when Marguerite was three months pregnant, they separated. Marguerite's sister Lillian would tell the Warren Commission that the separation happened because, according to Marguerite, he had lied to her about his salary. She also said that Edward didn't want children. On January 17, 1932, their son John Edward was born, into a city and country in free fall.

In April of that year, Huey Long delivered a speech on the Senate floor. It was called "The Doom of America's Dream," and it was all about the collapse of the cotton exchange in New Orleans, the stock market in New York, and the need for wealth redistribution. "The great and grand dream of America that all men are created free and equal," he said, "endowed with the right to life and liberty and the pursuit of happiness—this great dream of America, this great light, and this great hope, have almost gone out of sight in this day and time, and everybody knows it; and there is a mere candle flicker here and yonder to take the place of what the great dream of America was supposed to be."

Locked out of that dream, Marguerite would tell friends that she was reluctant to finalize her divorce, lest her husband refuse to pay child support. A year after the divorce was finalized in 1933, Marguerite would claim that John Pic did stop paying child support, and said so to her son John Edward for eighteen years. After

John Edward Pic was a year old, his father never saw him again until Marguerite sent him a photo of their son in his Coast Guard uniform. It was around that time that John Edward began filing his own tax forms and found out for himself that his father had, in fact, been paying forty-dollars-a-month child support for all of those years. It was not a large sum, but it wasn't nothing, and the discovery that Marguerite had lied to him about the matter only added to a litany of other problems that had sent him out the door. "Marguerite was a nice girl," Edward John told the Warren Commission, perhaps offering a gallant assessment. "We just couldn't get along, you know, so we finally decided to quit trying and call the whole thing off."

Years later, on November 22, 1963, when John Edward Pic learned that the man in custody for the assassination of John Fitzgerald Kennedy was his half brother Lee, he of course was shocked. By then, following a stint in the Coast Guard, he had become a staff sergeant in the Air Force. Overcome with shame and anger and grief, he nevertheless contacted his superiors at Lackland Air Force Base in San Antonio and told them of his connection. They in turn passed him on to the Secret Service, which then turned him over to the FBI. Over time, he would tell the story of his family to the Warren Commission, and one thing that began to stand out in all of the ensuing coverage was how he and his brothers all wanted to escape from their mother, locked in her endless striving for money and a nice house in a middle-class neighborhood, and destroyed by her own pathology.

One day, shortly after Marguerite was separated from Edward John Pic, a friend of her sister Lillian's saw Marguerite and her baby coming home from a park and picked them up in his car, and they began dating. This friend was a door-to-door insurance premium collector by the name of Robert Edward Lee Oswald. He had met Lillian, perhaps via this endeavor; she was by then married to Charles "Dutz" Murret, a steamship clerk on the wharves who years later would

be revealed to the House Select Committee on Assassinations as a
bookie and an associate of mobster Sam Saia, himself a friend of New
Orleans mafia chief Carlos Marcello, a target of Robert F. Kennedy's
crusade to bring down the mob when he was the attorney general of
the United States, appointed by his brother. These are the elements of
a conspiracy theory about the JFK assassination—how did it come to
pass that Lee Harvey Oswald, the nephew of an associate of Carlos
Marcello, a known enemy of the Kennedy brothers, whacked the
President? The question has been asked and maybe answered elsewhere many times; for our purposes, it's important to understand
that Lillian and Dutz were important figures in Lee's life. Lillian was
a thoughtful matchmaker for her sister Marguerite and, as we'll see
throughout this story, an aunt who was most concerned about Lee.

Like Marguerite, Robert E. Lee Oswald was separated from a
previous marriage when they met. After their divorces became final,
they married on July 20, 1933. Because he was previously divorced,
he could not marry in his own Catholic church, so the couple tied the
knot in Marguerite's Lutheran church on Canal Street. "He wanted
to adopt young John Edward Pic," Vincent Bugliosi has noted, but
Marguerite was opposed, fearing that child support payments would
then come to a halt.

On April 7, 1934, she gave birth to her second son, Robert E. Lee
Oswald, named after his father. The couple was able to buy a small
house at 2109 Alvar Street in the Upper Ninth Ward, and they even
had a car—both rarities for that time of great economic turmoil. On
August 19, 1939, Robert was stricken by chest pains while mowing
the lawn, and keeled over. He asked his wife to get him some aspirin,
and then she fetched the pills and rubbed his arm. Within a couple
of hours, he had died of a heart attack—incurred by landscaping!—a
death that seems quintessentially middle-class in the world of this
hardscrabble story. In a speech a few years earlier on the Senate floor,

Huey Long had talked about the plight of the American worker, for whom one dollar was then worth sixty cents. "Senators," he said, "you have allowed the property of the country to be concentrated in the hands of a few. You did that in the face of the warning from every teacher of religion and every teacher of government since time started . . . In 1916, President Woodrow Wilson, through a commission of his own, said that a calamity was heading for this country . . . We have reached the point of stagnation. We have reached the middle of the stream. The abyss yawns."

Later that very same day, to the dismay of her husband's family, she buried Robert E. Lee Oswald at the Cypress Grove Cemetery. There was no time for a proper funeral or any sort of official grieving; it was an act of desperation and haste. Over the years, some of those around her would note that this was the way she did things: when something was upsetting, she would quickly put a lid on it—in this case, literally—and move on. Later, Marguerite would remember the six years that she was married to Robert as "the only happy part of her life."

After his death, she collected the insurance premium and remained in their house with her two sons. In 1967, Robert Jr. published a book called *Lee: A Portrait of Lee Harvey Oswald by His Brother Robert*. He recounts a prevailing memory of his father: "Sometimes he would put a hand into his back pocket," he wrote, "with three fingers tucked in and the thumb and little finger out. Then he'd say to John and me, 'Grab ahold!' We would hold on and he'd swing us around." Robert comments that this memory may seem "trivial," but what he recalled was a moment of tenderness, and we can guess that to him it clearly meant the world. Two months after his father died, on October 18, 1939, Lee was born. He would miss out on moments like the one that Robert never forgot, until Marguerite remarried for a while in 1944 and he acquired a caring stepfather.

While Marguerite was in the old French Hospital on Orleans Avenue giving birth to her third son, John and Robert were staying with their aunt, Lillian, who lived nearby. They had been there often and liked to visit her and her five children. "Two of our cousins were almost exactly our ages and we often played together," Robert wrote. "When Mother brought the baby home, she told us his name was Lee Harvey. He was named for my father and our grandmother, whose maiden name was Harvey."

Both parents had decided on the name Lee Harvey Oswald. The nomenclatural importance of both the father's name and Lee's should not be discounted, and in fact it was said that Lee's father—and therefore Lee himself—was a distant relative of Robert E. Lee. In any case, the reference has not been discussed beyond minor notice in the myriad works about Oswald. Yet in the South, naming boys after the Confederate hero was a signifier of identification with the mythical "lost cause" and a heritage that harkened of ancient honor codes and decorum—everything that Blanche DuBois longed for in *A Streetcar Named Desire*, as was revealed whenever she recalled Belle Reve—Beautiful Dream—the family plantation that is long gone by the time the play unfolds. In the lives of the Oswalds, about to embark on years of crisis-driven moves from rental to rental, school district to district, the South that Lee's name invoked was a dim memory of a past that was never really theirs.

Yet it must be noted that this tale bears a hint of the old saying that "the South shall rise again"—Oswald from deep in the heart of Dixie taking out the head of an iconic family from the North, a fine representative of old (and ill-begotten) money destroyed by a man whose mother once complained about being treated like trash, and having to stand in line with "Puerto Ricans and Negroes" at a youth house for truants in order to visit Lee. Though outwardly defiant (the coin of the American realm, when you get down to it), Oswald himself was embarrassed by his origins—and so was his mother. Once she was fired from a job for body odor. "I use an anti-perspirant," she told her son John Edward after it happened. "If it doesn't work, what can I do about it?" It was as if she was being rebuked for her standing in the American class system by her very essence, perhaps afflicted by what Norman Mailer called "spiritual disruptions." There was nothing—not deodorant, nor a coat of arms from Burke's Peerage—that could cover that up, and she never forgot it.

In the end, being named like his father before him after a father figure for what was once half of the nation—Southern royalty, after all—didn't make up for the fact that Lee did not have one—a factor that his various truant officers and teachers and social workers noted with concern when he came to their attention. During the final years of his life, Oswald would talk about his mother's bitterness regarding her situation and said that she was a worker who was exploited by capitalism. That language came from Karl Marx, whose works he sometimes checked out of the library and studied closely. However, although Huey Long had been killed by the time Oswald was born, it is almost a certainty that the seeds of his beliefs were passed on by his mother, who was—in today's parlance—"validated" by Long and his oft-repeated slogan. In fact, everyone was. As Stanley Kowalski says to Blanche in *A Streetcar Named Desire*, "Remember what Huey Long said—'Every man is a King!' And I am the king around here, so don't forget it!" And then he wrecks Blanche's birthday party, hurling plates to the floor.

Shortly before his death, Long wrote a song named for that very statement with the leader of the band at the Roosevelt Hotel. It was recorded by the Louisiana Ramblers a few weeks after Long died, and then more recently by Randy Newman. Played across the airwaves, the song carried Long's legacy forward, an anthem that was tailor-made for someone like Marguerite Oswald. She traveled under it throughout her life, wearing a figurative crown.

> Why weep or slumber America?
> Land of brave and true
> With castles, and clothing, and food for all
> All belongs to you
> Every man a king! Every man a king!
> For you can be a millionaire
> But there's something belonging to others
> There's enough for all people to share
> When it's sunny June and December too
> Or in the wintertime or spring
> There'll be peace without end!
> Every neighbor a friend
> With every man a king!

PART TWO

ROAD TRIP

"The American community is an overnight camp."—Wallace Stegner

"Take a chance."—Dale Carnegie

"Lee Harvey Oswald's childhood did not take place in any one town or city," Peter Savodnik wrote in *The Interloper*. "He was always provided for, but he was also, in a way, homeless—without a stable backdrop of buildings or even people. By the age of seventeen, he had moved twenty times. Almost all of these moves happened because of his mother, Marguerite. Often he shuttled between Dallas, Fort Worth, and New Orleans, but he also lived in New York. His briefest stay, in Manhattan, lasted six weeks; his longest, in Fort Worth, four years. He averaged 10.2 months per address . . . nearly all of these homes were rentals or places owned by others, and [move number] twenty-one, when Lee was of school age, took place when Lee was in school."

For a while after Lee's father died, Marguerite and her sons remained in the house on Alvar Street. John Edward and Robert attended William T. Frantz Elementary across the street. This was the school that years later, on November 14, 1960, would make headlines when six-year-old Ruby Bridges became the first black student to attend, greeted by mobs of angry white people and escorted by federal marshals. The scene was famously depicted by Norman Rockwell in a painting called *The Problem We All Live With*. Of course, that was true, and especially in New Orleans, center of the slave trade during the 1800s, with its notorious Congo Square as ground zero for many of the country's slave auctions. The Oswald family itself was not immune; their connection to that era was not just reflected in the invocation of Robert E. Lee in the names of its men but also via their little-known ancestor, Colonel Thomas Hepworth Oswald, Lee's paternal great-grandfather. On November 10, 1835, he posted a fifty-dollar reward for a runaway slave in several newspapers, including the *Courrier de la Louisiane*. She was a "mulatto girl nam'd JANE," the ad said, rendering her name in uppercase letters, "about twenty-four years of age, of a lively intelligent appearance, and is generally quite talkative. I purchased her in New Orleans in February last . . . Said girl once resided in Vicksburg, where she is well-known. The above reward will be paid upon her apprehension and delivery to the subscriber, or her commitment to jail, so that I may get her." Such is the history of many (though of course not all) families in the South, and some in the North, with a connection to Dixie, a heritage that was often not spoken of until recent years, or to some not even known. Sixteen years before it was integrated, at the age of six, Lee too would attend Frantz Elementary. Sometime later, he was excoriated by several white friends for sitting next to black people on a streetcar, oblivious to the offense.

In January of 1940, Marguerite sent John Edward and Robert to a Catholic boarding school called the Infant Jesus College across the river in Algiers. World War II had just begun, and Algiers was the site of a burgeoning Navy base, which made it a place that could be called "where the boys are." Marguerite was working as a receptionist in Algiers and liked to dance at local taverns, later earning the scorn of those who did not approve of widows, however young they may be, having a good time. How can she pack her kids off just so she can go out and have a drink? was the idea, though the fact is that over the years, as her son Robert noted, he could hardly think of a time when his mother did not convey the sense that the boys were a burden, and Lee, the youngest and home alone with her more than his brothers who were long gone by the time Lee was in high school, bore the brunt of her resentment.

It wasn't long before Marguerite began to run out of funds from her late husband's insurance policy, so she rented out the house on Alvar and the family moved to a smaller one on Congress Street in the St. Claude neighborhood, a now-hip enclave offering yoga and filled with cafes and bars featuring alt bands, then a scene of furniture stores, houses that needed a new coat of paint, and residents on weekly salaries. Linked to the rest of New Orleans via the Desire streetcar line, "it's still referred to as the 'old neighborhood' by locals who lament the ongoing trend of gentrification," according to a local real estate blog.

Feeling like outsiders at their boarding school because they were Lutheran, Robert and John Edward soon returned home. About the school, Robert wrote that the nuns were strict and beat the boys who broke rules with a broomstick. "It was gloomy and cold," he continued, "and I guess we must have told Mother that we hated it."

In September of 1940, Marguerite applied for assistance from Aid to Dependent Children. She sold their house and bought a smaller one at 1010 Bartholomew Street in Bywater—like St. Claude, a gritty district that John Edward recalled as "upper lower class," noting that the move was a "step down." In recent years, Bywater has come to be appreciated by hipsters for its run-down and "authentic" nature. The small house cost $1,300, or about $28,000 today. Here, Marguerite tried to make a go of it as an entrepreneur, opening up Oswald's Notion Shop in the front room. The term "notion" refers now to a

kind of quaint or even ironic enterprise; at the time it was a reference to any purveyor of sewing materials such as needles, thread, and
ribbon and other assorted items like candy, soap, and a variety of
spur-of-the moment necessities. It wasn't exactly a scenario of Joan
Crawford as Mildred Pierce baking pies, and Marguerite didn't go in
for that sort of thing anyway. But there were similarities. She was just
as attractive as any number of stars at the time, some would observe
in the aftermath of JFK's murder, and she had these piercing blue eyes
that everyone remembered, and you could see those eyes with their
dark lashes in Lee years later, some remarked, and that's the kind of
thing that can take you places—up to a point. Moreover, she was
self-employed and didn't have to report to a boss—"every woman
a queen," which Huey Long had sometimes said as well, and why
not, I deserve it, do I not? And so she sat in her front room, trying
hard to peddle her wares, letting her friends and family members and
neighbors know what they could acquire for not very much; she had
longings and hopes and dreams that could come true someday, after
all, if things worked out like they should if everything weren't rigged.
But the selling of notions did not facilitate the payment of bills and
consequently she sold the house, and thus did the family tread water
for a little while longer.

Once again, the older boys were shipped off, this time to
Bethlehem Children's Home, fully known as the Evangelical Lutheran
Bethlehem Orphan Asylum. Of course, those particular children were
not orphans; the home also took in boys and girls with just one parent.
Marguerite had wanted Lee to join his brothers there, but he was not
yet three years old at the time, which made him too young to qualify.

It's difficult in New Orleans to not be aware of the past, unlike,
say, in southern California, where time is often obliterated by nice
weather—the kind that is featured on Chamber of Commerce postcards featuring beaches and palm trees—and this particular children's

home conveyed a lot of history. It was originally established in the post–Civil War nineteenth century to care for destitute children orphaned by the war, and then later, by yellow fever. In the 1880s, its headquarters became an old plantation building on the banks of the Mississippi in the Lower Ninth Ward purchased by church leaders, and that's where John Edward and Robert lived for a time. On Facebook, a student who lived there in 1932 recalls a great teacher who was also a strict disciplinarian, using the edge of a twelve-inch ruler to rap students on the back of the hand when things got out of control. Robert remembered it as "a cheerful place," not nearly as harsh as the Catholic boarding school in Algiers. They didn't have to wear uniforms and could decide on their own what to wear. The rooms where they slept—boys in one wing and girls in the other—were big and open. There was only one rule—that they had to eat everything on their plates at mealtime.

It was January of 1942 when Marguerite sold the Bartholomew Street house back to the previous seller for a profit of $800 and moved again, to an apartment at 831 Pauline Street back in the Bywater district. She had found a job as a switchboard operator, and problems with Lee began to surface in their new home. Two-year-old Lee was ill-tempered, and according to a babysitter at the time, he threw a toy gun at her and broke the chandelier in the bedroom. Marguerite turned to her sister Lillian, who agreed that Lee could live with her family, which included her husband Dutz Murret and five children, all older than Lee. Everyone got along well and enjoyed each other's company. Sometimes, Lillian would take him into town in a little boy's sailor suit, and he would say hi to everyone and people would say, "Oh, what an adorable child." At times he could be troublesome, especially on mornings when Lillian was busy getting her own kids off to school. There were problems at night as well. "He could slip out of the house like nobody's business," she later told investigators searching for information about Lee's childhood, "even if you had everything locked up. We had gates up and everything else." He would then surface down the street at a neighbor's house, sitting in their kitchen, wearing his pajamas.

When Lillian would raise various issues with Marguerite, Marguerite insisted on getting her own way. "She was always right," Lillian said, just like she was when they were growing up. She was ungrateful as well, never acknowledging that anyone was actually helping her, including Lillian when it came to the matter of Lee being a temporary member of the Murret household so that Marguerite could keep working. At some point—the time that Lee lived with his Aunt Lillian varies from a matter of months to two years, depending on the memories of various family members—Marguerite decided that Lee should be back in his own home, even if she had to hire someone to take care of him while she was at work. She advertised in a local paper, and a couple applied for the job. She hired them at fifteen dollars a month, and to make up for the low salary, she permitted them to live in the house rent free. That situation lasted for two months, ending when Marguerite came home from work one day to find that Lee was crying. She discovered large red welts on Lee's legs. A neighbor told her that the babysitters had been mistreating the toddler, whipping him to keep him quiet. Marguerite immediately fired the caretakers, though they protested that Lee was a "bad, unmanageable child." "How could a two-year-old baby be that bad?" Marguerite had said, soon quitting her job rather than leave Lee with strangers.

Shortly after that incident, she moved with Lee to 1111 Sherwood Forest Drive, a modest home where her sister lived with her family, in the City Park section of town. Later that year, in October of 1942, Marguerite again petitioned the Bethlehem Home for Orphans to admit Lee. He had just turned three. Robert and John had come home for Christmas in December, and when they went back to the orphanage, Lee joined them. A happy period for the boys unfolded, with Lee living there for about a year. It involved tender family things such as Marguerite bringing them clothing, and there was a big communal dresser with a drawer full of socks, all sizes. In the mornings, they would fish around to find the right pair, and Robert would "always look for the smallest pair for Lee"—a touching image of an older brother looking after the little boy in the family.

Alone with his brothers, without their mother around, Lee began to develop a real bond with them, the first time for all of them, according to what John Edward and Robert later recalled about that time. Marguerite seemed to flourish as well. She found work at the Princess Hosiery Shop on Canal Street, and once a week during the summer, every Wednesday, Robert recalls, the boys would take the streetcar to Canal Street and visit their mother at work. Then they'd all have lunch—po' boys maybe? gumbo?—and the family would go to a movie. On weekends, she would visit her sons at the Bethlehem Home, and one weekend, she brought a friend. This was Edwin A. Ekdahl, a nice guy with a Yankee accent who had a way of talking to the boys. He was an electrical engineer from Boston who was working for the Texas Electrical Service in New Orleans. He was much older than Marguerite, had a 1938 Buick—a car, a nice one, which was important to Marguerite—and he was "a ten-thousand dollar a year man with an expense account," also important. He and Marguerite had been dating for several months, and he had asked her to marry him. She was considering it, and one day in 1944, she arrived at the home to take Lee away. Edwin had been transferred to Dallas, and she was weighing the pros and cons of joining him. Although he earned quite a good salary for that period of time, he was a lot older than Marguerite, he traveled frequently, and he had a bad heart. Soon an emissary from Ekdahl's family arrived in New Orleans; this was Ekdahl's sister, coming to convince Marguerite to say yes to her brother. He's lonely, she said, pressing his case, and shortly after that visit, Marguerite moved to Dallas with Lee.

She purchased a two-story duplex on Victor Street with money from the sale of her last house in New Orleans and, according to educated guesses that came later, Ekdahl helped her with the down payment. The idea was to rent out one of the floors while she and Lee settled into the other, laid out "railroad-style" in a linear progression—living room, bedroom, bathroom, bedroom, and kitchen—with room for John Edward and Robert when they arrived later that year after finishing up their classes at Bethlehem. They were then twelve and ten years old, attended summer school, and in the fall were enrolled at Davy Crockett Elementary School three blocks away. The school was named for the legendary "King of the Wild Frontier" and rifleman who died in battle at the Alamo. The image of Crockett that is etched in American history is of the young Davy in a coonskin cap brandishing his rifle—later replicated by actor Fess Parker in the eponymous TV series. At the height of the popularity of this series, many a child in the 1950s—including this writer—sported a coonskin cap and was photographed thusly. Strangely, the famous photo of Davy Crockett is almost a forerunner of the image of Lee Harvey Oswald posing with his rifle in his backyard in Dallas, the one that surfaced after the assassination of JFK and was, and continues to be, published everywhere.

At the time his brothers attended Davy Crockett, Lee attended nursery school, and Marguerite would drop him off on her way to work in the morning and pick him up at the end of the day. Ekdahl would stay with Marguerite and the boys on weekends, and the prevailing winds were favorable; she decided that she would marry him. Yet she soon tried to send John and Robert back to the children's home in New Orleans, explaining to school administrators that although they would now have two parents, Ekdahl's job required frequent travel, so the boys in effect had one parent. Her argument was unsuccessful, and she then enrolled her sons in the Chamberlain-Hunt Academy, a military school in Port Gibson, Mississippi, paying the tuition from remaining proceeds from her house sale. John Edward and Robert remained at home for a short period, awaiting their move to Mississippi for their first semester in military school. And so began a period in Lee's life in which he would have a father in the house for the first time. He took to this man, and the man to him, like actual blood relatives, and the older boys flourished as well. Marguerite herself seemed happier than ever, and for a while, the whole arrangement seemed like a match made in heaven.

On May 7, 1945, Marguerite Oswald and Edwin Ekdahl tied the knot and began living in the house on Victor Street in Dallas. "Call me Ed," Edwin had told the boys, and it made them feel grown-up and most likely not intimidated by the prospect of having to suddenly call a stranger "Dad." He seems to have been kind of a fun dad, taking the boys out for excursions and for ice cream—minus Marguerite, it sounds like, judging from various accounts, providing John, Robert, and Lee with the opportunity of having this new father figure to themselves. In September of that year, Marguerite and Ed drove Robert and John to Port Gibson and dropped them off at Chamberlain-Hunt where they would live, except for visits home, for the next three years. The older boys thrived at the military academy, receiving individual attention from the commandant, a former Marine officer, who regaled them with tales of life in the Corps, perhaps furthering the idea of someday entering the armed services (which they would do, with Lee following suit), a tradition observed by many in the South—and of course Robert Sr. was a war veteran, and Marguerite's older brothers had served in WWI as well. Then again, there was that undeniable linkage in various family names to Dixie's most famous general.

While Robert and John Edward were in Port Gibson, Lee often traveled with Ed and Marguerite on his stepfather's business trips. The first one happened right after the older boys had been dropped off at school. With Lee in tow, the newlyweds continued the family's road trip and headed for Boston to visit Ed's son from a previous marriage. Over the months there were other excursions, and Marguerite made sure to send snapshots to Robert and John Edward at school in Mississippi. In Robert Oswald's book about Lee, there is a series of pictures of Lee as a young boy at various ages. There is one of Lee at about six and a half, hands on hips, standing with a leg crossed and looking very happy right behind Marguerite, who is looking kind of jaunty in a kind of fedora hat with a scarf around her shoulders, seated on a rock next to a large agave plant in a park in Arizona. There is one of Lee at about two and a half, lying prone on the ground at his Aunt Lillian's house, smiling and playing with his locomotive. There's another one of Lee, about six or seven, smiling, hands on hips again, looking satisfied as can be. And then there's Lee on a pony in front of the house in Dallas where he lived with his mother and Ed. Who brought the pony? one wonders, and what was the occasion? Maybe it was a neighbor's, and the idea was to have the pony come over and give Lee a ride. Not a big deal in Dallas in the 1940s, yet nonetheless something of a treat.

Then there's one of Lee sitting on a couch in the family living room, ankles crossed, wearing a striped T-shirt and white jeans and Robert's hat from military school, which he always wanted to try on when Robert came home on vacation. He has a mischievous look, and he is pointing a toy pistol. Behind him is a guitar on the wall. Was someone making music there? If so, who was it? Although we certainly don't associate Lee Harvey Oswald with being steeped in music or even experiencing enjoyment of it, despite having been born in and spent a great deal of time in New Orleans, this is an early hint that someone in his family was involved enough in music to display a guitar. As we shall see, Lee did in fact incorporate music and even melody into his life—and guns, as suggested not only by the early image with the pistol but another one of Lee, on leave from the Marines, standing with a .22 while squirrel hunting—and, surprisingly enough, the two would come together in a kind of Wild West–Ennio Morricone convergence shortly before he killed John Fitzgerald Kennedy when he posed for what may be the most well-known picture of a man and his rifle.

When Marguerite and Ed returned from their trip to Boston, Ekdahl leased a house in Fort Worth, Texas. Although not generally regarded as figuring as prominently as Dallas in this story (understandable, as Dallas is of course where JFK was shot and where he had numerous and powerful enemies), Fort Worth informed Oswald's life just as surely as did New Orleans and later, New York City. If you had to pick a physical location as the birthplace of the Wild West, you could say that *X* marks the spot in Fort Worth. In fact, the city's founders did just that when they decided to describe the town as "Where the West begins." They were not being hyperbolic or acting simply as Chamber of Commerce–type boosters. There was a method to the madness and it went like this:

In 1843, Sam Houston, then a general in the Texas Army (before the state was annexed to the United States) and also President of the Republic of Texas, led a historic peace parley with Native American chiefs representing such tribes as the Apache, Wyandotte, and Chickasaw on the Grape Vine Prairie of Texas. The idea was to formulate some sort of agreement regarding conflicts between settlers and Indians and soon after the conference ended, the Treaty of Bird's Fort was signed. It did bring a modicum of peace in a region that was fraught with tension and bloodshed involving not only the parade of newcomers who believed that the land was theirs due to a Biblical mandate and Native Americans who had been there for tens of thousands of years, but also Mexicans who considered Texas as a territory that belonged to their own country, Mexico. The peace parley was commemorated with a medallion depicting a handshake, a peace pipe, and a tomahawk, and the whole thing was memorialized years later in 2021 with a ceremony at the site of the treaty signing wherein statues of the various chiefs at the original event were unveiled, a replica of the medallion was given to representatives of each tribe, and the grounds were cleared of forces that did not belong with sage and prayer, followed by the beating of Comanche drums. The primary act of the old treaty was to demarcate a zone where Indians could live without harassment and that was to the west of a line passing through the future site of Fort Worth, where the oak trees stopped and it was pretty much red rock, mesas, and canyons. Well-intentioned treaties of that era were rare and rarely honored, but nevertheless, for all intents and purposes, that line of demarcation entered the national conversation as the place where the West begins.

There was much else that amplified the claim that Fort Worth was a city worthy of such tribute. In 1867, the Chisholm Trail opened up, the storied frontier path ferrying cattle from San Antonio northward through Austin and Waco and then into Fort Worth. There, the cowboys would stop for a spell, gather supplies, rest the longhorns, gallop their horses into saloons to announce their arrival, fire guns, drink, revel—all the things for which that rowdy era is known. A lot of it happened in a certain part of Fort Worth known as Hell's Half Acre. This was the equivalent of Storeyville in New Orleans and, like Storeyville, it was a red-light district. It was also a hangout for notorious outlaw gangs such as the Fort Worth Five, aka the Wild Bunch, whose members included Butch Cassidy and the Sundance Kid. Then there were the Fort Worth Stockyards, the place where herds that had been driven up from the South converged and then were driven on to slaughterhouses in Chicago or, later, placed on railroad cars for the same destination. The stockyards are now a national historic district that has long maintained its original features, but with museums (a new one for John Wayne), reenactments of cattle drives featuring famous longhorns with names like Jake that kids can ride through the dusty streets, and replays of shoot-outs involving frontier rivals in period costume ("It's 3:00 p.m. Watch someone get shot. At 6:00 p.m., watch it again"). Although the cattle drive era came to an end in 1884, that part of the American story of course endures in a million different ways, including when young Lee Harvey Oswald posed atop a pony in his front yard, dressed in Western regalia with a bandanna around his neck, and entering a stream that lures boys and girls everywhere. "Howdy partner," the traveling photographer behind the camera might have said—"ready to hit the trail?"—and then the wannabe cowboy looked at the camera and smiled. It was soon after this that Marguerite, her new husband, and Lee hit the road to meet Ed's son, off on an American adventure.

In 1917, Boston newsman Arthur Chapman developed a fascination with the West as he traveled across the land and proceeded to broaden the concept of Fort Worth as its progenitor, writing a poem in response to various Western governors who could not come to an agreement about which states should be considered "the West." It was called "Out Where the West Begins," and its first verse goes like this:

Out where the handclasp's a little stronger,
Out where the smile dwells a little longer,
That's where the West begins;
Out where the sun is a little brighter,
Where the snows that fall are a trifle whiter,
Where the bonds of home are a wee bit tighter—
That's where the West begins.

The poem became an instant hit, reprinted in many venues and on colorful postcards bearing frontier scenes depicting wide open spaces, cactus, mountains, buffalo—any elements that conjured the land of the national dream, advancing the idea that neither latitude nor longitude signified the launch point of the West but that it was a state of mind. Yet Fort Worth was not to be outdone by this lofty idea. Amon Carter, prominent citizen and vice president of the *Fort Worth Star-Telegram*, took note of the poem's popularity and reattached his city's centrality to this concept, suggesting that the Chamber of Commerce adopt "Out Where the West Begins" as the city's slogan. In 1957, in one of her varied parade of jobs, Marguerite Oswald became a greeter for the Fort Worth Welcome Wagon, a nationwide organization that did exactly that: roll out a station wagon and welcome newcomers to a particular city. In her position as greeter, Marguerite would drive up to meet the freshly arrived in their just-purchased homes in a car that said "Bob's Buick" or the name of some other dealership on the driver's door, with the phone number below. She would present a gift basket bearing goods and certificates from local merchants, no doubt forcing a smile that may have seemed authentic, and in fact maybe was, because, after all, America is the land of starting over! There's always a second chance right here in the US of A! Haven't you heard? and then say something along the lines of "*Welcome to Fort Worth! If you stand in front of your house, I'll take your picture. Can you smile and say 'Land of the free'? Of course you can. There . . . that looks perfect. Did you know that this is where the West begins?*" And then she would drive off and her mood instantly soured and she would wonder why her son Lee hardly ever spoke to her any more, was he going to turn out like the other boys and leave as soon as he had the chance, what was wrong with them—she put food on the table, ok maybe it wasn't steak dinners—but what did they expect from a woman in her station? Maid service? Do I look like some sort of servant? "*Lee-boy is a good son,*" she'd tell herself. "*He won't move away. He loves me, I know he does.*"

Let us now spin the wheel and watch as another version of the West was playing out six years later. On November 21, 1963, the President was in Fort Worth, where he would spend his final night. He was heading through Texas en route to Dallas as a way to advance his campaign for a new frontier. Now the frontier was outer space—not the forests and canyons and rivers of the Great Plains and beyond—and Texas, with Fort Worth's Carswell Air Force Base as headquarters for the Strategic Air Command during the Cold War, was a critical component of the program.

That night, Air Force One landed at Carswell, and the President was greeted by much pomp and circumstance as well as a large and admiring crowd. At 8:45 the following morning, he addressed a crowd of about eight thousand people or so who had gathered in the rain in the parking lot in front of the Hotel Texas where he and his wife were staying. "There are no faint hearts in Fort Worth," he began, as his local advance man Jeb Byrne later recalled in *Prologue* magazine, "and I appreciate your being here this morning." Ever the master of repartee and one-liners, he remarked that "Mrs. Kennedy is organizing herself. It takes longer, but, of course, she looks better than we do when she does it . . . We appreciate your welcome." After noting the importance of Fort Worth and its defense contractors, such as Bell Helicopters and General Dynamics, in protecting the security of the nation, he then headed inside for a breakfast in the ballroom, feted by national and local officials from Texas. One of them presented him with a pair of cowboy boots and a cowboy hat. Not that much of a showman, he thanked the presenter but did not don the hat (and of course not the boots), and then asked a Secret Service agent to let Mrs. Kennedy know that it was time to make her entrance. Two Secret Service agents escorted Mrs. Kennedy down from their suite, and as per the President's instructions, the hotel orchestra struck up "The Eyes of Texas Are Upon You" as she crossed to the dais before a tumultuous welcome. She was wearing the pink suit that would soon bear the national stain. Within hours, Lee Harvey Oswald, an ordinary young man out of the South by way of the West, would commit the ultimate act of defiance, blowing the head off the President of the United States, in this case, an American king. Later that day, Governor John Connally of Texas, riding in the limousine with John Fitzgerald Kennedy as it passed through Dealey Plaza, had planned to honor JFK at a celebratory dinner in Dallas. He too had a gift for the President—a Stetson—once known as the Boss of the Plains and "the hat that won the West."

It was in Fort Worth that Marguerite and her family would experience a taste of the American birthright—living the full-on middle-class dream and then some. They were in Benbrook, a suburb just north of Fort Worth on a rural mail route, in the house that Ekdahl had leased. It was said that President Franklin D. Roosevelt's son lived nearby. Shortly after the family moved in, for whatever reasons, Lee got into a fight with another young boy; the child threw a rock at Lee, wounding his left eye. On April 6 of that year, 1945, he was taken to the emergency room at Parkland Hospital, where he was treated with ice packs and then released. (This was his first visit to Parkland, though it would not be his last; when that hospital later moved from Fort Worth to Dallas, it was where JFK was taken after the assassination and died, and Oswald himself died there as well, after he was shot by Jack Ruby while in the Dallas County Jail.) Regardless of that incident, life in Benbrook was mostly tranquil for a while.

On October 31, a few days after his sixth birthday, Lee entered first grade at the Benbrook Common School, and there he did well, receiving As and Bs, including an A in citizenship. At Christmas, John and Robert returned home from military school for their first visit. Robert was immediately impressed, and it's from his description of the house that we know the dwelling was a radical departure from all of their previous homes. "It was the largest and most comfortable house we had ever lived in," he wrote in his portrait of Lee, "a spacious, low house of native stone surrounded by some acreage. There was a creek about four or five hundred yards behind the house. Lee took me out there to show me where he had found a skunk a few days earlier. He said he hadn't known what a skunk was before, but he found out!" Robert further reported that he and Lee would wade and fish in the creek during his visits, and Lee liked it when the two would head into the woods and play Cowboys and Indians. "I thought I was too old," he said, "but I found myself enjoying it with Lee."

For that initial vacation from military school, Robert and John had returned with their wooden practice rifles. The rifles didn't fire, but the boys had been taught how to hold them. In turn, they taught Lee how to hold a rifle and how to follow commands. "He had a fine time," Robert recalled, "right-facing and left-facing and marching around with my rifle." This image of Lee marching to and fro in formation while carrying a rifle at the age of six—combined with Robert's recollections of hunting adventures with Lee and John—is at odds with the countless assertions from many quarters over the years that Lee didn't know his way around guns except what he learned in the Marines (itself not inconsiderable), and that even *that* wasn't sufficient to have enabled his apparent facility with firearms on that terrible day in Dallas when he killed not only the President but also J. D. Tippit of the city's police department as the officer tried to nab the fugitive on his beat in the Oak Cliff neighborhood. On that day Oswald kept running, hiding out like Butch and Sundance in a hole in the wall, acting inside his own private reel of the Wild West—America's address, after all. Instead of a remote canyon, the hideaway was now the Texas Theatre—where Officer Tippit himself had also once worked as a security guard. Like many establishments in the Lone Star State, the theater conveyed instant history. It was named in honor of San Jacinto Day, the day that Texas won the battle that led to its independence from Mexico. In yet one more convergence of moment and myth, there was a double bill of war movies playing that day. One of them was *War Is Hell*, set in the Korean War with decorated World War II army hero and cowboy actor Audie Murphy narrating the prologue. "In combat, there's the external battle, war with the enemy," the handsome war veteran says, looking into the camera. "There's the personal war, sometimes even more deadly, that each man has with himself." The other film was *Cry of Battle*, set in World War II, with Van Heflin as Joe Trent, a rough-and-ready merchant marine who rapes a teenager and participates in a massacre of townies. For that era, the film was strange indeed, presenting the darkest aspects of masculinity, with a major star enacting them.

What might Oswald have been thinking as this film played out? Certainly he was deeply amped up, having just killed the President and a policeman. Or maybe he was simply hiding, having completely disassociated and entered some sort of fugue state. Acting on a tip from a shoe salesman in a store next to the theater, a cop entered through a fire exit in the dark and crept up the aisle towards Oswald. This was Maurice "Nick" McDonald, World War II veteran and member of the Dallas Police Department. He did not know that he was approaching the man who had just killed the President, believing only that his quarry had moments earlier gunned down Officer Tippit. As he neared Oswald, McDonald was acutely aware of the Van Heflin movie on the screen behind him. The two men were about to converge in a life-or-death struggle as reality converged with Hollywood and Oswald starred in his own matinee, complete with an audience and a soundtrack. As fifteen cops waited nearby, McDonald made a move towards Oswald. Lee hit back, instantly entered fight mode, and punching him between the eyes in the forehead. Then he grabbed his Smith and Wesson from his belt—the one he had used to kill

Tippit—aimed it at McDonald, and pulled the trigger. He was about to make his third kill of the day.

But McDonald jammed his thumb and forefinger between the hammer and firing pin, and the gun didn't go off. The fight spilled out onto the street, with the burly McDonald finally overpowering the amped-up though smaller Oswald and wresting away his gun. The episode had concluded. McDonald walked away with his life and a four-inch gash on his face, incurred when Oswald struck him with his gun. Oswald was taken in with bruises and a black eye. "Police brutality," he called out as he was taken away. This was nearly the last time he deflected blame in a violent act—and it was no small one at that. It was an attempted homicide. But of course, not nearly as foul as the killing of the President, an act which he also disavowed.

Such proclamations were part of a pattern, a thing that he did whenever he was in trouble, starting from his early years in elementary school; his mother would always back him up in his protestations, never saying "you're grounded" or issuing any sort of punishment or even a warning, never asking him to apologize to anyone, always insisting that he would never do such a thing, yet secretly hoping that things would change, and seeing that they never did. She continued to engage with her son in this pattern of behavior right up until the very end and throughout its aftermath, which became a time when she made another escape, an inner move we might say, into a better neighborhood as a more than ever outwardly righteous mother who saw—yet again—an opportunity to cash in. She just couldn't help it; it's how she was wired, how she connected with people, like Burt Lancaster working a flimflam in the movies, and like anyone running an effective con, she had these flashes of longing and desire, you see, she really meant it.

The marriage between Marguerite and Edwin began to crumble about a year or so after they had tied the knot, and there would be breakups and attempts to reunite for several years. Lee treasured these tries for harmony. Throughout most of this period, John and Robert were away at military school, and Lee was home alone with his mother and stepfather. John and Robert liked Chamberlain-Hunt, their military school, and it was there that Robert himself found a new father figure. This was the Commandant, an ex-Marine, and Robert sparked to everything the school offered: arithmetic, English, and history, along with military science, training, and field drills. Robert knew that someday, he'd follow the Commandant into the Marines, and this was something that he passed on to his younger brother. One of the things that he and John most enjoyed about Chamberlain-Hunt was weekends. "There were private lakes for fishing," he wrote, "and the woods around Port Gibson were full of small game—foxes, birds, rabbits and squirrels. In those woods my hunting instincts came alive." Along with his goal of one day joining the Corps, he passed on his zeal for hunting to Lee. A few years later, Lee would follow his brothers into the woods, learning to hunt and shoot.

While away at school, Robert found further contentment in the assumption that Lee was benefiting not just from the idyllic surroundings in Benbrook but also from the dynamic that appeared to be unfolding when Ed would take Marguerite and Lee on road trips across the country. There were letters that Marguerite would send, and then there was that snapshot of Lee and Marguerite in Arizona, looking happy under the desert skies. Perhaps the prevailing factor in Lee's apparent new feeling of calm was that, as Robert and John well knew, their mother was easier to be around when she herself was around Ed; her happiness changed the mood in the house and Lee seemed to take to the new arrangement like a plant to the sun. But actually, as the months unfolded, there was a degenerating scenario that involved numerous arguments and recriminations, and John and Robert were oblivious to the escalating turmoil.

Marguerite was a nag, Edwin later complained to friends and

relatives, using a term that today might be viewed as derogatory when it comes to the behavior of women who "demand" things—another term that is not in favor—but the fact was that Marguerite *was* kind of a nag, *was* demanding, and gave no quarter to those around her when it came to her wants and needs. In *The Glass Menagerie*, Amanda Wingfield berates her son Tom for things that were little and large—his posture, his plans for the future—and in various films of the era, there are harridans and "divorcees" —yet another term deployed to dismiss and mock women, often played by Barbara Stanwyck—who are constrained by the strictures of that time, alternating between haranguing their husbands or cajoling them, walking a tightrope that permitted a narrow range of behavior and getting the short end of the stick, regardless of the situation.

But by all accounts coming from inside the Oswald family, Marguerite tended towards the haranguing side of this equation, and was pretty relentless. What was it that Marguerite really wanted Edwin tried to fathom, and Marguerite herself, hard to please except when overcompensating for Lee's troublesome behavior over the years, seemed in her heart of hearts to not want this marriage. All in all, she lived in the uncomfortable terrain of an inability to accept satisfaction of any sort, and she did not make compromises, except for when the behavior was mostly a quid pro quo, like the very marriage itself. Soon Edwin was spending more time on the road, and she began to suspect him of having affairs. She had also taken note of his tightness with money, or at least an unwillingness to provide her with enough—a situation she would often accuse others of over the years, including her own sons. "Even though they stayed in good hotels when they traveled," Bugliosi wrote in his book, "and lived lavishly because of his expense account, he gave her only a hundred dollars a month for household expenses and demanded a strict accounting of it. She continued to use her own dwindling supply of money for the boys' expenses at the military school." When Marguerite and Ed had first tied the knot, she had written "Happy—though married" on the back of their wedding photo for her sister Lillian, making kind of a typical marriage joke of the time. But putting it on the back of a wedding photograph? Wink-wink throwaway that it may have been, the line would prove to be a wish and a loaded statement. She was not a person who found much happiness in life, and a caveat like this one suggested that she had her doubts about this marriage and perhaps the entire institution in general.

Amid this period, Lee was diagnosed with a middle ear bacterial infection on his left side called "acute mastoiditis." Common in children, it caused fever, headache, and temporary hearing loss in the affected ear. In other words, he was tuning out household noise, or at least that was the result of this condition. He was admitted to Harris Hospital in Fort Worth, where he underwent a mastoidectomy, or removal of part of the mastoid bone, to drain the infection. There he remained for four days, an unexpected break from the troubles at home. Several months later, Ed and Marguerite separated, and one day, with no advance notice, she showed up with Lee at Chamberlain-Hunt. "Time to go," she said, or something along those lines, and then she told John and Robert that they were moving to Covington, Louisiana, for the summer.

Using Peter Savodnik's math, this was move number seven for Lee, and soon he would be entering first grade for the third time. Covington was a resort town on the shores of Lake Pontchartrain near New Orleans where Marguerite used to take the kids on weekends. It was linked to the Crescent City by the Huey P. Long bridge, known to locals as "the Huey P." Opened to much fanfare during the Depression, it was a masterwork of engineering, perhaps the most famous of Huey Long's accomplishments, a fulfillment of one of his key promises that he never got to see; he was assassinated two months before it was launched. Now listed on the National Register of Historic Places, it is considered an engineering marvel in the same vein as the Statue of Liberty and even the Eiffel Tower. Marguerite may have attended the opening of the Huey P. in 1936. Everyone did—marching bands, circus acts—it was a very big deal, and it started with a party across the Mississippi River. Now New Orleans was linked with the riverbank to the east, and the bridge transformed the region by opening up new paths of commerce and permitting locals to easily access remote areas of Lake Pontchartrain and its enclaves.

Lake Pontchartrain has long been a haven for all manner of travelers, pilgrims, outlaws, seekers. In 1947, Hank Williams with the Drifting Cowboys released "On the Banks of the Old Pontchartrain," a tune that captures the spirit and allure of the place. The song is about many a Pontchartrain regular, and you could say it well conveys the plight of Marguerite Oswald, who was traversing a well-known circuit during the time that she brought her boys there. The song recalls a journey from Texas to "old Louisanne," across mountains and plains, its teller tired and with aching feet, stopping for awhile on the shores of the old saltsea and praising that moment—and the fiddler plays on.

It is said that Lee loved fishing, and this was the place. But it was really because of Covington that Marguerite brought her sons there. A big draw was that it was less expensive to live in than any number of other places, and with her separation from her husband, Marguerite needed to find a new home. Also, Covington was centered around the idea of well-being—although that term was pretty much nonexistent at the time, at least in its current iteration. It was a charming and restful town known for its healing waters, situated in the heart of the "Ozone Belt," a term cooked up by realtors and local boosters in the 1880s who decided to promote the therapeutic vapors emanating from local pine forests along with "highly medicinal" waters at dozens of artesian springs nearby. At first, the region was a refuge for residents of New Orleans who were fleeing the yellow fever and malaria epidemics. There was a rest home called Ozonia and numerous hotels and spas. One brochure described the area as "cool and shady in summer, surrounded by grand old oaks and health-giving pines. Alluring in autumn, when the bracing air invites to walks through bright-hued forests." Another proclaimed that "according to the United States health statistics at Washington, Covington is the second healthiest spot in the United States. The natural springs are highly medicinal and especially helpful in the healing of all kidney troubles, liver diseases, dyspepsia, chronic diarrhea; catarrh, constipation, nervousness, general debility, and almost any unnatural condition." Ozone boosterism proliferated quickly and soon was all over the region. Maps depicted "The World Famous Ozone Belt," and a local paper ran a headline that said, "Ozone Belt Gained World Fame for Unusual Healthful Climate." Indeed, it did attract an international crowd, along with dedicated locals who came for the "ozonated atmosphere" and the miracle pools. The reputation of the place persisted through the 1950s, with various ozone-related products being proffered and promoted along with events such as the Miss Ozone beauty pageant in nearby Ponchatoula. In the 1970s, of course, scientists determined that ozone was a health hazard and it went out of fashion, legally banished, something that damaged the lungs rather than healing them. But what people had been inhaling all of those years in the Ozone Belt was actually terpene, an emission from evergreen trees. Who doesn't feel good when walking through a pine forest? Such was the atmosphere that Marguerite entered when she first separated from Edwin, and perhaps she was hoping that all of her boys would breathe in or bathe in the town's palliative air and springs, and that, when she and Lee returned to Fort Worth, they would be cleansed and new.

She rented a house on Vermont Street, and her friend Myrtle Evans observed that they were very happy. They went swimming, ate watermelon, and had a couple of dogs, Evans later told investigators.

Lee seemed to prefer his own company to that of his brothers or any-one else. In the fall, the two older boys returned to school in Port Gibson according to the original plan, but Marguerite decided to re-main in Covington with Lee. He enrolled in Covington Elementary School, in the first grade yet again, not because of poor grades but be-cause he hadn't finished his first year. And now, let us visit a scene that unfolded during the Christmas season of that year, 1946. The town is bedecked with decorations, and the local Lutheran church is full. Two of its attendees are Marguerite Oswald and her son Lee Harvey. The pastor beckons for seven-year-old Lee to come to the lectern. He clears his throat and sings "Silent Night," without a choir or accompanying music. Its melody soothes congregants and so do its words, especially coming from a young boy in an innocent timbre. It's a story about Lee that is rarely fleshed out or even recounted in its barest form. As we shall see, this is not the first time that he sings; there would be others later in his life, and whistling, too, all such expressions buried in an avalanche of coverage about conspiracies and plots, and what he sang later may also surprise you, and all such exuberances must be added to the deck of cards that comprise his life.

Two years later, the noted novelist Walker Percy moved to Covington. There he would write *The Moviegoer*, which went on to much acclaim and import. About a disaffected young man named Binx Billings, the novel followed the protagonist's life in New Orleans and rendered a deep disconnect from the lovely and profuse gardens and the ornate courtyards of the city, the enveloping and sometimes overwhelming sounds and scents and the memories they evoked, even if you didn't want to have them. It told of despair and loneliness, of get-ting lost in the movies in order to find yourself, becoming the charac-ters and living inside their dreams, and what happens when you emerge from the dark and face life for real. Although Billings was an academic, and much more prone to introspection than someone like Lee Harvey

Oswald, or his mother Marguerite, there are parallels between the lives. "Losing hope isn't so bad," Percy wrote. "There's something worse; losing hope and hiding it from yourself." Certainly that was a condition that could describe Lee later in his life—and actually very soon, even if he wouldn't have thought of it that way. And Marguerite as well was always trying to run out the clock, hide the desperation that erupted as rage or excoriation, or oozed through as unwelcome bodily scents, putting on a public face of "welcome to Fort Worth, you'll love it here, take it from me, Marguerite Claverie Oswald."

For the moment, things seemed pretty good. Marguerite and Ed had reconciled, and in the New Year of 1947, on January 23, to be precise, she withdrew Lee from Covington Elementary. The pair headed back to Texas, probably taking the Huey P. for New Orleans and stopping there to visit familiars, and then continuing north for Fort Worth in a reverse journey of the Hank Williams account, this time going from old Louisanne to the Lone Star State, but no longer "footsore and weary," having healed in the waters of Covington and the pine-infused air. They settled into a second-story apartment that Ekdahl had been renting while they were away, and Marguerite enrolled Lee in first grade—yet again, due to all of the moves—at Clayton Elementary School in Fort Worth. In spite of the upheavals, he continued to do well with his studies, earning Bs, mostly, and As in physical education and health.

One day, Marguerite was hanging laundry downstairs in the yard. She encountered a neighbor and introduced herself as "Mrs. Ekdahl." The neighbor was surprised, telling her that Mr. Ekdahl had been living there with another woman whom she assumed was his wife. There is nothing in the record that tells us if Marguerite confronted Ed about what she learned. But according to various accounts there seems to have been another round of fights and separations around this time. One night, John came home from his job at a local ice cream parlor and was happily surprised. His mother and Ed were inside Ekdahl's Buick, on their way to a hotel for an evening of reconciliation. John then told Lee, who was elated. Of the three boys, it was seven-year-old Lee who was the most heavily invested in parental accord.

But marriage could not bear the weight of this particular husband and wife. There came a day towards the end of that summer that Marguerite received a telegram from Ed. He was still on a business trip, it said, and wouldn't be home for a few more days. She then called his secretary to relay the news, but the secretary told her that Ed was out for lunch. At this point, Marguerite drove to his office; he was leaving as she arrived and didn't see her. She followed him to a nearby apartment, where he was visiting another woman.

And thus were Marguerite's early suspicions confirmed; her husband was indeed the cheating type, and while she never trusted anyone anyway (*"everyone's out to get you, don't you know? give 'em an inch and they'll take a mile, what'd I tell ya?"*), finding out that Ed was disloyal, on top of already knowing that he was cheap and had a heart condition (*"do I need this again?"*) propelled her into mounting an operation that could be viewed as a classic noir scenario. It has all of the elements portrayed in the literature of alleys and the furtive acts that transpire there, and it came together quickly, in the moment—when the mind and heart are most vexed and answers seem to present themselves out of nowhere (not unlike JFK crossing Oswald's path in his rifle sight years later at the Texas Book Depository). It went like this:

When Marguerite returned home, there was John with several friends, all of whom lived in a world of diminished hopes and too much time on their hands. The group included Sammy, a resident of a downtown hotel, and a young couple named Marvin and Goldie. Marguerite knew them from previous visits; they felt comfortable in each other's company, and they spoke freely. "Ed is having an affair," Marguerite told them, or something along those lines. "And I know where he's having it. Let's go!" The compatriots agreed and got into Marvin and Goldie's car, heading for ground zero. "Telegram," Sammy said upon arrival, knocking on the door and pretending to be a messenger. "Slide it under," came a woman's voice. "You have to sign for it," Sammy replied, and the woman opened the door in a negligee. Marguerite pushed her way in and there in the living room on the sofa sat a surprised Edwin. His sleeves were rolled up and his tie was off. "Marguerite! You've got it all wrong," he said, trying out the time-honored protest. "Listen to me!"

But the marriage was over for Marguerite; she had seen enough.

Mrs. Ekdahl and crew then left and Marguerite consulted her pastor, a man who seems to have known a fair amount of her history with Ed. "Should I get a divorce?" she asked. He didn't think so, he said, reminding her that Ed had a heart condition. Soon after this conversation Ekdahl was hospitalized, and they had a shouting match at his bedside. For another few months, that's how things proceeded back at home; there was a great deal of heated interchange, and sometimes Marguerite would throw things. Yet her fear that she would lose financial support prevented her from filing for divorce, and on the pair faltered, with Marguerite no longer "happy"—though still married. "Indeed, the whole scene had an ancient, almost classical ugliness to it," James M. Cain wrote of a similar relationship in *Mildred Pierce*, "for they uttered the same recriminations that have been uttered since the beginning of marriage, and added little of originality to them, and nothing of beauty."

In the fall of 1947, John and Robert returned to Chamberlain-Hunt, and Lee returned to Clayton Elementary, still in first grade. One of his classmates remembered Oswald quite distinctly. This was the late *Fort Worth Star-Telegram* reporter Phil Vinson, who recalled that the boys in his class, about fifteen of them, would break down into what they called gangs when they were out on the playground. These weren't "gangs" in a gangster sense, nor were they menacing; the scenario was boys "horsing around" without supervision, and Lee was the leader of his own little gang, comprised of two, maybe three, boys. He was a year older than his classmates, due to his frequent school transfers and not having completed first grade at the usual time. He was also stocky and well-built, Vinson recalled, though not tall, and the combination of being a bit older than everyone else with his size made him kind of an imposing figure. The other boys would tease Lee about being big and strong, and when asked how he got that way, Lee would joke about eating his spinach, like the cartoon character who was on the radio and in early animated films. "I'm strong to the finich cause I eats my spinach, I'm Popeye the Sailor Man!" the cartoon figure would sing, in some weird dialect that seemed to invoke New England whalers, street types in Brooklyn, or Irish immigrants, and then he'd pump up his biceps and take a puff on his pipe. Lee himself spoke in a dialect that Vinson associated with New England or Brooklyn, saying things like "give me dat" or "dis," and that confirmed his tough guy status because it reminded Vinson of gangster movies. But, of course, Lee was from New Orleans, and later, when Vinson found that out, he figured that that was probably the source of the accent. But maybe the embellishments were all part of Lee making himself up as he went along, one can now say in retrospect: a little of this, a little of that, and of course pretending was not so unusual for a child his age.

Of course, pretending would become something that defined Lee; it was just what he did, until the pretending merged with real aspects of his true personality and it became hard to tell the difference, even for himself. In fact, when he began getting into trouble in New York, he was diagnosed as having various behavioral disorders, including early signs of schizophrenia. We can look to these early years as a time when this began to take shape. He was one of those people who preferred his own company, and alone with himself he could brew and fester. Even in spite of being a kind of gang leader, he did not hang out with other boys off the playground, and he had no friends that anyone remembers. One thing he loved to do during his elementary school years was listen to *Let's Pretend* on the radio, and later, when Marguerite bought her first television and Lee had become a teenager, he would watch *I Led Three Lives*.

Let's Pretend—with the tagline of "radio's outstanding children's theater"—was broadcast every Saturday from a studio in Duluth, and across the land kids tuned in for one of the most popular shows of the era. It was prefaced by the well-known cereal jingle for Cream of Wheat ("Oh cream of wheat / it's so good to eat") and hosted by a genial character named GI Judy (the show had started during World War II, and there were plenty of patriotic references and acknowledgment of players who had joined the service or just returned). The show offered classic fairy tales such as "Cinderella," "Jack and the Beanstalk," and "The Enchanted Frog," presented by a cast known as Uncle Bill and the Pretenders. "Are you ready for another fun-filled show?" a narrator asked the boys and girls who were assembled in the studio in that sincere, old-time radio voice that enthralled millions, including the young Lee Harvey Oswald. Yes! came the response and cheers, and then Uncle Bill would say something like "once upon a time," and the play would begin. Each character came to life with vivid voice portrayals, including horses and ducks and turtles, and for a certain time on Saturday afternoons, a lot of parents found comfort in the fact that their kids were not running around with "riffraff out there," to use the day's vernacular, but sitting before the radio and listening to *Let's Pretend*.

Lee's devotion to *Let's Pretend* is hardly ever mentioned in commentary about him, even though it's the understory, or one of them, for much of his life. During the week between shows, he would pretend to be one of the characters in the previous episode, and his brothers, or John at least, was his audience and he often spoke of how intently Lee acted the parts. On the other hand, the TV show *I Led Three Lives* is frequently cited—and not just because it's interesting background.

I Led Three Lives was based on the book of the same name written by Herbert A. Philbrick about his real-life adventures during the Cold War when he was first an ad executive, then an FBI agent who had infiltrated the Communist Party and become a figure of influence who then reported back to American intelligence operatives. It was a sensational book published in 1952 portraying the underbelly of international espionage in a time when Russia and the United States were locked in a battle for world domination, and when there was talk of Russia invading America either for real or by way of spies who were said to be lurking everywhere. These fears heated up during the Red Scare of the 1950s with Congressman Joseph R. McCarthy cooking up a list of names, including prominent citizens, that led to hearings in which the representative shook his fist at the accused and shouted, "Are you now or have you ever been a member of the Communist Party?" The series based on this book first aired in 1953, and it was in the vein of *Dragnet* or *Highway Patrol*, opening with a scary music sting that blasts you out of your seat and followed by the interruption of a menacing voice: "This is the story of a man who spent nine frightening years living three lives fighting the secret enemies of our country who often attempt to hide behind our respected institutions. In a moment," he says, "you will see the Communist Party attempt their deadly subterfuge on a college student." Now the series is high camp, worthy of an *Ed Wood*–style remake with Tim Burton directing (if only Russians hadn't already recently entered through the front door via Donald Trump and his presidency, this time on a different side of the American equation). At the time, however, *I Led Three Lives* was deadly serious, and one can see how the teenage Lee Harvey Oswald, already appropriating bits and pieces of personas from cartoons and the Wild West and his older brothers, who were Marines, got caught up in the drama. "Hey, let's pretend!" was the message. "You too can head off the bad guys at the pass."

Did Lee Harvey Oswald, in fact, lead three lives? The question has propelled various conspiracy theories, and the answer is he did, and maybe more but probably just one, and whether one or many, they were in service not to shadow agencies but to his own inner directives, memos, and urgings.

Outside of Lee's fantasy world, drama on the home front was escalating. "The hand that holds the money cracks the whip," Mildred Pierce had said, but for Marguerite, the prospect of continuing to live with the wayward Ed Ekdahl finally outweighed the fear of having no means of financial support. And it wasn't just the support, a small allowance of one hundred dollars per month, but to Marguerite, it was something. She would also be giving up a lifestyle that she and Ed enjoyed when they traveled together on his business trips. "We lived in the finest hotels," she later said. "We had the finest food. It was all charged to my husband's expense account." That was a new experience for Marguerite, and it told her that she mattered. The pending loss of such affirmation must have made her very needy, creating a situation or conversations in which she continually sought out something, anything, that kept her at sea level. When John and Robert came home for Christmas that year, 1947, it was not a festive time at all in the Ekdahl household. Ed was absent, and when he showed up later, Marguerite followed through on her plan and told him to leave. She soon consulted a lawyer about how to proceed, but the following spring, she received a surprise notice: Ed was the one who actually filed for divorce. "I was 'sitting pretty,'" she later said. "I had him on adultery and everything. I didn't have any idea that he could sue me for a divorce."

Divorce proceedings shake out in all manner of styles. Sometimes they are routine, with each party simply identifying themselves after being sworn in, agreeing to the problem or problems asserted by the other party, working out terms of the separation, and calling it a day. Other times the proceedings are violent, with one or the other party assaulting the partner who has allegedly done wrong, going after the judge, or making a move on the bailiffs. In this case, the proceedings were sordid and shabby, maybe with some histrionics or rage here and there, but nothing that required the judge to gavel anyone down, nothing that stands out in the record as alarming. The strange thing about the proceedings between Edwin and Marguerite was that there was a jury trial—an unusual occurrence in such matters. What happened was the fear of finding herself without support was so great that Marguerite ended up contesting the divorce. And at the time of this trial, there was no such thing as "believe all women." There was not even such a thing as "believe some women."

The jury was comprised of twelve men. The cards were stacked against Marguerite, and regardless of the tenor of the times, she didn't have much in her favor. Yes, Ed had been messing around with other women. It was true that she "had him on adultery." But he had some legitimate complaints. Plus, she was now on the defensive, having to respond to his quest for divorce. The record is mostly spare, but from the language in the verdict, there seems to have been testimony regarding cruelty and physical violence on the part of Marguerite towards her husband. He said that Marguerite once threw a bottle at his head and another time scratched and hit him. Marguerite herself alleged violence, as her son John Pic later recalled, testifying that "if Ekdahl ever hit her again, she'd have to send me in there to beat him up, something I doubt that I could have done." John too was called as a witness—for which side it is not clear—but later told members of the Warren Commission that he didn't remember much of his testimony. Strangely, although underage, Lee was also called to testify, and in language that sounds as if supplied by a lawyer, he said that "he wouldn't know right from wrong or the truth from a falsehood," and he was excused.

At some point, in the words of Marguerite, "a very big businessman" took the witness stand to testify on behalf of Ekdahl. This was George Levine, an associate of Ed's through his job. Marguerite had met him just once, she said, when she and her husband and Lee had gone out to dinner with him, and then to the circus afterwards. He relayed how Marguerite nagged Ed. The term "nag" was loaded at the time, more so than nowadays, and judging from the verdict, there were other allegations that constituted something more menacing: "excesses, cruel treatment, or outrages," meaning physical violence, as well as "conduct, demeanor and language of one party toward the other of such a cruel nature as to affect the mind or sensibilities of the other to such a degree as to affect the physical welfare of the person subjected to such conduct."

From the record, it's not clear whether Marguerite was able to recount Ed's adultery at trial. Somewhere along the way, she had learned that the woman in the negligee was the one he was living with during their earlier separation. In the end, the jury found her guilty of the charges, and the culpability was sufficient to render their living together "insupportable." Aside from Marguerite herself, the only other person who might have been able to refute Edwin's claims was Lee, and of course that did not happen. One suspects that Marguerite's lawyer did not want him to testify because what he had witnessed of the tribulations between his mother and stepfather would corroborate Ed's claims. Or perhaps he himself really did—at the age of nine—decide that testifying in this trial would have been too much to handle. Whoever made the decision, or however it was made, it seems to have been the right one. Can you imagine what would have happened if Lee had been questioned by his stepfather's attorney? "Young man, did you ever see your mother throw anything at Mr. Ekdahl? Yell at and berate him?" Even if Marguerite's lawyer had countered with a cross-examination that reversed course, helped him recover from having to answer those questions in public, before his mother, the experience would have caused considerable damage for the young boy—and he was already in serious trouble.

In the end, Marguerite was awarded a paltry sum: a final settlement of $1,500 and $250 for attorney fees. Once more, her fears were confirmed, and she and her sons would move again. This time it was to a much less desirable neighborhood and a house that was very small. As John would tell the Warren Commission, they were "right back in the lower class again"—a place from which escape options seemed to diminish as time went by. For the boys, it would soon be the military, which provided a steady and respectable income, the idea that you were part of a team, and, perhaps most importantly, the adherence to the family legacy of serving in the armed forces. It is human nature to live inside a story; this we know because when stripped of their stories, people and cultures wither and die. For two of the Oswalds, Robert and Lee, bearing the name "Robert E. Lee" on your own in one way or another carried a lot of weight, don't forget, and once back in New Orleans, they were surrounded everywhere by reminders of their heritage. For instance, there was Robert E. Lee Square, Robert E. Lee Boulevard, and the Robert E. Lee Monument in the middle of Lee Circle, the most imposing of memorials. It was a large bronze statue of the Confederate general astride a horse atop a marble pedestal, and it presided over the city. If you carried the same name as the man in the saddle, there was a subtext that you lived inside of a real-life fable that was always with you; when someone met you for the first time, hearing your name generally impressed them, and it was said that young Lee liked telling people where his name came from, not its connection with his father and brother, necessarily, but its conveyance of

American history—and that meant that he mattered.

John and Robert would later tell investigators and anyone else who asked that the divorce of Marguerite and Ed clearly took its toll on young Lee. Having a father figure in the house, someone who served as a role model and guide, a provider of fun and adventures—ice cream! road trips!—was something that served as a center of gravity. As we see in far too many instances today, such figures are absent from the lives of many boys and young men, and girls as well. In the wake of this absence has come an endless wave of violence in many forms— unchecked aggression, pervasive cruelty, mass shootings—and there is no better cautionary tale of this than Lee Harvey Oswald. In our close look at the young man who has long been portrayed as an American cipher, we can see exactly what happens when certain circumstances are present in a family, and then personal pathology is both formed and amplified by those circumstances, at which point the language of the national mantra becomes the costume in which it all travels—"It's a free country, I know my rights"—which Lee began uttering as an excuse and storyline as early as sixth grade.

BACK AT CHAMBERLAIN-HUNT FOLLOWING THE divorce of Ed and Marguerite, John and Robert were expecting to spend the summer there. They liked the school and by this time, in spite of the upheavals at home, had more or less settled in. Most of the boys had already left, Robert recalled, and he was packing up various school items, including some old Springfield rifles, for storage. He and John received another surprise visit from Marguerite. This time, it wasn't for a vacation in Covington; although they'd be leaving again, it was to head back to Fort Worth. "I just can't pay the tuition anymore," Marguerite said, telling the boys something they were actually expecting, but were hoping would somehow change and they could stay in Port Gibson until they graduated from military school.

The small house in the lower-class neighborhood of Fort Worth that Marguerite had rented was next to the railroad tracks. It was "drab and closed-in," Robert recalled. "The train tracks were about sixty or seventy yards behind the house, so the furniture would rattle every time a train passed by." Soon after the brothers had returned, Marguerite bought another house in Benbrook, the area where the family had lived before with Ed Ekdahl. On a remote rural road that didn't have a name (later it became San Saba Street), this was a small house with just one bedroom, "pleasant enough," Robert said. He and John shared a screened-in porch, where they slept on studio couches, and Marguerite and Lee shared the bedroom. There has been much talk over the years about the effect that sharing a bed with his mother had on the young boy. This situation would continue until he was ten years old. While this bedroom arrangement happened out of economic necessity, it's noteworthy that Marguerite didn't set up the space such that there were two single beds. Perhaps she liked having the company—not in a sexual sense, but strictly in the sense of "there's someone sleeping next to me, and it's a warm body, and he happens to be my son." But for Lee, who had already demonstrated that he liked being alone, this had to have been an unwelcome experience. It meant that while at home, he had little time to himself, could not regroup at night from the day's activities, could not lie in bed reading, for example, or not comfortably, at least, could not listen to the radio—things he liked to do, according to the recollections of those around him—lest he disturb his mother, someone with a volatile temperament who was easily provoked or roiled. Perhaps this became a time when he regressed further into his fantasy life, imagining himself as characters on *Let's Pretend* (which he did anyway, acting out moments from that show between episodes as theater for his brothers). Perhaps it drove a wedge between him and his mother, causing him to shut down and go into a deep sleep, not at ease in such close proximity to the woman who smothered him with love as compensation for the disdain and disapproval that was the opposite of that equation. However it shook out, it was not healthy, the kind of thing that psychiatrists generally cite as a negative contributor to a young boy's sense of self.

At some point during their stay in this house, the family acquired a dog named Blackie. Marguerite was working at Leonard Brothers Department Store, a respected emporium in Fort Worth that was kind of an early Walmart, selling groceries, fresh produce, dry goods, medicinal items, hardware, auto supplies, and seeds. During the Depression, the Leonard brothers, the store's owners, offered check cashing and low-priced bread. When the banks were closed, they continued to cash checks, offering Leonards' Scrip for cash, and local merchants accepted this cash as payment for goods and services, and sooner or later they shopped at Leonard Brothers, redistributing the wealth. At a time when cash was scarce, this was one of the things that kept Fort Worth afloat; the store's practices were exactly the kind of thing that Huey P. Long was trying to bring about in Louisiana—a fair shake for the common man. By the time Marguerite worked there, the store was selling furniture and appliances and had added air-conditioning, a welcome feature for Fort Worth summers, along with a second floor. When this new part of the store opened on September 1, 1948, you could take the escalator to get there. The moving stairway was the first one in the city, so noteworthy that a piece of it is now featured in Leonard's Museum, a shrine to the superstore. On one Saturday alone shortly after it was unveiled, forty thousand customers rode the escalator, perhaps waited on by Marguerite Oswald. Unbeknownst to shoppers, getting to work was an ordeal for this beleaguered mother (although it's quite possible that if anyone struck up a conversation, she'd find a way to tell them). Often her ten-year-old car wasn't working, and she would task the boys with flagging down neighbors to help push it into the street and give it a jump start.

Other times, she would get a ride to and from work, and at Leonard's she may have once again deployed the deferential "Welcome Wagon" voice, *"Nice to see you in Leonard's Department Store! We have a special on sewing machines today! And Black Angus steaks!"*

The steady job at Leonard's did little to tamp down Marguerite's edge. She often complained to a neighbor that "society was against her," and that it was hard for a widow—harking back to her first marriage—to make enough money for her family. Moreover, observed the neighbor, Lee did not take well to discipline. And the older brothers got along better with other neighborhood kids than Lee did. One night, according to Bugliosi's *Reclaiming History*, Marguerite asked another neighbor to come over and estimate what her house was worth, in case she might want to sell it. Although he was a teacher, not a realtor, she insisted that he make a ballpark guess; sitting in the living room and looking around, he told her $2,750 for the house and lot. (Apparently Marguerite said, "I'll take it," for he soon bought the house.) Strangely, amid the conversation about the worth of her property, Lee was chasing John through the kitchen door with a butcher knife. He threw the knife at John but hit the wall instead. It was almost a cartoon scenario in which the main action is in the foreground but Yosemite Sam is chasing Bugs Bunny in the background, but a real weapon was used. "Oh, they have these scuffles all the time," Marguerite said. "Don't worry about it."

Perhaps she was offering the advice that she herself followed. From the time of her divorce and the many moves that followed it, there was a series of moments and acts involving Lee—all cause for minor or even major alarm—that she constantly excused. Maybe she was secretly concerned, but if so, it didn't last long; once there was any hint of a problem with Lee's behavior, gaslighting and obfuscation would take over and a dark mother-son cloud front would emerge, not according to an agreed-upon plan, but according to the Marguerite

Oswald playbook in which she was always the victim—of course!—
unless the victim was Lee—which of course he always was—at which
point she would hold him accountable for nothing, and that was how
she displayed affection. What a conundrum that was for the young
boy, even if he didn't know that he was afflicted in such a manner.
*What must I do to win my mother's love? I can't do THAT again. I'm
sure something will come along . . . it always does.*

On February 21, 1964, three months after JFK was assassinated,
Life magazine published its widely circulated issue with the infamous
photo of Lee with his rifle and handgun on the cover. This was the
first time that image had been presented so prominently, in one central
location, to millions of people. The headline said, "LEE OSWALD
with the weapons he used to kill President Kennedy and Officer
Tippit." The accompanying piece blazed the trail for the deluge of
Oswald reporting that was to come, relaying details on a national
level about Oswald, his family, and people who could shed light on
Lee and Marguerite's behavior, which had been attracting attention
long before the President was killed. A Fort Worth neighbor who lived
three doors down from the Oswalds in the Ridglea district when Lee
was nine told the reporter, Donald Jackson, that Lee was "quite vi-
cious with other children," becoming angry at very little provocation.
"I saw him chuck things at other kids several times," the neighbor said,
and his wife added that she "didn't think he was anything but a high-
tempered kid." There was also an accountant who lived nearby and
seems to have readily issued an opinion. "I'll tell you the way I got
acquainted with that little squirt," he told Jackson:

> I came home from work one day and picked up the phone. It was
> dead. I figured what the hell, so I asked into the receiver if anyone
> was on the phone. A kid's voice says, "You're goddamn right
> there's someone on the line." This stopped me for a minute, then

> I asked the kid if he'd mind releasing the line. So he says to me,
> "I'll release it when I'm damn good and ready." Well, naturally, I
> was a little burned . . . my wife told me it was the Oswalds on
> our party line. I knew them slightly—every single night she'd
> get off the bus at my corner and walk across my lawn. Well, this
> night I stopped her and told her what happened. She asked me to
> quote exactly what was said and I did. She said, "I don't believe
> Lee would say anything like that." Then Lee walked up and said,
> "What's the matter, Mother?" She told him that I had accused
> him of using profanity on the telephone. She asked him what
> about it and he denied it. So then she said, "I guess you must be
> mistaken, Mr. Simmons."

He was not mistaken; in fact he knew "damn well" that it was Lee on the phone. That was his first and last contact with Lee Harvey Oswald. And then one day the reporter from *Life* came calling and it all came back to him, clear as a bell.

And then there was Mrs. Clyde Livingston, Lee's first teacher at Ridglea West Elementary School. In the words of the *Life* reporter, Mrs. Livingston was "warm and lively," and had taken a special interest in Lee. "Lee left an empty home in the morning," she said, "went home to an empty home for lunch, and returned to an empty home at night. I once asked him if his mother left a lunch for him, and he said, 'No, but I can open a can of soup as well as anyone.'" You never know how the adjustments we all make in childhood prepare the way for whatever comes up in life. Perhaps Lee's early lessons were good training for the Marines (and he eagerly read the handbook before enlisting years later). Or maybe they served as groundwork for Russia, to which he would later defect (although when he returned, one of the things he complained about was the limited range of food there). In any case, his house was kind of like boot camp or Communism:

rations were doled out, only, in this case, he got to boss around the person in charge because she felt guilty about the conditions.

Sometime during the Benbrook period of Oswald's life, when he was about nine years old, his next-door neighbor Mary Smith became his babysitter. Mary was married with several children, and she was at home every day. Her husband was in the Air Force, stationed at the nearby Carswell base, the same one that JFK would visit the day before he was killed. Marguerite was then working at Stripling's, another department store (though it's not clear from the record at which store or exactly when she was working at them during those years, and of course people's memories differ when it comes to such details; some were interviewed many years after encountering Marguerite and her family). But with Mary Smith, we can be sure of where Marguerite was working because she used to drive her neighbor to work and pick her up every day, taking care of young Lee, who walked over to her house when Marguerite was leaving and going home when she returned. On those twice-a-day trips, Mary got to know Marguerite pretty well. For the fiftieth anniversary of the JFK assassination, she was interviewed by Stephen Fagin for the Sixth Floor Museum in Dallas, the site of the book depository where Oswald was working when he shot the President. How strange the feeling was, she acknowledged, to have such a conversation at the very site of the terrible act committed by the grown-up boy she once tried to nurture. She recalled Marguerite as "overbearing" and "not a pleasant person." Her neighbor's presentation was one of "poor me"; she had trouble paying bills and complained of having no support from the fathers of her children (though let us recall that she was in fact receiving support for John Pic from his father Edward, unbeknownst to John himself until he was eighteen). Marguerite was very focused on herself and was "not the kind of person who would say thank you for the ride" or for any help at all, ever. Almost every interaction was beyond transactional; the exchange was generally one-way. What's in it for me? was the prevailing question, and the answer was never enough. In terms of Oswald family dynamics, Mary never saw any affection from Marguerite towards her sons, or the boys for each other; in fact, they fought a lot, knocking down furniture, with Lee often instigating the altercations. The Oswald house kind of reflected the chaos; it was messy, Mary said, and she added that "there wasn't that much food."

Further deepening the story of Lee Harvey Oswald are indicators of a serious problem. "He was different than a typical boy that age," she recalled, as others have observed as well. "He couldn't sit still. He was quiet. He was a loner." Yet there was something of greater concern. "He had an inner meanness in his body and his mind," she remembered. "He never showed emotions other than anger. He always seemed to want to destroy things." One day, he knocked on her door and, when she opened it, he said, "Look what I did," and he was brandishing a handful of rose bushes. The bushes were a gift from Mary's husband, and she had planted them in their yard. Mary told Lee not to do it again, and then she told Marguerite what Lee had done, and Marguerite in turn said nothing. But that was minor compared to another aggressive act of Lee's. As per their daily program, Lee was in her house, and one of Mary's children, a newborn, was in a bassinet. "I caught him spraying the baby's eyes with deodorant," Mary recalled, and she then took the baby to Carswell for treatment. The baby recovered, has good eyes, and today is a pilot for American Airlines. The incident became something of a family joke; Mary's sons told her that she was the worst babysitter in the world.

Was Lee reenacting in some way what his babysitters had done to him when he was two or three and they whipped him on his legs until he had welts? Of course, we do not know, but such is the beginning of patterns. Perhaps more importantly, there do not seem to have been any consequences for him, or any that we know of, beyond an internal response to the reality of what happened and its reverberation over the years, especially when combined with the myriad of other disruptions, and when Marguerite and her boys moved yet again, Mary was happy to see them go. Or Marguerite, at least; she was "always asking for things," Mary said. Yet Mary maintained a fondness for the older brothers; John was handsome and Robert was kind. In their next neighborhood, a friend of Mary's became Lee's babysitter, and the pattern of behaviors may have repeated in one way or another. What stories that friend has, or may have had, are lost to the ages; she passed away some time ago.

Written just three months after the assassination, the momentous *Life* magazine article preserved a number of other recollections from Oswald's classmates and teachers about his years in elementary and junior high school. At the fourth-grade class party in 1949, Lee surprised his teacher, Mrs. Livingston, with the gift of a puppy, the offspring of the family dog, and her name was Lady. He would visit on weekends to see how she was faring, though Mrs. Livingston suspected that he was coming over for another reason. "He'd stay around and talk"—but not very much. He seemed to crave the company. In class, his interest turned towards girls. He was interested in a little girl named Nancy, and Mrs. Livingston seated him next to her, hoping that he would stop being so messy. The strategy seemed to work; he slicked his hair down and straightened up his desk. At some point, her attention was drawn to another boy. In subsequent grades, one admirer recalled that Lee "had muscles" and "was strong." Another asked him to kiss her while they were walking home. But there was another girl with them whom Lee preferred, and he ended up kissing them both. Once he wrote a love note to a classmate named Pat. She wasn't interested, and he "hated" her back. In other words, in some ways, he seemed to be doing all right; he liked puppies and girls in the usual ways, and his actions around them showed some attempt to get beyond the world of "let's pretend" and into actual contact with those who could return affection.

The boys who were his schoolmates recalled that in class he was sometimes "brash," although the behavior some reported suggests "class clown" might be a better description. "Sometimes he'd scoot his desk chair across the floor to the pencil sharpener," one said, "just to get attention. Of course, the kids would snicker and the teacher would get mad." Other boys spoke of his dominance when they played ball and in other activities, or his predilection for starting brawls. In retaliation, Oswald was roughed up by classmates one day and there was another pile-on, according to Joe Shannon, now the district attorney of Fort Worth. He still has a scarred knuckle to show for it—along with his third-grade class photo with Lee. "He fought dirty," another boy remembered. "He was pinching and biting, but Lee would have licked me anyway." Strangely, just as the fight was breaking up, Marguerite arrived, and started to laugh. "She was real proud of him," the boy said, and that seems to have wrapped up the episode.

Over the years, a number of other Fort Worth residents have come forth with tales of Lee Harvey Oswald. After all, he lived there for nine years, counting the period that followed his return from Russia when he landed right smack-dab in the heart of the Wild West. Marguerite herself is remembered by many; she was the nanny to the children of a parade of local residents, one of the various jobs that was part of her occupational resume—and one of the only ways that she came into contact with those who were well-off, a situation that fueled her ongoing resentment. "Every Fort Worth native has a personal story about [Lee Harvey Oswald] or his overbearing and manipulative mother," wrote reporter Bud Kennedy in the *Star-Telegram* on a recent anniversary of the JFK assassination. "This is mine."

> In 1966, when I was eleven, my wallet was stolen at what is now
> Stripling Middle School in the Arlington Heights neighborhood.
> A woman who lived nearby called our house and said that it had
> been tossed in her yard. I bicycled to her home on Byers Avenue
> and thanked her. 'Your name is Kennedy?' she asked, peering
> sternly through the door, and I nodded. She did not smile as she
> said, "Well—I'm Mrs. Oswald."

Why the name "Kennedy" would elicit a response from Marguerite Oswald is plain to see. But there was more to it than mere mention of the name. This encounter occurred three years after the assassination, and it may have aggravated her paranoia. By then she was deeply embroiled in trying to prove her son's innocence, and she was touring the country with attorney Mark Lane as they both advanced the theory that Oswald had been set up as the fall guy for a cavalcade of nefarious players who dwelled in the shadows.

In his memoir about his brother Lee, Robert wrote that there was always something eating away at Marguerite, the feeling that an unnamable person or pair of eyes or god knows what was around the next corner. At some point during Lee's high school years, when Marguerite had moved yet again, he tried out for the Yellow Jackets junior varsity football team at Arlington Heights High School. One day during practice, the coach told him to start running wind sprints, and he refused. "I don't have to," he said. "It's a free country." He was kicked off the team, and the only repercussion that can be discerned is that he now had a new story of defiance to add to his growing repertoire. It invoked the thing that Marguerite would often speak of when it came to how Lee was treated following the assassination in his two remaining days and in the aftermath of his execution by Jack Ruby. It was all about a violation of rights, and it proved once again that someone or something was out to get the Oswald family, especially

Marguerite and her youngest son, Lee. Is it any wonder that in the immediate hours following the death of JFK when she and Robert and Marina—Lee's widow—were held in custody by the FBI at a motel in Fort Worth that she had a bayonet in her suitcase?

Yet this story is racing ahead of itself, by several road trips, including a few to various other addresses in Fort Worth, and one that in the annals of American migrations must be one of the strangest to have ever transpired. Around fourth or fifth grade, amid the ongoing moves and general turmoil, it appeared that Lee was becoming more agitated. Once again, Marguerite was running out of money—a subject that was discussed at least once on any given day for as long as the boys could remember. It was time yet again to relocate. But where? And when? The answer would present itself as it always did, but how long could she hold out? One day in 1950, August 15, to be precise, in violation of the rule to only call Marguerite at work if it was an emergency, Lee phoned her to report some big news: Queen Elizabeth had just had a baby—an important person has been born!—and of course the fact that he was relaying the news would make him important in her eyes. And so, the time had come—a new address awaited her arrival, if only she knew what it was, exactly, but without a doubt an upgrade was in the cards; she and Lee should live where royals lived, and over the next few months, there came an answer. Marguerite's eldest son John Pic had enlisted in the Coast Guard and was stationed on Ellis Island—away from his mother at last! Robert had dropped out of school at seventeen like his mother, was working as a checker in a supermarket and giving most of his salary to her for household expenses and getting ready to join the Marines. With John and Robert no longer under her care, there was no better way for Marguerite to start over—to heed the calling—than to visit John and his wife and their baby in the Bronx where they were living—in New York City, home of our very own royals—so she and Lee packed up a few things, piled into her 1948

Dodge, and hit the road. Using the Savodnik math, they had just left the home that was their thirteenth address, joining the parade of no-mads without end, entering the stream of American zen, moving fast through time and space and really going nowhere.

"Lee Harvey"—yes, that's what she and the boys sometimes called him—*"when we get to New York, we'll show everyone"* is what I imagine her saying, and here is a mash-up of some things that are real and some things that are reality based; I'm pretty sure this is how it went between Mother and son: *"I'm going to show you everything like it's nobody's busi-ness, and it will be a thing to remember . . . " And they did go to the Museum of Natural History with John as their guide, wandering through the Hall of Minerals or dinosaur exhibit and marveling at the wonders, and then went on to Rockefeller Center where the rich people worked on the upper levels and The Today Show was televised with the chimpanzee sidekick J. Fred Muggs and all of the famous people came to talk about their accomplishments; "maybe someday you'll be on that show too, son, I'll be watching!" and then they probably ordered the lobster at the exclusive restaurant on the top floor and Marguerite promised that they'd come back someday and see the Christmas tree that was world-renowned and all of the beautiful ice skaters, princesses, after all, and then it was on to other popular locales; they went to the automat and watched the food whiz by, and they did walk down Fifth Avenue and look in store windows, which prompted Marguerite to remark, "Of course, we'll never have anything like that; only rich people do, and they don't like us, do they Lee Harvey?"*

"Of course they don't, Maw"—for that's what the boys called Marguerite, Maw—*"we're not like them. We're different than everyone else,"* and then perhaps there was a moment of responsive recitation, a duet of sorts—

MARGUERITE: Where did we grow up?
LEE: South of the Mason-Dixon Line.

MARGUERITE: And why don't people like us?

LEE: Because we don't have any money.

MARGUERITE: That's right, son. But this will change soon.
When we get to the Big Apple and take our bite. Oh the places
we'll go. Everyone will be so jealous. They will worship us
when they find out how well we are doing. Won't they, Lee
Harvey?

LEE: Yes they will, Maw.

MARGUERITE: Now repeat after me . . . I'm special.

LEE: I'm special.

MARGUERITE: There's no one else like me.

LEE: There's no one else like me.

MARGUERITE: The world is my oyster.

LEE: The world is my oyster.

MARGUERITE: And we're going to be just like the
Rockefellers and live like kings.

LEE: Maw, that's weird.

MARGUERITE: Say it, Lee Harvey.

LEE: We're going to be just like the Rockefellers and live like
kings.

And then maybe he fell asleep as the car headed through the night,
with Eddie Fisher and Patti Page on the radio and Frankie Laine,
too, and Frankie was singing "High Noon," which Lee Harvey would
whistle hours before he whacked John Fitzgerald Kennedy, and on the
car went towards the Big Apple where all of the fancy people lived
and experienced fine dining every night of their goddamn lives and
then somebody would turn down the sheets on their beds just like in
the movies.

But when they got there, the understory prevailed, and here are
some things that really happened: Lee attacked his sister-in-law with

a knife and started hitting Marguerite, and Marguerite got a job selling notions on Canal Street. The upper levels of society became more
unreachable than ever and Lee Harvey Oswald found refuge in the
subways and the zoo, where he seemed to find a modicum of contentment. In spite of the chaos, there was a moment when an intervention
involving psychiatrists and social workers was almost at hand and the
tragedy at the end of his path might have been dodged.

Marguerite had not seen John for two years when she and Lee
arrived at the apartment at 325 East 92nd Street where John, his
wife Margaret, and their baby boy, John Edward Pic, Jr., were living.
Things did not get off to a good start, with Marguerite and Lee, now
thirteen, walking in with a number of suitcases. The original plan was
for a brief family reunion in which Marguerite would get to meet her
new grandson. Now it seemed like she was up to her old tricks; maybe.
she was planning a long visit, or, something that John Pic absolutely
did not want, a move that would bring her into close proximity, let
alone into his own dwelling, which wasn't really his anyway; it belonged to his mother-in-law, who was away on vacation.

"On their first day," Robert wrote in his book about Lee, "Mother
came out of her room crying." She said that Lee had slapped her when
she asked him to look out the window to check on the car. Now the
fact that there was violence inside the family had begun to leak out,
past Lee's babysitter and her family in Fort Worth and anyone else
who saw Lee's brawling on playgrounds, which was not something
that in and of itself would send up a red flag, though some people
had taken note. John conveyed the story of this slap to the Warren
Commission years later, and it did come to serve among mental health
experts as an indicator of what was coming. When Robert's book
about Lee was published a couple of years after the Warren Report, he
responded to the view that had emerged. "I had never seen Lee strike
Mother," he wrote, "but I don't think I would have been alarmed by

his behavior. Knowing how Mother could nag, I think I would have assumed that she goaded him into slapping her." It wasn't the first time that Lee would slap Marguerite. Throughout their visit, there were other such eruptions, and, one presumes, they continued when they moved into their own succession of places in New York.

John's wife Marge, meeting Marguerite for the first time, was of course made to feel uncomfortable in her own apartment, forced to act as hostess for physically battling in-laws and carrying out the related tasks: preparing meals for them, making sure that a welcoming atmosphere prevailed—or at least not something that would ruin what was supposed to be a happy reunion. She was just eighteen and taking care of a baby, after all. And sure enough, there came no indication of a departure date for Marguerite and Lee, and this further added to Marge's discomfort.

Yet in spite of the disturbance in the household, the reunion between Lee and John was at first a good one. John took some time off from work, and the brothers went for a ride on the Staten Island Ferry, to Lee's delight, and they partook of other things that New York offered: a trip to the top of the Empire State Building, a visit to the Natural History Museum, and stops at other wonders of the city. Back in the apartment, Lee "enjoyed playing uncle," Robert wrote. "Marge said he was very gentle with the baby and could be genuinely helpful around the house." This aspect of Lee again manifests later when he has his own wife and baby; by all accounts, he doted on the little girl June Lee, who was born in Russia and was five months old when he returned to America with her and his wife Marina.

Still, none of this was enough to quell the hostility that was escalating. With the arrival of Lee and Marguerite, John was now supporting five people on a Coast Guardsman's salary, Robert wrote, not to mention "paying his own daily transportation to and from Ellis Island and trying to provide a few treats for the visitors. The money disappeared so fast that he hardly had time to put it in his pocket. Mother had made no offer to help with expenses, and when John casually mentioned the budget problem to her, she blew up."

As always, this became another situation permitting Marguerite to play the victim and deflect attention from what the aggrieved parties were trying to address by placing them on the defensive. From the very beginning, she would say later, she and Lee were not wanted. As soon as they set foot in the house, her daughter-in-law asked what they planned to do. Marguerite insisted that she had made it very clear to John Edward that the idea was to get her own place and that she and Lee were just stopping temporarily. But "she made no move to find an apartment or a job," Robert wrote, "and began talking about enrolling Lee in the school there in the neighborhood."

And then came the incident that we might call "the thing with the knife." It is repeated over and over in the annals of Oswald coverage, as well it should be, yet it has various iterations. They range from not that big of a deal to something that could have led to a serious injury. Regardless of how the story appears in the record, it was one of those moments that people have looked to over the years as a demarcation, a precursor of much more violent behavior, a more direct hit than slapping. Anything that involves a knife and a personal attack is seriously problematic on its face, for it involves direct contact with something that can cause fatal damage, and the person wielding the instrument has no fear of getting up close and personal with rage and anger; all boundaries have been crossed.

One afternoon, John came home from work and the household was in an uproar, Robert reports. Lee had been watching television, Marge had told John, and she asked him to turn it down. Instead, he pulled out a pocketknife and opened the blade, making a move for Marge. Frightened, she moved away, possibly calling for Marguerite, who immediately responded. When she told Lee to put the knife away, he hit her. When John entered in the immediate aftermath of this scene, Marguerite dismissed it, telling him that it was "just a little argument. Lee had been whittling," she said, and therefore was using the knife. Maybe Marge misunderstood when she saw it and thought that Lee was threatening her, so she reacted accordingly. Weighing both sides of the story, John believed his wife, but asked Lee to recount his version. "He wouldn't talk to him," Robert wrote, Lee apparently feeling from then on that everybody was against him, an echo of his mother's prevailing worldview. "He began keeping more and more to himself," Robert added, "refusing to talk with anybody." John told him that he was never able to get to the kid again.

But that's just one version of the story. There's another one that's far more menacing, and it surfaced later, when the various involved parties, namely Marguerite and John Pic, testified before the Warren Commission. It goes like this. Marguerite and Marge were arguing over the television set, the story went, but it was really about who mattered more to John: his mother or his wife. Marguerite enlisted Lee, who pulled out a pocketknife. That's what John told investigators, and Marguerite herself relayed it this way, taking advantage of the moment to blow a smoke screen—or a negative personality profile—regarding her daughter-in-law: Margy, as she called her, "didn't like me," she said, "and she didn't like Lee. So she—what is the word to say—not picked on the child, but she showed her displeasure. And she is a very—not, I would say so much an emotional person—but this girl is a New Yorker who was brought up in this particular neighborhood, which I believe is a poor section of New York . . . And this girl cursed like a trooper. She is—you cannot express it, Mr. Rankin—but not of a character of a high caliber."

Marguerite further elaborated that the whole thing was Margy's fault. Yes, Lee had a knife, a pocketknife, not a kitchen knife as was suggested; after all, he was whittling with John. They were carving little ships out of wood blocks and the chips fell to the floor. Margy was upset about the mess, and "she hit Lee," Marguerite said, and "now, I remember this distinctly, because I remember how awful I thought Marjory was . . . Lee did not use the knife," adding that he could have—with the underlying suggestion that he was actually not a menace but a magnanimous fellow who had refrained from responding to a personal and physical attack from someone who should know better. Marguerite did not mention the television set, or, more importantly, that Lee had hit her—and thus are family patterns concealed and advanced. It was shortly after the knife dispute that Marguerite and Lee moved out. Marguerite had gotten a job as assistant manager at one of the Lerner Shops, the chain for which she briefly worked in Fort Worth, and found an apartment in the Bronx at 1455 Sheridan Avenue, just off the Grand Concourse. It was one big room in a basement, Robert reported, and Lee hated it. Soon there came another move, to a larger apartment in a five-story building at 825 East 179th Street, just south of the Bronx Zoo. "For the first time in his life," Robert made a point of noting, "Lee had a room of his own."

But that may have been too late to head off any further troublesome behavior; privacy is just not something that cures deep-seated problems, although it was a nice idea. In October of 1952, after having attended a private Lutheran school and then P.S. 117 Junior High in the Bronx, Lee was transferred to a school in his new district, P.S. 44. It was there that he first encountered people making fun of his accent, classmates who belittled his Texas drawl—and probably its New Orleans inflections made him suspect as well, although it's not likely that anyone would have noticed that particular origin. He spent a lot of time alone in his bedroom, watching television, and engaging in fantasy interactions with his favorite shows, escaping to another world populated by a strange man who led three lives.

Sometimes he'd spend the day riding the rails. He had been used to the streetcar in New Orleans, so it wasn't exactly a new experience, but it was different and exciting, mostly underground unless you were on the El, and sometimes at the big destinations like Times Square or Grand Central or Staten Island Ferry you could slide easily on or off the cars, carried by crowds rushing to one place or another. Lee Harvey Oswald became part of the stream, the flow of humanity, something he never felt on the streets of the Crescent City except maybe at Mardi Gras, but he hated costumes so that was never an occasion in which he participated. Once, while he was living with John, he and Robert traveled together on the subways when Robert was on leave shortly after enlisting in the Marine Corps. Lee kept subway maps in his pocket, and he delighted in showing off his knowledge of the system, Robert recalled, and we can imagine Lee tracing the different colored subway lines with a finger and saying hey, let's take the F train and go to Brooklyn . . . It rattles when you cross the bridge and it makes this sound, you gotta hear it . . . One day they even visited Marguerite, then on the job in the Empire State Building. She was not the kind of woman who took to surprises, but we can imagine that when her boys walked in unannounced, this made her happy, and she might have taken great pleasure in introducing her coworkers to her sons. After the visit, Lee and Robert took the elevator up to the roof, and Lee began to map a tour of the city for his brother, pointing out sights on their itinerary.

One day during Robert's vacation, Lee took him to the Bronx Zoo, his favorite place in the city. They walked over from the apartment and arrived just as the gates were opening, entering a zone where you could leave the honking and sirens of city streets behind and the only sounds became roars of wild creatures, or squawking raptors, or people walking and talking their way through the grounds, perhaps seeking an escape from the things that haunted them at home, playing their own game of "Let's Pretend" and conversing one way or another with their animal friends.

Throughout the seventeen months that he and Marguerite lived in New York, Lee was absent from school for many days at a time, more days than he was in class, and that brought him to the attention of school authorities, who frequently cited him for truancy. "If only Lee had a father in the house," Marguerite would say to a neighbor, confiding her sadness regarding her son's behavior and sometimes crying. But that wasn't the half of it. On the fiftieth anniversary of the JFK assassination, *The New York Times* published a report about a strange oral history that had surfaced thanks to a reporter trying to track down the neighbor to whom Marguerite confided upon learning of her existence in an FBI report.

It was a kind of convoluted journey into that part of Lee's life that led him to the neighbor. Looking up the names of other residents of the Oswalds' building at the time they were living there, he came across the name of Gussie Keller. She had long since passed away, but the FBI file that her name appeared in also listed the owner of the building, one Philip Jacobs. He too had long since passed away, so the reporter started tracking down members of his family. Soon enough, he found a son, who told him that his daughter, the granddaughter of Philip, had recorded an oral history of her grandfather's life for her social studies class in 1974 when she was eleven years old. It was all about life on the Lower East Side, and it included an account of the building their forebear owned in the Bronx. Someone with a BB gun had been shooting at his building, "pinging the dark brick, piercing the windows, even targeting the elderly women who sat and gossiped in front of the building, on the sunny side." Judging from their trajectory, he suspected that the shots had come from a building across the street, but when he started asking around, a boy in that building told him that they were coming from one of his own tenants, a teenager

by the name of Lee Harvey Oswald. Lee had recently received the BB
gun as a gift, the landlord learned, and he decided to speak with both
Mrs. Oswald and Lee rather than causing a more serious problem by
calling the police. Marguerite was "tight-lipped," he recalled, and Lee
offered "snappy answers, just like any teenage boy." But the shooting
stopped, and Philip Jacobs's oral history of that era, including his tale
of a brush with a future Presidential assassin, lay buried in family storage as a curio, its weird story about Oswald recounted every now and
then, generally on an anniversary of the assassination, as in "the time
that Grandpa told Lee Harvey Oswald to stop shooting at his tenants."

While BB guns don't generally kill people, they can, but what's
more likely is that the pellets pierce the flesh and cause wounds or
perhaps more serious damage. In the annals of "Hey, I met that guy
and lemme tell you what happened," this one isn't the most harrowing. You'd have to include members of Lee's own family, specifically
his sister-in-law and his mother, in that record, and then add his wife,
Marina, whom he was beating upon their return from Russia, and
then add myriad others who had all manner of encounters with Lee or
knew him pretty well, including two people who inadvertently helped
him conceal and transport the rifle used to kill the President shortly
before he did so. But the incident does show that Lee had no respect
for the elderly, for the lives of vulnerable people, and perhaps delighted
in their torment. Wanting to keep the story of a teenage hothead who
was the son of a tenant between himself and the Oswalds, Philip
Jacobs did not speak of it until the day his granddaughter recorded
the account of his life, not even telling the FBI. With volatile people
such as the Oswalds, he believed that it was best to handle the matter
privately. Long before ubiquitous conversations about "toxic masculinity" and how to raise boys, this was an era in which secrets prevailed.
And thus did the story remain stored away on a cassette until a reporter learned of its existence years after the Warren Commission and

other investigative bodies had carried out their work. Nowadays the signs of pending deadly acts are known, though still often hidden or ignored; in retrospect, this episode on East 179th Street in the Bronx, combined with other eruptions, outbursts, and aggressive behavior, was a clear warning.

In the early days of Lee's problems at school, the attendance board at P.S. 117 called Marguerite to a meeting. She was instructed to do something about Lee's ongoing absences. It's not clear from the record exactly what she told her son about this problem; perhaps she warned him that a suspension was en route, though given his predilection for zoo visits and his passion for riding the subways, such a punishment would have only resulted in more frequent trips to both. Around the time of the warning from the board, Marguerite had started selling insurance, driving from house to house, with Lee waiting in the car as she made her rounds. Meanwhile, he had been transferred to another school, P.S. 44, which sent a teacher to check on Lee at home follow-ing another absence. "I'll think about it," he responded to the emissary when told that he'd have to show up for class lest he face suspension. "I haven't made up my mind." Since the warnings had begun, two more hearings before the attendance board had come and gone with Marguerite and Lee failing to appear. On January 27, 1953, Lee was placed on probation until the end of the school year on June 20 and told that this was a last chance to show up for school before truancy charges would be filed. One time during that period, John Pic, along with his wife and baby, visited Lee and Marguerite for Sunday dinner. This is one of the few examples in the record of the Oswalds having a family meal together; in other words, there is not much known about such things as Marguerite preparing a meal, if she did in fact prepare this one—perhaps the Pics provided it—and in any case, just as the Pics arrived, Lee walked out, probably, Marguerite later told investiga-tors, on his way to the zoo. For the first time, with her family minus

Lee gathered round the table, she told them about the truancy problem, confessed that she couldn't control Lee and that he had refused
to see a "head shrinker or nut doctor." Clearly, it seemed to John, Lee
was now in charge and shortly thereafter John's next Coast Guard
assignment took him out to sea. As for Robert, something seemed
off during his visit, but unaware of Lee's truancy problems, he really
didn't know what was going on and hesitated to ask. Soon it was
time for him to ship out as well. Lee accompanied him to the bus
terminal—perhaps via subway!—and Robert told him how much he
had enjoyed the sightseeing and thanked Lee for showing him around
New York. "He seemed to me a normal, healthy, happy thirteen-year-
old boy who was enjoying himself," Robert wrote—and with Robert,
the brother with whom he shared a father and a name, perhaps he was.

It was the truancy that led to a battery of official reports that were
actionable, along with behavior in the classroom when he was there
that was viewed as problematic but that might have been overlooked
without the truancy, such as flying paper airplanes around the room
and refusing to salute the flag. And so began the shuttling of Lee between various agencies and homes for wayward youths, all of which
involved situations that were increasingly harsh and not helpful. But
there were one or two psychologists who offered encouragement and
outlined possible paths out, pointing the way towards possible rehabilitation, if only Marguerite had listened.

As a result of the various failures to appear at hearings, combined
with his ongoing truancy and the recommendation of a psychiatrist
who noted his schizophrenic tendencies, Lee was remanded to a juvenile
detention center called Youth House, a drab building in the Bronx with
barred windows. Suddenly he was living with boys who used dope—he
told Marguerite—and were killers. He wanted out but he was undergoing continuing evaluation. On April 16, 1953, social worker Evelyn
Siegel interviewed Lee and wrote up the following report:

This is a seriously detached withdrawn youngster who has
preserved some ability to relate but is very hard to reach. He
is laconic and taciturn and while he answered questions he
volunteered almost nothing about himself. Toward the end of
the interview he occasionally would say something gratuitously
without my asking him but on the whole everything had to be
pulled from him. What is really surprising is that this boy has
not lost entirely his ability to communicate with other people
because he has been leading such a detached, solitary existence
for most of his life . . .

Despite his withdrawal, he gives the impression that he is
not so difficult to reach as he appears and patient, prolonged
effort in a sustained relationship with one therapist might
bring results. There are indications that he has suffered serious
personality damage but if he can receive help quickly this
might be repaired to some extent.

A big part of the problem was Marguerite herself, social workers
observed. "Mrs. O. is a smartly dressed, gray haired woman, very
self-possessed and alert and while making a superficial appearance of
affability I felt that essentially she was defensive, rigid, selfish and very
much of a snob," Evelyn Siegel wrote.

According to Mrs. O. she had never had any difficulty with Lee
while they were living at Ft. Worth at all and disclaimed any
knowledge of the fact that he had played hookey there. She felt
that if he had said this it was really only to rationalize his playing
hookey up here. She told me that he had always been an extremely
quiet boy as was John and she felt both of these boys were like her.
Even as a little kid Lee had never mixed freely with other children
and she told me she felt this was in response to her teaching. She

had always been a working woman who didn't have to worry about his wandering off or association with other children in their houses so she instructed him to stay within the yard and he always did so. If other kids came to play in his place it was all right but he seemed never to go to other boys. She said that as a matter of fact when other boys did approach him to play he usually preferred to be by himself and she felt that this was in his nature and that one couldn't change people's natures very easily. She herself found nothing wrong with this and told me that Lee's probation officer had remarked to her that the boy seemed to be completely without feeling and that he withdrew from others. She herself did not see anything strange about this and told me that she herself was not a very gregarious person either and had never felt the need to make friends . . .

When I offered that it must have been rather difficult for her to have to be both parents and bread earner at the same time, she told me very proudly that she had never found it so. She said she was always a very independent, self-reliant person who had never wanted any help from anyone, had always had "high fulutent" [sic] ideas, which she felt to a large measure she had accomplished, and she always was able to pull herself up by her own bootstraps.

When I asked if hers had been a good marriage, she said yes and went on as if I hadn't said anything but questioning revealed that she had come from a family where her mother had died when she was only two years old. The father raised six children with the help of housekeepers and she said she was brought up in an extremely poor neighborhood in New Orleans where she was forced to mix with Negroes and other people but even though she played with them and made friends with them she always had again "high fulutent" [sic] ideas and managed to make something of herself . . .

Mrs. O. railed and railed against NYC laws which she felt in a large measure were responsible for the way Lee acted. She said that when he first began to truant, the truant officer picked him up in a police car and took him back to school and she thought that was just atrocious. She felt that the boy had been given a criminal record for no good reason at all and told me that she felt that had she been allowed to handle things in her own way she felt she could have gotten around it. She said she had had a problem in truancy with John too and to a lesser extent with Robert and had been able to handle it with both these boys . . .

I now explained to her the purpose of Lee's being at Youth House in terms of a diagnostic study and the fact that while our psychiatrist here was free to make recommendations actually it was the court's decision . . .

The thing that made her exceedingly angry was that she felt if the boy were given another chance and sent home it should be what she called a real chance and should not involve having to report to a P.O. or "talk to a stranger" which was the way she felt about his going to a social worker. She was adamant however, in her feeling that she really did want him to have one more chance with the knowledge that if he played hookey for even one day he would have to be put away in a home.

I had the feeling that the basis of this was a need to assert her own volition as it were against the authority represented by the court, rather than any real understanding of Lee's welfare or his needs . . .

I honestly don't think that she sees him as a person at all but simply as an extension of herself. Interestingly enough by the way although Lee was a planned for baby because her husband, herself wanted a girl, I take it that she was rather disappointed at having a third boy . . .

I discussed with her what actually would change for Lee if he went home again and the truancy started. To her way of thinking she could not see the truancy as symptomatic of anything and apparently thinks of it as an act of defiance which in a sense of course is really true but she doesn't mean this. I have some real question at this point about just how much Mrs. O. could offer Lee since I feel that her own attitude about social worker's probation, etc. would inevitably communicate itself to the boy and that if he started showing improvement in therapy I have the feeling she is one of these mothers who would have to break it up.

On the other hand Lee himself is so averse to placement at this time that I have some question too as to what would be accomplished by sending him away. He has withdrawn completely here at Youth House . . ."

At some point, Lee was released and returned to school. His behavior had improved, and he was even saluting the flag! This may have been a result of Marguerite taking more of an interest in him, or simply that he wanted to follow the rules lest he have to spend more time at a place that he hated. But soon enough, his behavior became problematic, and he was now mired in the bureaucracy of juvenile rehabilitation. Social workers referred him to the Berkshire Industrial Farm for further treatment, a last-stop upstate residence for the most troublesome youth. However, there was no room, and Marguerite agreed to another hearing, asking the judge for leniency, fearing that life in such a place would only aggravate her son's behavior, and also that he'd disappear forever in the clutches of the New York state legal system. "This kind of thing doesn't happen in Texas," she had told a caseworker early on in this cascading series of punishments. "Playing hooky is not a big deal."

The judge extended Lee's probation, which meant that as long as he would meet with counselors from Big Brothers, he could continue living with Marguerite. Shortly thereafter, a Big Brother visited Marguerite and Lee in their apartment. She politely received him and then said that Lee no longer needed counseling. He had joined the Y, she said, which he attended every Saturday. But Lee said that he didn't care about the Y, at which point Marguerite announced that she and Lee were returning to New Orleans. "You need the court's permission to take Lee out of its jurisdiction," the caseworker said, and to arrange this, Marguerite had to meet with her son's probation officer. Appointments were arranged and missed, and arranged and missed again.

Ten days after Lee's fourteenth birthday, Marguerite telephoned Lee's probation officer and said that she could not come for the next hearing. The probation officer said that it was time to transfer Lee to a home. It was clearly not possible for Lee to improve while living with his mother. Marguerite seems to have relented, finally agreeing that her son would have a better chance if the pair lived apart for a while. So another hearing was arranged, but Marguerite was just buying time. The day before the hearing, she phoned the P.O. "I can't make it," she said to his assistant and apologized. But the officer was on vacation, she was told, and she'd have to wait until his return to reschedule. His assistant reminded her that she was not permitted to take Lee out of the court's jurisdiction. When he got back, the probation officer sent Marguerite a letter. It was returned, marked "Moved—address unknown."

"*Damn Yankees*," Marguerite may have said as they hit the road, heading back to New Orleans—home of the Lost Cause, her own birthplace, and Lee's. *Forti Favet Coelum* said the Oswald coat of arms, announcing the Medieval battle cry: Heaven Favors the Brave—"*Don't you worry son. It's all for the best. What happened is their loss and some-day, you'll show everyone, I know you will."* And then she floored it.

IF IT'S TRUE THAT THERE'S no place like home, what can you say about someone who had dozens of homes, and never really got the chance to settle into any one of them? Nevertheless, once back in the Crescent City, Lee did seem to have entered a period that was not quite so rough around the edges. He and Marguerite landed at Lillian Murret's house at 757 French Street. After the ping-ponging around lesser neighborhoods in New York, mired in a troubling situation that seemed to have no end, they were now in a nice, working-class district called Lakeview, near Lake Pontchartrain and its popular shorefront. Mother and son were surrounded by family—Marguerite's sister Lillian, her husband, their kids—and the kind of conversation that is a shorthand for a million things, the countless moments that they had all shared or heard talk of, for better and for worse, and while Lee had been long estranged from himself, there were times during this return that he did seem to connect with people and the city around him.

He was enrolled at Beauregard Junior High School, three stops from the end of the streetcar line called Cemeteries because of its proximity to the city's landmark graveyards. Soon after Lee and Marguerite had moved in with Aunt Lillian, they relocated to an apartment on St. Mary Street, rented from Marguerite's old friend Myrtle Evans. Because Lee was doing relatively well in school, Marguerite continued using Lillian's address in order to keep him enrolled at Beauregard rather than forcing another school transfer. Seventy was the passing grade, and he had scored a seventy-three in English, seventy in math and social studies, seventy-eight in industrial arts, seventy-two in physical education, and seventy-four in science. This was all below the average grade of seventy-nine to eighty, but he had clearly improved since his time in New York, and for the most part, he actually attended school. In fact, according to his brother Robert, he was getting acquainted with a few of his classmates. But he did find himself in another strange situation. Knowing that he had just moved to New Orleans from New York, some of the students began calling him "Yankee." Whether or not he was offended, we do not know. His association with New York did not get him into trouble the way being from Texas drew derision in the Bronx, even to the point of a truant officer mocking him for his clothes and accent when he was detained at the zoo, but it may have stirred up the feeling that he was an outsider no matter where he went; there was nothing he could do to belong—and belong to what, anyway?

Throughout this period, Lee would visit Aunt Lillian from time to time. He liked her company and indulgence, but he also resented it. "Why are you all doing this for me?" he once asked after Lillian and her daughter bought him new clothes. "Well, Lee," she said, "for one thing, we love you, and another thing, we want you to look nice when you go to school, like the other children." He replied that he didn't need anything from anyone, but of course he did. One day, he told his aunt that he wanted to try out for Beauregard's baseball team but didn't have a glove or shoes. Lillian gave him a glove that belonged to one of her sons and also asked a son-in-law if he could spare a set of cleats. He sent them to Lee from Texas. Lee evidently made the team, but then seems to have quit. From then on, he never said a word about what happened to anyone.

One thing that was kind of a routine for Lee was showing up periodically for Aunt Lillian's Friday night dinner, the traditional Catholic repast. It was mainly because he liked seafood, though the camaraderie was probably all right with him too. Sometimes he visited on Saturday mornings as well, and Lillian would give him money to rent a bike. "New Orleans is a great city for bicycling," Tom Piazza wrote in *Why New Orleans Matters*. "There are no hills to speak of, so it never becomes an athletic event." The Murrets lived near City Park, and Lee liked to ride alone through the park, perhaps visiting the historic train garden with its replicas of streetcars and trains from bygone eras like the one on which his grandfather was a conductor. Maybe on those Saturday mornings he availed himself of the city in other ways as well, biking through the Garden District for a view of how rich people lived, as Marguerite would have put it, and then through the French Quarter because of its verve and mystery and dangerous allure.

"One morning—it was December, I think," Truman Capote wrote of New Orleans in *Harper's Bazaar*, a few years before Oswald was bicycling around town, "a cold Sunday with a sad gray sun—I went up through the Quarter to the old market where, at that time of year, there are exquisite winter fruits, sweet satsumas, twenty cents a dozen"—did Lee stop and buy some?—"and winter flowers, Christmas poinsettia and snow japonica. New Orleans streets have long lonesome perspectives; in empty hours their atmosphere is like Chirico"—a surrealist painter of forbidding cityscapes —"and things innocent, ordinarily (a face behind the slanted light of shutters, nuns moving in the distance, a fat dark arm lolling lopsidedly out some window, a lonely black boy squatting in an alley, blowing soap bubbles and watching sadly as they rise to burst), acquire qualities of violence."

At the apartment on St. Mary Street, things between Marguerite and Lee remained customarily loud and weird. Marguerite's friend Myrtle, who lived in another apartment in the building, would later tell investigators about a disruptive pattern of behavior. As soon as Lee got home from school, for instance, if his mother was downstairs visiting Myrtle, he would stand at the head of the stairs and shout, "Maw, how about fixing me something to eat?" Marguerite would immediately leave and make something for Lee. Myrtle felt that Lee was spoiled and overindulged. Myrtle's husband, Julian, was partial to Marguerite and said that Lee was "arrogant and no one liked him." He even had a terrible fish story about Lee, one that was all too true. One day, he took Lee on a fishing trip to the far side of Lake Pontchartrain, where he was visiting some relatives who had a private fishing pond. Lee wouldn't speak to the other boys and went fishing by himself. He caught some fish and threw them on the bank. After they piled up, he walked away. Julian was puzzled. As Bugliosi reported in *Reclaiming History*, Julian felt that you should eat what you catch or throw the fish back in the water. It was a disturbing image that he recounted, and he said that Lee was "a psycho." He agreed with his wife that Marguerite was spoiling the very demanding Lee, who was generally "very loud and insolent," though sometimes with other people, he employed a civil tone. But the prevailing problem was Lee's frequent yelling; because of it, everyone in the building's twenty-seven units would know when he was home.

Finally, after he and Marguerite had lived there for six months, a month in arrears and unable to keep up with a rent increase, although Marguerite was already paying a reduced friends' rate, Myrtle kicked them out. Mother and son moved yet again, this time to 126 Exchange Place, a second-story apartment overlooking Canal Street in the French Quarter. "This part of town looks like the Devil," Marguerite later told the Warren Commission, referring to her particular location. "But very wealthy and very fine citizens live in [the French Quarter]," she added, wanting to assert proximity to the upper class as was her custom. But wealthier people did not live on Exchange Place. According to the city crime commissioner, the street was "the hub of some of the most notorious underworld joints in the city." Marguerite had gotten a job at a nearby department store and the rent may have been within her range because of the apartment's location, above a pool hall. Nevertheless, the place was airy and somewhat spacious, with a bedroom, bath, large living room, and a breakfast room as well. Lee got the bedroom and Marguerite slept in the living room on a studio couch.

At the time that the pair were living on Exchange Place, the street "was one den of iniquity after another," said G. Robert Blakey in a *Frontline* interview on the fiftieth anniversary of the JFK assassination. As chief counsel to the 1977 House Select Committee on Assassinations, the inquiry that followed the Warren Commission, Blakey led the investigation and said that Oswald had grown up in a community and environment of crime and corruption. "Strip joints, gambling joints. It was a place where every hustler and pimp in New Orleans plied his trade." These operations were affiliated with Carlos Marcello, the mobster who allegedly supervised the fellow for whom Oswald's uncle Dutz Murret worked. Not that proximity to establishments run by the underworld meant anything beyond the surface; there were probably others who lived in the French Quarter with relatives in the Marcello circle. To put it another way, "This city is famous for its gamblers, prostitutes, exhibitionists, anti-Christs, alcoholics, sodomites, drug addicts, fetishists, onanists, pornographers, frauds, jades, litterbugs, and lesbians, all of whom are only too well protected by graft. If you have a moment, I shall endeavor to discuss the crime problems with you, but don't make the mistake of bothering me." These are the oft-quoted words of Ignatius Reilly, the hero of *A Confederacy of Dunces*, a novel about New Orleans that's a tale of a mother and a son; although prizing education more than the Oswalds, they bear a distinct resemblance to Marguerite and Lee Harvey, both hopeless devotees of themselves and, in a complicated way, one another, both caught up in a circuit of the desperate and the flailing with few prospects of escape.

The question from this period of Lee's life is whether or not the joints on Exchange Place offered any sort of way out, whether he started hanging around the pool hall, meeting its denizens, the sort of folk who could have led him into a promise of easy living now and trouble later. Nelson Algren had written about such characters in *Walk on the Wild Side*—later invoked by Lou Reed in the eponymous song—or in that Eric Burdon and The Animals rendition of "House in New Orleans," the growly tune about an infamous brothel that was "the ruin of many a poor boy, and God I know it, I'm one." The record tells us that in fact Lee and a classmate, Edward Voebel, did sometimes visit the pool hall for an occasional game; Lee taught Edward how to shoot pool and they played darts, too. After the first couple of games, Ed started to beat Lee and Lee chalked it up to "Beginner's Luck." But Lee wasn't accomplished enough as a pool player to make fun of Ed for beating him because he got lucky. As Ed told the Warren Commission, "I am really not that good at playing pool." Moreover, they just weren't well versed in the ways of the pool hall. They didn't really hang around the establishment all that much, Voebel recalled, never talked to any of the regulars when they were there, and always left when their game was over. Still, someone had to have taught Lee how to play pool before he taught his friend—not that that's so terrible—and what teenage boy would refrain from visiting the pool hall downstairs anyway, especially a lonely kid like Lee?

There were other, more problematic things going on throughout this period in the French Quarter and at Beauregard Junior High. Once again, trouble seemed to find Lee. One classmate told the reporter from *Life* magazine that Lee had a number of fights and didn't have any friends. "Lee believed in self-defense," Robert recalled, "as John and I did. All three of us made it a policy never to start a fight—but never to run from one, either." On the aforementioned day when Lee was attacked by white boys for sitting in "the Negro section" of a segregated bus, he fought back mightily, said Robert, with "fists flying in all directions." Since he was outnumbered, he was badly beaten up. Another incident involved an altercation with two brothers, "notorious troublemakers of the neighborhood." Lee had "picked on the younger one," the brothers said, and a fight erupted. Just like in the movies, it moved down the street, "from front yard to front yard, from driveway to street, watched by an expanding group of boys and girls on their way home from school."

One of the spectators was Voebel. According to his recollection of the proceedings, the crowd was rooting for Lee because he was the underdog, one boy taking on two others. But crowds are fickle, and when Lee punched the younger boy and made his lip bleed, their allegiance quickly shifted. A couple of days later, a possible retaliation occurred. Lee was walking out of the schoolyard, and "some big guy" approached him out of nowhere and punched him in the mouth. He knocked out a tooth or several, and they cut through Lee's upper lip; then, Robert said, the guy "turned and ran." Edward and a couple of other boys took Lee back to the school restroom and washed up his bloody lip. His Aunt Lillian paid the dentist bill. And that was the start of the friendship between Edward and Lee, possibly the only classmate who ever visited Lee at home. One thing that the boys had in common was that neither liked to smoke, unlike many of their classmates, and Ed regarded that as evidence of "a bum-type nature." Beauregard Junior High in fact had a student population that was a kind of New Orleans version of *Grease*, filled with Danny Zuko types—the character played so memorably by John Travolta with his ducktail haircut—and of course, unbeknownst to everyone at the time, it was the quiet, privately seething Lee Harvey Oswald who would one day become the real rebel.

After that bruising fight in the schoolyard, Ed seems to have found a kindred spirit in Lee. He felt that the pair had a lot in common, and he liked his personality. Plus, as he would tell investigators years later, he admired how Lee stood up for himself. If you didn't belong to a gang, you had to prove yourself, which is exactly what Lee did. It was just like Robert had described the brothers in his memoir: don't mess with the Oswalds. Ed himself had been involved in a similar incident, which probably accounts for his bond with Lee. One day at school, the overweight boy was taunted by a classmate, trying to force him into a fight. Finally it worked and Ed "beat the dickens" out of him. When word about what happened got around, he was approached by a gang at school one day but was able to talk his way out of it. Later, the gang came over to his house, piled out of cars, and started yelling vulgarities. The idea was to get Ed to come outside. But Ed's uncle ran them off, and that was the end of the trouble. "Lee didn't take anything from anybody," Edward said, and then—adding to the chorus of many around Lee during his school years—Ed recalled another aspect of his friend's personality. Evidently, aside from getting up close and personal in schoolyard battles, Lee simply had no interest in people. "He was just living in his own world."

For someone who had an active fantasy life, hanging around with imaginary characters from radio and television shows, he was often found doing things that solitary types favored. Lee frequently favored libraries throughout his life. There could be found legions of make-believe characters and plenty of figures from the annals of history, writing of their philosophies and beliefs and the courses they charted.

One day while Lee was walking through New York City, perhaps as he had just emerged from or was about to enter the subway, someone proffered a leaflet. It was "an old lady" who gave it to him, as he recalled of the moment after he had defected to Russia during an interview with an AP reporter by the name of Aline Mosby. After being besieged by requests from various American correspondents in Moscow, he had asked Mosby to come to his hotel room in the Metropole, hoping to clear up misunderstandings about his defection that stemmed from a UPI report circulating in the United States. Mosby was a rival of the UPI representative. On November 13, 1959, a little more than four years before Lee killed the President in

Dallas, the pair met in Oswald's large room overlooking the Bolshoi Theater. With "its ornate furniture and blue walls," Lee looked out of place there, Mosby thought, "like some Oakie from the boondocks." Oswald talked "nonstop" for two hours, she later told another journalist. "He struck me as a rather mixed-up young man not of great intellectual capacity or training"—not somebody that would interest the Soviet Union.

But he did tell her one thing that later became of note to American investigators following Kennedy's assassination. When she asked how he became a Marxist, he told her that when he was around fifteen and in New York—apparently misremembering the date, for he was back in New Orleans by then—the elderly woman had handed him that leaflet, and that's when he became "ideologically interested." The flyer depicted Julius and Ethel Rosenberg, the married couple who were facing execution for giving atomic secrets to the Soviets during a time when America and Russia were locked in a race for nuclear domination. The leaflet read "Save the Rosenbergs," and it had images of them along with pictures of their young sons. It was the first time that he had been introduced to socialist literature, and thereafter, he told Mosby, he started to observe the "class struggle" in New York, the "luxury of Park Avenue, and workers' lives on the Lower East Side." Having already been influenced in the nature of "class struggle" by way of Marguerite—although that was not her language; her style had more to do with overt statements about being at the mercy of rich people, a serf among kings and queens—he began reading up on Marxism and Communism, philosophies out of Russia that had gained broad currency among the American left, including the Rosenbergs.

Back in New Orleans, he spent a great deal of time at the library, withdrawing books such as *Das Kapital* by Karl Marx and works on Communism, studying up on the "worker's paradise" to which he would soon escape. But what was it about that flyer that propelled him along his strange journey? Perhaps it was the portrayal of a mother as a martyr, the journalist who later interviewed Mosby posited, reminiscent of how Marguerite presented herself, and the fact that her sons appeared to be persecuted like he was. Could "Save the Rosenbergs" have resonated such that it meant "Save the Oswalds"? Quite possibly. And soon, the Rosenbergs were executed; spies they may have been—a married couple leading dual lives, Julius in particular—but for Lee, they were unfairly accused figures who were denied their rights and strapped to an electric chair, leaving their sons to pick up the pieces. It's strange to think that a chance encounter on the streets of New York—though where else? when you think about it—revved Lee up to the point that he would one day flee his own country for another one, the land that was said to treat workers fairly. But combined with Marguerite's feeling that she—a have-not—was taken advantage of by the haves, it was a potent formula. And strangely enough, Lee seems to have been handed the leaflet portraying the Rosenbergs on Mother's Day, according to the calculations of the journalist who later interviewed Mosby; she had put a few things together and realized that groups in New York that had been lobbying on behalf of Julius and Ethel had called for actions on the Sunday that was devoted to mothers, not to make a point, but out of sheer coincidence. Such are the ways that things reverberate through the ethers, and for Lee, there was no way of getting around Marguerite and her resentments, no matter how much he may have tried.

But let us also recall that Lee was open for business, a teenager afflicted by a swarm of unhinged neurons floating around in his mind and spirit, and they could have attached themselves to any gripe or obsession or whim and gone from there if the time and place were in alignment. It was in the stacks at his local library in New Orleans that ideas began to formulate and take root, long after a senior citizen had handed him that pamphlet. He'd be leaving this country soon enough, for the country that the Rosenbergs were trying to help, but really, the destination was not clear. The plan wasn't formulated yet, but running away was a family tradition, at least for Marguerite; to be more specific, running away to start over somewhere else was an American tradition—do we not have millions of people on the road at any given time, furniture in a U-Haul, heading to a scenic overlook or a parking lot or maybe a new address? For Oswald, some sort of seed was planted, and until it came to fruition, he'd continue playing "Let's Pretend," communing with few people, keeping mostly to himself, and imagining himself far away from Marguerite.

Sometimes Lee had his head in the stars and not books. He liked stargazing and through a coworker at a dental lab where he had gotten a job as a delivery boy learned of an astronomy club, and he began attending meetings at the home of William Wulf, a young man with a telescope and knowledge of the heavens. "We were all nuts on rocketry at the time," Wulf told investigators by way of conveying the atmosphere of the era, and gaining knowledge of the skies was certainly in accord with that passion. Lee himself had a "fledgling" knowledge of astronomy, and this was off-putting to Wulf; members of his club were serious students of such matters and did not want to spend their time instructing a novice about the right way to use a telescope and what exactly they were seeing. Wulf felt that Oswald and his coworker, Palmer McBride, both lonely boys whose families were financially strapped, found common ground in their fascination with stars—McBride himself wanted to pursue a career in rocket engineering—and would talk about what was going on in the skies as they made their rounds "delivering dentures." This jarring juxtaposition wasn't offered as a disparagement of the job; he was simply describing to investigators how he had met Lee and the probable way that McBride and the teenage Oswald had come to share their interests.

In the heat following JFK's death, such inquiries often involved lines of thinking designed to elicit information about how Oswald had come to anyone's attention and what the nature of it was, and Warren Commission documents are filled with weird details such as this image of Lee carrying out one of those "somebody's gotta do it" tasks in order to help Marguerite pay the rent.

After maybe his second or third astronomy club meeting, Oswald and Wulf got to talking about other things, and at some point the conversation turned to Communism. This was a subject that Lee liked to talk about, and once even showed off his library copy of *The Communist Manifesto* to Palmer, praising Russian Prime Minister Nikita Khrushchev for taking up the cause of exploited workers in the Soviet Union. He even predicted that one day, the workers of the world would unite and throw off their chains—just like Karl Marx and Friedrich Engels had written at the end of their manifesto. He was hardly alone in expressing these beliefs; across the United States, "Workers of the world, unite!" was something of a war cry among various constituencies, and it was published on posters and newspaper broadsides with images of laborers breaking free of their chains. But in New Orleans, for a teenager to express such sentiments was peculiar; this was not the language of Huey Long, although similar in intent, and Lee certainly did not have the gravitas of a wildly popular governor or senator.

In declaring such statements, Lee drew a lot of attention to himself—but maybe that was the idea. At Wulf's house, Lee was drawn to certain books in his friend's library, the ones about Communist doctrine and so on, and told William that he had been looking for a Communist club to join. Communism was the only way of life for the worker, he told William, and he was dismayed that he had been unable to find the appropriate organization to join in New Orleans. This was triple-alarm language for Wulf, a history major with a deep

interest in the course of human events. To him, the idea of joining a
Communist group was not a good one, and it raised the disturbing
possibility that Lee was a security risk. Because of widely watched
shows such as *I Led Three Lives* and other pop culture renditions of
international affairs, anyone who associated with Communists at
that time—even a teenager—was viewed as a possible spy. Moreover,
William had grown up in a German household that opposed what was
going on in Russia; his father had served in the American Navy during World War I after emigrating from Hamburg, where he had seen
what the Communists were up to and he didn't like it.

Such was the nature of the era that the conversation between Lee
and William became quite heated, and we can imagine how Lee's
fight-or-flight mechanism must have kicked in when anyone seemed
to impugn workers and their beleaguered state, which really translated
into an attack on his mother. Overhearing the argument from another
room, William's father entered and joined in, and judging from Lee's
outburst, it occurred to William that Lee could become violent when
defending something that he fervently believed in. He was "loud and
boisterous," and as the argument escalated, William's father took Lee
by the arm and escorted him out of the house. Looking back on the
episode, William felt that Lee wasn't really interested in astronomy,
per se, or even Communism. The boy that many would later describe
as a loner simply wanted to belong—to what, it wasn't clear, something or anything. But the situation wasn't reciprocal, William said.
There was no entity or individual person who wanted Lee to join their
circle and thus did Lee remain isolated and cast aside. The day of the
argument was the last time that William saw Lee Harvey Oswald, until his picture appeared all over the front page in newspapers around
the world. The teenager who was drawn to the stars had grown up and
killed the President, and now belonged to the ages.

WILLIAM WULF WAS NOT ALONE in noticing that Oswald had violent tendencies during his junior high school years. The problem was that no one was able to put the full picture together until after the fact, and even now, the elements of the picture have been obscured by the endless fog of conspiracy theories. (Today, the problem persists, in many different iterations.) From family accounts and from his Marine record involving incidents with weapons, we know that Oswald messed around with guns from time to time, and his childhood engagement with *Let's Pretend* led him to cook up a break-in scheme in pursuit of a firearm, and he tried to enlist the aid of a friend to steal it.

This friend was his pool hall buddy, Edward Voebel. Sometimes Lee went to Ed's house and was especially interested in a collection of foreign guns that Edward's uncle had brought back from wartime travels. Ed was interested in guns, Robert reported in his memoir, particularly their history and how they worked. He had learned to shoot when he was about seven years old. "Lee, too, had always showed an interest in guns," Robert said, "but Mother hated them and would not let us have them around the house. John and I, of course, had our rifles at military school, and when we were living in Fort Worth I used to borrow a rifle from a friend when I wanted to go hunting." As we have seen, Lee sometimes went hunting with Robert, and one day he told Ed that he wanted a pistol. It was during a concert at Warren Easton High School that some students from Beauregard were attending that Lee told Ed he was going to steal one. He had seen it in a shop window on Rampart Street, he said, and figured out how to get it.

"I can't remember the pistol," Ed told investigators, "to tell the truth, but I don't think it was a collector's piece. It might have been a Smith and Wesson. It was just a weapon. I think it was an automatic, but I don't remember. I really didn't pay too much attention to it . . . it was maybe the following week that I was up at his house and he came out with a glass cutter and a box with a plastic pistol in it, and I think he had a plan as to how he was going to get in there and get this pistol."

Ed didn't know what to tell Lee, so Lee continued pressing his friend, asking him to come with him to the store, check out the gun, and tell him what he thought of the plan. Ed relented, and they walked over to Rampart Street and beheld the firearm behind the window. "What do you think?" Lee said. Ed thought that stealing it was a bad idea and didn't know how to talk his friend out of it. And then he noticed a metal tape around the window and realized it was part of a burglar alarm, so he told Lee that if he cut the window, it would break the band and the alarm would go off. Yet Lee really wanted to go inside and look at the gun; one way or another, the idea was to get his hands on that weapon. Ed remembered that there had been some robberies of jewelry stores on nearby Canal Street, and the robbers had cut the windows to break in. Surely, Lee would get caught if he tried to carry out such a theft. Lee finally relented and that was the end of the conversation.

For what, if anything in particular, Lee wanted that gun we do not know. Strangely, he had told Palmer McBride around this time that he wanted to kill President Eisenhower. Palmer didn't take it seriously, though certainly considered it noteworthy because of its outrageous nature. Over the years, this statement has baffled many students of the Oswald story, and it's often cited as one of those weird anomalies about Lee's life. Why on earth would he want to kill Eisenhower? the question goes. It just doesn't add up.

But this is a riddle that has an answer. Some digging around reveals that Oswald's declaration didn't come out of nowhere. World War II hero and general Dwight E. Eisenhower was often a subject of conversation around New Orleans; the University of New Orleans is home of the Eisenhower Center for American Studies, which includes the study of three major historical epochs that comprise Eisenhower's career. One of them is the USA-USSR rivalry of the Cold War, which

Lee knew all about, at least on the surface and somewhat beyond, and certainly any local examination of such would have attracted his attention. On October 17, 1953, when Oswald was fourteen years old, President Eisenhower visited New Orleans for the 150th anniversary of the Louisiana Purchase. There was a festive, Mardi Gras–style procession through the French Quarter, with Eisenhower in an open sedan followed by thousands of servicemen in uniform. At Tchoupitoulas Street, gaily bedecked royals belonging to various Fat Tuesday krewes joined in the military procession and headed past the reviewing stand at Jackson Square, where none other than Cecil B. DeMille was watching the spectacle. DeMille later narrated a reenactment of the transfer of Louisiana Territory from France, land of Oswald's progenitors, home of the language his grandfather spoke to his mother and her siblings when they were growing up. All in all, it was a festive and celebrated occasion, and one that Oswald might well have been drawn to, if only because of the presence of Eisenhower, defender of America against Russia in the emerging dispute between the two superpowers, soon to reach a boiling point under John Fitzgerald Kennedy.

The parade was in close proximity to Oswald's apartment, which perhaps even provided Lee with a view of the President. Or perhaps Oswald was in the streets nearby. Did this image of Eisenhower heading through New Orleans and greeted by throngs of admirers lodge in his memory bank and replay itself when JFK's motorcade went right past his vantage point at the Texas Book Depository years later, with Kennedy himself in an open limousine? Who knows, and it certainly wasn't possible that Lee would have been able to kill the President, or anyone, in a moving parade with a .45. He might have known his way around a few guns by then—even his brother Robert said later that he had "very rapid reflexes" and was "much stronger than he looked"— but this was long before he had Marine marksmanship training and had run out of options, as they say.

Edward Voebel told investigators that Lee probably wanted to be talked out of stealing that gun. "It was just some fantastic thing that he got in his mind," he said. "I think maybe he was thinking along the lines of if he went through with it, he'd look big among the guys but I'm just speculating." Having a gun, in particular one that he stole, certainly would have made Lee feel powerful, fueling fantasies of who knows what—leading workers to salvation?—or maybe it was all about keeping demons at bay. This was New Orleans, after all, where dark spirits lurked in the mists and alleys, in the cemeteries behind all of the mausoleums, waiting to possess the vulnerable, ready to enter canals that would carry their whispers. As we shall see, in the days before he shot JFK, Lee was visited by a song that had been calling him, "High Noon," regarding the famous showdown in which only one would return, and he whistled its catchy tune; the lyrics—"Do not forsake me oh my darling"—were on his mind, and on the very night before he shot JFK, he was still looking for a way out, making a plea to his wife, just like the song said, and she said no. On the next day, just before high noon, he was locked and loaded and there was no one to tell him it was a bad idea, step away from the gun, and the opportunity at hand prevailed.

There is nothing in the record about Marguerite learning of Lee's plan to break into a store and steal a gun. But she did know that he was spiraling down once more into some private netherworld, getting into fights at Beauregard, and she wanted to keep him off the streets however that would play out. Plus there was the fact that she needed him to pitch in on the rent; with John and Robert gone, there was a shortfall, and John's child support had run out for real. Starting to take on dead-end jobs that were generally the domain of high school dropouts like Marguerite, Lee worked at Dolly's Shoe Company for about ten weeks during eighth and ninth grades, reporting in on Saturdays, mostly. Marguerite worked there, too, as a cashier and clerk, and had asked her employer if they would hire her son. Later filling out a personal history statement for school, he wrote that he had been a "retail shoe salesman," when in fact he was a stock boy. It wasn't a big lie in the scheme of things, or certainly on its own accord, but it added to what would soon become a mountain of exaggerations and falsifications, and it must be taken into account as legions of people continue trying to decipher his later lies.

Quite simply, it was easy to to pretend, and he did it all of the time, whether saying that he didn't start fights when witnesses saw that he did, pumping up his work history to attract better job offers, or announcing that he was a patsy in the assassination of John Fitzgerald Kennedy. His lying was so prolific that it consumed much of his energy and "complicated his life," the writer Patricia McMillan said years later; by that point, his Russian wife Marina had even codified his prevarications. "Lee told three kinds of lies," she revealed to McMillan, author of *Marina and Lee*, the story of their life together. "One was vranyo, a wild, Russian, cock and bull lying that has a certain imaginative joy to it; another was lying out of secretiveness; and still another was lying out of calculation, because he had something to hide."

For one reason or another, the stock boy position didn't work out, and there came a mysterious episode involving his time in the Civilian Air Patrol, an auxiliary Air Force group that he joined, for a minute or two, in eighth grade. The CAP was comprised of people who liked to fly; they wore uniforms and met regularly, sometimes carrying out search or rescue missions, kind of like today's Cajun Navy that we all see on national news whenever there's a disaster in the region, but an official branch of the military. Oswald was recruited by classmate Frederick S. O'Sullivan, who sat behind him in class due to the fact that their surnames both started with the letter *O*. The air patrol was having a recruiting drive for the New Orleans squadron while O'Sullivan was at Beauregard, and there were three students who attracted his attention as possible candidates for cadet. They included Lee's pool hall buddy Ed Voebel and Lee.

The reason that he wanted Lee to join up was that the patrol had a drill team of note, and O'Sullivan felt that Lee would be a good fit because of his posture. (Had Marguerite ever nagged him to stand up straight, young man? If so, this is one instance that proves that maternal exhortation to do so, annoying though it may be, is not necessarily a bad idea). Oswald was erect in his carriage, O'Sullivan told the Warren Commission, and looked like he could be marching, was in fact marching, with his eyes straight ahead, head straight, and shoulders back. These qualities suggested that he had the makings of a drill team cadet and, if he got into the squadron, would make a pretty good leader. So Frederick explained what the CAP did at the airport, marching and flying on the weekends, and invited the three potential recruits to visit. They did, and one of them joined the squadron. For some reason, Voebel decided to join the team at another airport in the vicinity of New Orleans, and because of their friendship, Oswald joined along with him.

It's not clear whether Oswald officially signed up, but he did attend a few meetings. His squadron was led by David Ferrie (or maybe it wasn't—the record varies), a peculiar man with a high-pitched voice and an ill-fitting toupee—remember Joe Pesci in Oliver Stone's *JFK*? That was Ferrie—who came to figure prominently in conspiracy theories because of his alleged involvement in anti-Castro activities that presumably emanated from the swamps of Louisiana and ranged into the failed Bay of Pigs campaign in Cuba, the one where a kind of Dirty Dozen of American military and intelligence operatives tried to take out the Castro regime but failed, due to, they said, lack of support from John F. Kennedy. Ferrie was a good pilot, everybody agreed, graduating from remote runways near the Gulf of Mexico to commercial flights in big cities for Eastern Airlines.

Among the zillion questions that arose following the assassination of the President was whether David Ferrie flew Oswald to Dallas to take him out. By then a detective in the New Orleans Police Department, Intelligence Division, O'Sullivan was tasked with finding out. He and another cop went out to the airport and examined Ferrie's plane. It had flat tires and instruments missing and needed a new paint job. Not flyable, the detectives determined. Nor was there evidence that Ferrie had rented another plane with which to fly Oswald to Dallas. While neither observation could be viewed as infallible or proof of anything, really, Oswald's contact with the CAP was nevertheless brief; he was in it and then he wasn't, and he appears to have left little impression on fellow cadets. The Civilian Air Patrol was one more thing that Oswald dabbled in, that he wanted to be part of, and this time, it even wanted him back.

There was another military outfit that was calling, and that was the US Marine Corps. He wasn't old enough to sign up just yet, but it had been on his mind for years. On July 11, 1955, after completing three years in the Corps, Robert was discharged and returned to Fort Worth. He wanted to live and work there, and after visiting old friends and making plans, he headed for New Orleans two days later, arriving the following morning. He stayed with Marguerite and Lee for about a week, he recalled, in their apartment on Exchange Place. "I noticed no unusual resentment between Mother and Lee," Robert wrote, "and they did not quarrel when I was there. Perhaps they were trying, as they did in New York, to make things especially pleasant for me. Mother tried to persuade me to stay with them in New Orleans, but I had made up my mind to go back to Fort Worth, where I felt at home."

At the time, school was out, and Lee didn't have a job. The brothers had a lot of time to spend together. They would visit Audubon Park and City Park, wander around the French Quarter and along the waterfront. "We talked a lot," Robert said. Lee had endless questions about the Corps, and Robert told him all about it, perhaps describing the places he'd seen, the people he met, the good and the bad of it. Mainly he was on his own, away from their mother—something that may have been unsaid but was nonetheless front and center. As the brothers ambled along the waterfront, familiar scents of goods from the Caribbean stacked up on the docks were in the air, coffee and bananas mainly, and the fragrance was both comforting and alluring, hinting of other places and inviting escape, and perhaps the scents added to Lee's wanderlust and confirmed the way out—the sea, the skies, the world. Someday, sooner rather than later, Lee knew that he'd join the Marines; he told Robert that he was going to enlist as soon as he was old enough. It wouldn't be long before he got out of Dodge.

In the fall of 1955, Lee enrolled in tenth grade at Warren Easton High School, where many students from Beauregard transferred for the remaining three years of education. He was almost sixteen and getting good grades in reading and vocabulary, an eighty-eight and eighty-five, respectively. His scores in English, math, and science were lower, but it was almost time to drop out. Three weeks after the start of the semester, the principal received a note in Lee's handwriting, signed with his mother's name, and dated October 7, 1955. It wasn't the usual sort of fake note that students have sent down through the ages—"my son was not in school yesterday due to a headache"; it was something a little more dramatic.

"TO WHOM IT MAY CONCERN," it began. "Because we are moving to San Diego in the middle of this month, Lee must quit school now. Also please send by him any papers such as his birth certificate that you may have. Thank you." And then the sign-off was "Sincirely"—Lee never could spell properly, due to his dyslexia—"MRS. M. OSWALD."

San Diego was referenced because Lee's idea was to go to the base at Camp Pendleton and enlist. A few days later, the principal called Marguerite to verify the note. Receiving the call at Keeler's Specialty Shop where she was working, she was surprised but covered for Lee, and later that afternoon, he rushed in and announced that he was dropping out of school and wanted to join the Marines. Would she falsify his birth certificate? he inquired. She said no, but because Lee kept asking, she contacted an old friend who was a lawyer; he too thought it was a bad idea and advised her not to do it. But she soon went ahead with Lee's wishes and signed an affidavit that said Lee was born in 1938, not 1939, and that she had lost his birth certificate. With the statement from Marguerite and a packed duffel bag, Lee proceeded immediately to Camp Pendleton—next stop, boot camp; that was the idea, but it didn't work. For some reason, the recruiter rejected the affidavit and sent him home.

More resolute than ever, Lee lost himself in the Marine Corps manual that he had gotten from his brother, reading it over and over again and asking Marguerite to take the book and give him a quiz. She later said that he knew it by heart, and it sounds like they had a tender mother-son moment, one of the few that we know of, with Marguerite paving the way for Lee to leave. Three days after Lee had written the forged note, he dropped out of school and got his first full-time job.

Marguerite had asked her brother-in-law Dutz Murret about finding work for Lee, and he was able to secure employment for him at Tujuage's Shipping Company (not to be confused with the famous restaurant with the same name, as many have done over the years— the one that was known for its historic stand-up bar, dedicated locals, discerning gourmands from around the world, and being a hangout for mobsters). Uncle Dutz secured a job of messenger and office boy for his nephew at a salary of $130 per month. For two months, Lee delivered shipping papers to the US Custom House export office, steamship lines, and foreign consulates. He didn't have much to do with other employees and went home for lunch because his apartment was nearby. Some have said over the years that Lee was actually running numbers for his uncle, a bookie, going from ship to ship along the wharves of the river and taking bets in an underground lottery with headquarters in a local casino. It promised huge wins if you picked the lucky number, which hardly ever happened, and it was a racket that was streaming through the Big Easy at that time. When questioned about Lee's history later, Marguerite told investigators that he had been working for "steamship people," and her sister Lillian did say that Oswald had indeed "worked as a runner," though what he was delivering was not made clear. He never mentioned it in any sort of personal history, and the associations he may have formed at that time are known only to those people, now long gone.

In any case, Lee seemed to thrive in his new position, perhaps in anticipation that he'd soon be leaving. He was "eager, animated, and genuinely enthusiastic," Robert said later. "He liked the idea of working for a shipping company" and excitedly told Robert that they were about to send an order to Portugal or had just received a shipment from Hong Kong that morning. With his first paycheck, he bought presents for Marguerite, including a coat and a parakeet in a cage with a planter, and he paid his room and board. He opened a savings account and bought some things for himself, including an electric football machine, a bow and arrow, and, finally, a gun. The gun was a Marlin bolt-action .22 caliber clip-fed rifle, Robert recalled, and it had cost Lee eighteen dollars. It didn't work because the firing pin was broken, and Robert bought it back from Lee for ten dollars and had it fixed. But as excited as Lee was about working at Tujuage's in his first days, he soon grew tired of it. The high had faded, and the reality that he was just another errand boy settled in. Two months after he had started the job, he quit.

Shortly thereafter, he and Marguerite moved to Fort Worth, where Robert was making his home. Knowing that it was Lee's desire to join the Marines when he turned seventeen, she was hoping that Robert could talk him out of it, especially if they were all living together. So she rented an apartment for the three of them on Collinswood Avenue in a working-class section of town. Robert had been planning to get married later that year, in spite of the fact that Marguerite didn't approve of his fiancée because she had a club foot. And he certainly did not fancy himself living with his mother ever again. But he agreed to move in until he married in order to help Marguerite and Lee with bills.

In the fall of 1956, Lee enrolled in the tenth grade at Arlington Heights High School. It was his second time in tenth grade, and once again, he was starting over and had to make new friends—or at least engage with people he had never met before. But he did have the good fortune of running into a boy he knew from grade school who was now attending Arlington Heights High. This was Richard Garrett, who remembered the moment distinctly. "He walked up to me in the hall," Richard told the reporter from *Life* magazine. Richard had to look down to Lee to talk, and that seemed strange because in grammar school, Lee had been the tallest, the dominant boy in their group. "He looked like he was just lost," Richard said. "He was very different from the way I remembered him. He seemed to have no personality at all. He couldn't express himself well. He just hadn't turned into somebody. He hadn't turned into anybody. I've read where people say he was a loner. Well, he wasn't in the sixth grade, but he sure was in high school."

Not surprisingly, Lee began to have problems in school, including the time he told his coach that "it's a free country and I don't have to run if I don't want to" when asked to run sprints. It was the refrain that we all know, and one that Lee had picked up from his mother, the call of personal rights, and it was one that he would use over and over again, until the day that it didn't work anymore and the game was over. The coach told Lee to hand in his cleats, and it was soon after that he dropped out. To bide his time until he would try to join the Marines again, he wrote a letter, dated October 3, 1956, addressed to the Socialist Party of America in New York. "DEAR SIRS," it began, and once again his writing had some grammatical and punctuation errors due to his dyslexia. "I am sixteen years of age and would like more information about your youth League, I would like to know if there is a branch in my area, how to join, ect., I am a Marxist, and have been studying socialist principles for well over fifteen months I am very interested in your Y.P.S.L. Sincerely, LEE OSWALD."

There is no record of a response. About two weeks later, Lee turned seventeen and told Robert that he was ready to enlist in the Corps. Robert did try to talk him out of it, as Marguerite had hoped, telling him about the importance of a high school diploma when it came to finding a job—and Lee had already gotten a hint of the dreary life as a low-level worker—but there was nothing Robert could say to deter him. "Would you mind if I enlisted right now?" Lee asked, "before your wedding?" Robert advised him to make up his own mind. "The sooner you go," he said. "The sooner you'll get out." In the end, Marguerite seems to have accepted Lee's decision. It was clear to all of the boys that she never placed much importance on higher educa-tion, let alone the necessity of graduation from high school. She had dropped out in ninth grade and never regretted it (or if she did, she never expressed it), and she always told her sons that finding a job and earning a living was the thing to do. When Lee was in trouble in New York, she had even told the social worker that while she be-lieved strongly in education, the belief didn't extend to the idea that "a mother should go out and work and deprive her children of a mother's home and love in order to make the extra money go give her children a college education . . . I happen to know that a college education is something not as important as wisdom. There are college graduates who do not know how to apply their ability . . . "

So we must ask: Why was Marguerite hoping that Robert would convince Lee to finish high school before joining the Marines? Perhaps in her heart of hearts, she knew that was a good idea and probably offered Lee the best way out of his circumstances. Every man might be a king, but not if he doesn't finish high school—and she had only to look around in her own world to see that the people who were stranded in it, generally without a standard education, didn't stand a chance. But she also wanted Lee to be happy, believe it or not; the military had worked for John Pic and Robert, so maybe it would be a good thing for Lee. He wasn't paying that much rent anyway, and maybe while he was in the service he'd start kicking back some of his salary.

"I just want to do something different," Lee said when he told Marguerite that he had dropped out of school and was leaving. On October 24, he headed for Dallas, signed up for three years in the Marines, and then proceeded to San Diego and shortly after Camp Pendleton. He was ready for boot camp. But was he? When you think about the prototype of the drill instructor, especially one in the Marine Corps, someone like the guy in *Jarhead* comes to mind. "Are you eyeballing me with those baby blues?" the man shouts up close and personal in a new recruit's face. "Are you in love with me?" How Lee Harvey Oswald at seventeen responded to the blistering verbal assaults that went with boot camp is anyone's guess, though he may have expected some sort of hazing, having heard about it from Robert. A year after he joined up, the movie *D.I.* was released; it featured Jack Webb of *Dragnet* as the iconic screaming and sweating drill instructor, Sergeant Moore. "Casco, your shirt is unbuttoned, your belt buckle isn't lined up, your feet aren't at a forty-five-degree angle, your head's not square, you're lookin' at the sky, what're you a bird-watcher? Get your head down!" he yells at a new kid in his platoon. This wasn't Ed

Ekdahl offering ice cream; this was a male authority figure who really *was* an authority, the kind of guy who could make or break you, someone who "didn't know he had a girlfriend—and neither did she"—like the poster said. *D.I.* summed up what Lee probably experienced, and to this day, it's considered an accurate and harrowing portrayal of what it's like for new recruits in boot camp.

How did Lee fare in this trial by fire? From the record, we can tell that he reverted to type shortly after becoming a Marine. "I remember him as quiet, serious and trying to find himself," a fellow recruit told the *Life* magazine reporter. "The rest of us would wrestle and horse around, but he would have his bunk in the corner and stay there, reading a book. He didn't have any friends."

"He was good with a rifle," said his section chief at Pendleton. "But he was such a hothead I was glad when he finally shipped out for radar training. He was always having beefs with the guys. Never could figure out what it was really about, really. Just to get into a fight and vent, I suppose."

"He was a real oddball," said a guy who bunked in the same barracks when they shipped out to Atsugi, Japan. "He used to bring up this stuff about his name, Lee. He was proud of it, because he said he was named after Robert E. Lee. He thought Robert E. Lee was the greatest man in history."

Soon enough, the world conjured by the shipping labels at Tujuage's was at hand, and Lee embarked on travels that would take him from San Diego to Jacksonville to Japan to Biloxi to the Philippines to El Toro. Everywhere he went, he left strange and unforgettable impressions. They called him Private Oswald because he was so private. They called him Oswaldovich because he was always reading about Russia. They said he started fights but didn't make out very well. They said he was a troublemaker; they said he baited officers so he could show off his superior knowledge; they said he hated people who bossed him around—and all of this was true. And then came the day that he was court-martialed after he accidentally shot himself with an unauthorized .22. He was court-martialed again for fighting with a sergeant he blamed for the shooting incident, so they busted him down from Private First Class to Private and threw him in the brig, briefly. And then they court-martialed him for the third time when he fired his rifle into the jungle while on sentry duty in the Philippines. It was a terrible record, and perhaps Marguerite sensed that he needed to come home.

In the summer of 1959, while she was working in a department store in Fort Worth, a box of glass jars fell and hit her on the head. She was confined to bed for six months and used up her savings to cover medical bills. She didn't want to tell Lee and cause him to worry. But finally, she sent a letter. She needed him with her, and he'd have his own bed; the landlord said she could bring in a rollaway. So he applied for a hardship release from the Marines, and they said he could return. But it seems as if he hesitated; he applied to the Albert Schweitzer College in Switzerland for its prestigious program at the small school that specialized in courses such as religion, ethics, science, and literature. On the application he said that he had a proficiency in Russian equal to one year of schooling and that he had completed high school by correspondence with an average grade of 85 percent. (Of course, he had no such degree.) He listed philosophy, psychology, ideology, football, baseball, tennis, and stamp collecting as special interests, and writing short stories "on contemporary American life" as his vocational interest, citing Jack London, Charles Darwin, and Norman Vincent Peale as his favorite authors. He said he was a member of the YMCA and the A.Y.H. Association, and that he had participated in a "student body movement in school" for the control of juvenile delinquency. Asked to give a general statement of his reasons for wanting to attend the college, he wrote:

In order to aquire a fuller understanding of that subject which
interest me most, Philosophy. To meet with Europeans who can
broaden my scope of understanding. To receive formal Education
by Instructers of high standing and character. To broaden my
knowlege of German and to live in a healty climate and Good
moral atmosphere.

In retrospect, the application is viewed by many students of Oswald
as a subterfuge, a cover for his pending flight to Russia. If he had the appropriate paperwork, the theory goes, he could have entered Switzerland
and then gone from there to the Soviet Union. He was in fact accepted
at the Schweitzer College. It was a sophisticated application, regardless
of spelling errors, which the college obviously ignored. As a possible
front for another plan, it certainly shows that he was adept at laying the
groundwork for an elaborate scheme. But by the time he received word
of his acceptance, Lee Harvey Oswald had already defected to Russia. It
was time to go, and he just couldn't wait.

But before that, he had gone home to check on his mother. Some
have speculated that she herself may have been running her own con,
and that the terrible accident in the workplace was actually some sort
of slip and fall that she had created in order to get time off and try to
convince Lee to return to her side. That certainly suggested a dramatic
scenario—and Robert himself noted that "Mother had been known
to cry wolf before. Truthful or not, it's not that difficult to imagine
her in repose as her son enters, forearm on brow, and weak of voice."
"Of all my sorrow," she later said, describing the scene herself, "I don't
think I will ever forget the shame I felt when my boy entered that
small place with a sick mother." Soon enough, she was up and about
as if nothing had happened. On the morning of September 16, three
days after Lee had come home, he emerged from the kitchen with his
suitcase. "Mother," he said, "my mind is made up. I want to get on a

ship and travel. I'll see a lot and it's good work."

And then he showed her his passport: "Look, Maw, I really mean it." Marguerite didn't know this at the time, but the plan had been in the works for months. To take care of his mother, he had applied for a dependency discharge from the Marines, and as soon as he knew it was coming, he applied for a passport in Santa Ana, California, where he was stationed. On the application form he said that he was planning to leave the United States by ship from New Orleans on September 21, 1959, and for "statement of purpose for travel," he said that he was going to attend the Albert Schweitzer College in Switzerland and the University of Turku in Finland, adding that he wanted to visit Cuba, the Dominican Republic, England, France, Germany, and Russia as a tourist. His plan was moving along quickly; six days after he applied, he received his passport, and when investigators looked back on the timeline of his request for a discharge from the Marines and his planned departure from the States, it became clear that he had no intention of staying in Fort Worth with Marguerite, or anywhere in this country with anyone. He had $1,600 to his name, savings from his Marine Corps salary, and he walked out the door and left.

About a week later, Marguerite received a letter from Lee that was postmarked New Orleans, the city of his origin, port of debarkation for points near and far. "Well I have booked passage on a ship to Europe," he began. "I would of [sic] had to sooner or later and I think it's best I go now. Just remember above all else that my values are very different from Robert's or your's. It is difficult to tell you how I feel, Just remember this is what I must do. I did not tell you about my plans because you could harly be expected to understand. I did not see aunt Lillian while I was here. I will write again as soon as I land."

He had embarked on another road trip of sorts—this time, a move that he had initiated. It was a big one and true to the promise of such adventures, it would change his life. He had set out for Le Havre, France, on the first leg of his journey, on a freighter called the *SS Marion Lykes*. Altogether, there were four passengers on board, and he shared a cabin with one of them, eighteen-year-old Billy Joe Lord, who was heading to France to study. The other two passengers were a lieutenant and his wife; they later said that Lee kept to himself throughout much of the crossing and didn't seem very friendly. The truth of it was that he was about to become another person, one who let loose and appeared to love life, although he himself could not have been aware of this at the time, and his early days in Russia—his actual destination—were fraught, as would be expected for any foreigner, especially an American who showed up unannounced in the heat of the Cold War. There was even a suicide attempt, as we shall see, a dramatic act which actually resulted in permission to stay in Russia. And after that, it all worked out for a while.

From Le Havre, Oswald traveled to England and then boarded a plane for Helsinki, staying for the weekend at the Torni Hotel and applying for a visa at the Soviet Consulate on Monday, October 12. He then purchased a train ticket for Moscow; later, his brother Robert deduced that he was in a hurry to get to Russia before his visa expired on October 20 and his money ran out. Heading out of Helsinki on October 15, he landed in Moscow the following day. For most of the two-and-a-half years that he lived in Russia, he kept what he called a "Historic Diary," clearly convinced—or trying to convince himself—that he was a figure of import (almost like a teenage girl trying to find her place in the world with a secret diary), or perhaps naming his account in jest (not likely, for light of heart he was not—although this too would soon seem to change). On October 16 of that year, he wrote the following in his personal account upon his arrival in Moscow, characteristically riddled with errors:

Arrive from Helsinki by train; am met by Intourist Repre and
in car to Hotel "Berlin." Reges, as "studet" 5 day Lux tourist.
Ticket.) Meet my Intorist guied Rimma Sherikova. I explain to
her I wish to appli. for Rus. Citizenship. She is flabbergassed,
but agree to help. She checks with her boss, main office Intour;
than helps me add. a letter to Sup. Sovit asking for citizenship.
Meanwhile boss telephons passport and visa office and notifies
them about me.

It was two days before his twentieth birthday, and perhaps he
was giving a present to himself, intentional or not; it was the ultimate
act of starting over, after all—on the very day when such things are
supposed to happen. And it was actually more than that, when you
think about it; here he was, really pursuing the American dream, doing it wherever and whenever he wanted to, reinventing himself as per
everything that he had ever learned: *It's a free country and I have the
right; from the halls of Montezuma to the shores of Tripoli . . . left, right,
left right left . . . watch me . . . here I go.*

WE ONLY KNOW WHAT WE see of people, of what we experience directly.
The Lee Harvey Oswald whom Ernst Titovets met in Russia is not the
Lee Harvey Oswald we have all come to know in the coverage of his
life. As Marlon Brando once said, "We're all acting all the time. We
couldn't survive a second if we weren't able to act. Acting is a survival
mechanism. A social lubricant. We act to save our lives every day."
Was Lee taking off one mask and putting on another for the purpose
of a new performance on a vast new stage? When it came to Oswald's
life in the Soviet Union, Titovets had a front-row seat and was even
behind the curtain. The presentation was exciting and something that
others wanted to be part of and if you saw it, you'd probably give
it four stars, a big thumbs up, or a zillion "likes"—whatever your

preferred method of ranking may be.

Lee's first days in Russia must have confirmed his every fantasy. He was greeted with open arms, and the Intourist guide who met him upon his arrival took him on a tour of Moscow. She took him to the tombs of Stalin and Lenin and other exhibitions, and for his birthday gave him a copy of *The Idiot* by Dostoevsky, the famous novel about a naïve and Christlike figure who gets caught up in a world of corruption. Oswald liked to read, and maybe, between the time of his arrival and his birthday, he had conveyed that to his guide. Or maybe she had just wanted to present him with a Russian classic as further indication of hospitality. Or maybe, just maybe, the gift had a deeper message; perhaps she detected in the newcomer a hint of the martyr, and the gift was a warning. As far as we know, he did not read it, for it is not mentioned in any of his subsequent writings.

In any case, reading was not really on his mind at that moment. On October 21 at 8:00 p.m., his visa was set to expire, and accordingly, he was called to the passport office. He answered a few questions, and to his shock, they told him to go home. Of course, he persisted, requesting an extension. Now caught up in Russian bureaucracy, he didn't get an answer, and was told by officials that they would let him know shortly. At 6:00 p.m., the phone in his hotel room rang. It was the police, and they said that his request was denied. But it was worse than that! He had to leave the country before 8:00 that evening. This ping-ponging in his life, the pattern of highs and lows (*"I'm gonna play football!"*) and then quitting when things didn't pan out (*"Why do I have to run sprints?"*) was taking its toll. In fact, this time around it seemed like there was no way back; it had become a life and death situation, and when his request for citizenship was denied, he tried to kill himself.

"I am shocked!" he wrote in his diary. "My dreams! I retire to my room. I have $100 left. I have waited for 2 year to be accepted. My fondes dreams are shattered because of a petty offial; because of bad planning I planned to much. 7pm I decide to end it. Soak rist in cold water to numb the pain. Than slash my left wrist. Then plang wrist into bathtub of hot water. I think when Rimma comes at 8 to find me dead it will be a great shock. Somewhere a violin plays, as I wacth my life whirl away."

The violin playing as he watches his life ebb into the waters was a strange note to hit, one that indicates not just a detachment from his final act but a desire to have a soundtrack—just like in the movies. Rimma did indeed arrive in time to save him, finding him in the tub and then calling an ambulance. He was rushed to a hospital, where his wrist was stitched and bandaged, and then taken to a mental ward for recovery. What happened next was this: he was not expelled, and a few days later, he visited the American embassy and said that he wanted to renounce his citizenship.

"I affirm that my allegiance is to the Union of Soviet Socialist Republics," he said in a written statement, one more incredibly dramatic moment. Recognizing that while Lee may have been unstable, and that in reality he was just a minor and something of a "sophomore party-liner," officials temporarily denied his request and that was all. Lee considered it a victory; to the desperate, anything that's not a no is a big win. Once again hyped up for his next move, he returned to his room at the Metropole and opened his diary. "I am elated at the showdown," he wrote. "I feel now that my energies are not spent in vain. I'm sure Russians will except me after this sign of faith in them."

News of his defection had hit the United States, and there were headlines everywhere, just as he may have planned it. It was from the *Fort Worth Star-Telegram* that Lee's brother Robert learned of it—directly from a reporter who had been tailing him in a taxi while he was on the job making milk deliveries. The reporter flagged him down and showed him the paper. "Have you heard?" he said. Robert, astonished, said he had not, finished his delivery, went home, and took a call from Marguerite. She too was besieged by reporters. Robert told her about the newsman who had stopped him as he was making his morning rounds. "Tell the reporters I am under a doctor's care," she said, "and all I have to say is 'No comment.'" It was a press-savvy remark, and one that suggests she may have been rehearsing for such a moment for a long time—not specifically one that involved her reaction to her son's dramatic renunciation of American citizenship, but something that would place her front and center in the eyes of the world. This is exactly what happened three years later when, in her own words, she became "a mother in history."

Do you believe that the squeaky wheel gets the grease? It may be a cliché, but clichés are often true; Lee's failed suicide attempt did indeed propel him into a new life in Russia, and it involved employment, a place to live, and, soon enough, a wife. In March of the following year, he was sent to Minsk for a job at the Minsk Radio Factory. The salary was 700 rubles a month, and he would also receive a monthly check for the same amount from the Red Cross (later viewed by investigators as a perhaps unwitting front for payment from Russian intelligence). For the first time in his life, Lee had his own apartment—a room with a kitchen and bath—and it was only an eight-minute walk to work. Even Russians had to wait for months, years, sometimes, to receive such accommodations, and it was as if he had entered a dream. As he wrote in his diary, "I'm living big." On his twenty-first birthday, one year after his suicide attempt, he felt good enough to throw himself a party. He invited friends over, and two of them brought him an ashtray. It was a joke, of course, but it was also a welcome. Everybody smoked in Russia, and even if he didn't, he had become part of the gang. And if he really wanted to fit in, shouldn't he at least be a good host and provide such amenities for his friends?

And now, let us make the acquaintance of one Ernst Titovets,

observer of Lee Harvey Oswald's good life in Russia—in fact, a critical part of it. Ernst was a fourth-year medical student at a college in
Minsk when he and Lee met through mutual friends. They immediately struck up a friendship. Both young men who were just beginning
to make their way in the world, they had much in common. Ernst
wanted to improve his English, which was pretty good; from Lee, he
hoped, he could learn more about nuances and American culture in
general, especially about the South. Lee's Russian wasn't bad, but he
too wanted to improve, and he was hoping that by engaging in a friendship with Ernst, he could practice his Russian and learn what was right
and wrong. Both men liked classical music and both liked to read.

Like many Russians, Ernst was proud of his country's literary heritage and was well versed in the great books. Lee, on the other hand,
had taste that may have been of a broader range than is conventionally
known (it included writers such as Hemingway and Jack London),
and with Ernst, he even discussed some of the less literary books that
Marguerite would send him at his request. These included *The Power
of Positive Thinking* by Norman Vincent Peale and *As a Man Thinketh*
by James Allen. Both books were filled with comforting bromides,
and it struck Ernst that these books may have provided some solace
to Lee, so far away from home. "Keep your heart from hate, your
mind from worry," Peale had written. "As you change, your world
changes also." "Tempest-tossed souls," said Allen, "keep your hand
firmly upon the helm of your thought."

Marguerite had also sent Lee a copy of *Time* magazine with John
Fitzgerald Kennedy on the cover as "Man of the Year." It was the issue
from November of 1960, and throughout the rest of his life, Oswald
would keep it front and center. Not yet president, the handsome fellow
from Massachusetts had already made a big mark, his charisma draw-
ing people in from quarters around the world. He had a beautiful wife
with international appeal. He dressed well, with a sophisticated flair.

In 1959, his statecraft nemesis Prime Minister Nikita Khrushchev of Russia had traveled to America with an itinerary including a stop in Hollywood. Of all the celebrities he could spend time with, the studio thought that it was important for him to meet the most glamorous of them all, Marilyn Monroe, and she joined him at a star-studded event that included Judy Garland, Elizabeth Taylor, Gary Cooper, and Sammy Davis, Jr. "In Russia," the studio's PR people had told Marilyn "America meant two things. Coca-Cola and Marilyn Monroe."

In a receiving line for the gala, Khrushchev inspected her closely as he shook her hand, reported *Time* magazine. "'You're a very lovely young lady,' he said. 'My husband, Arthur Miller, sends you his greetings,'" she replied, ever witty. "'There should be more of this kind of thing. It would help both our countries understand each other.'"

Of course, Khrushchev was not the only head of state infatuated with Monroe. While recovering from his back injury on PT 109 during World War II, JFK kept a poster of Marilyn above his bed. After they began their affair years later, he told her that she had helped him get through his recovery. The affair with Marilyn was one of many that Kennedy had over the years; he was notorious for the philandering and the behavior was not just viewed as "what's the big deal," but considered cool. His era of power—the 1950s and early '60s—was a heady and sexy period of time, in spite of the Cold War, or maybe the fears of nuclear doom fueled the passions of the moment. "Why shouldn't we sleep together?" was an oft-asked question on first dates, at least in the United States. "The world may blow up tomorrow and we'll always regret it."

Together, Ernst and Lee were two young men on the make, and they made the most of it. There were parties with girls and dances and romances and they confided in each other about many things. Much later, Titovets wrote about all of it in his book *Oswald: Russian Episode*, and it shows you what can happen when you are able to make a jailbreak and get free of the traps in which we are all mired at one time or another, which is to say, to cast off perceptions and expectations and other forms of restraint, and, in today's parlance, go for it!

Lee was exotic, handsome even, and his Russian was pretty good although sometimes it sounded funny—that was charming. He was the new kid in town and everyone wondered what was this American doing here anyway? They spoke of such questions among themselves, and they had to be careful, because maybe the KGB was listening, you never know. Whatever was going on, it all made Oswald seem more mysterious, and women especially were drawn into his orbit; would he marry them? they wondered, and get them out of there? And some of them secretly planned for a life in America, but not everyone; there was one girl in particular who was said to be the love of Lee's life, but she ultimately broke it off because whatever he was offering was not enough, and he kept dating, playing the field, as the saying goes, and Ernst kept watching and making a mental note, and one day it all painted an amazing picture.

There was the time, for example, that Lee Harvey Oswald actually played spin the bottle! You see, Lee and Ernst lived near a women's dormitory for a musical college, and one evening they were invited to visit with some of them in their room. "The rules were simple," Ernst wrote. "A bottle was given a spin in the center of a circle formed by the participants. When stopped, the bottleneck indicated to the player who was supposed to give a kiss to another selected on a second spin. Oswald got very enthusiastic about the game . . . any time the bottle indicated a coupling of Oswald with Anita, the mischievous girl would put up quite a show of extreme modesty or burning passion with Oswald playing a supporting role. This American did have a sense of humor and I wished I could have been as relaxed and easygoing with the girls as he was."

Room 212 at the dormitory of the Foreign Language Institute was a preferred site for hanging out with local women. The four who lived in that room—Nell, Tomka, Tomis, and Alla—adored Lee, and they became known to Ernst and Lee as "Lee's girls." One night before heading to their room, Ernst arrived at Lee's apartment to pick him up. "I found Lee in one of his high moods humming a pop song . . . He was in the process of giving a finishing touch to his person. It was a necktie he was fixing and he took his time to do it to his satisfaction. The song he hummed was about a girl called Bush and her steady Push, with lyrics such as 'Sugar Bush I love you so / I will never let you go / So, don't you let your mother know! Sugar Bush I love you so!'"

The whole thing was kind of a joke, an Americanized mishmash of some Russian references and it had a catchy tune. Ernst and Lee soon made its composite language into a secret code, which further cemented their friendship. Once, at a dance, Lee was engaged in deep conversation with a girl he was trying to bed. As Ernst recalled, he was "leaning leisurely against a windowsill with his legs crossed, looking straight into the girl's eyes, doing most of the talking," and the girl was seriously considering his presentation. Ernst approached but Lee signaled with his right foot that this was not the time. Ernst nodded and kept walking. Later, Lee wrote in his diary that "a growing emptiness overtakes me in spite of my conquest of Ennatchina a girl from Riga, studying at the music conservatory in Minsk. After an affair which lasts a few weeks we part." Ernst figured that Ennatchina was probably the girl he had seen Lee chatting up at the dance.

Over the months, Lee began to confide in Ernst about some of his past relationships. He was especially nostalgic for his time in Japan while in the Marines. "Those Japanese girls!" Ernst wrote of Lee's reverie. "Wee pretty girls! So meek and ever ready to please they were." They even washed him, Lee said, and later, when he returned to the United States with his Russian wife Marina, they would bathe together and she would wash his back, she told a reporter, and it was clearly something that he loved.

It was in 1961 that Lee met Marina Prusakova at a local dance. She was attending pharmacy school and was beautiful, a young woman two years his junior with many suitors. She lived with her uncle, a colonel in the KGB, having moved in with him at the age of sixteen after her mother and stepfather got divorced and she was sent away. She and Lee hit it off right away and got married six weeks later. "She is madly in love with me from the very start," he wrote in his diary. "Boats rides on the Lake Minsk, walks through the parks, evenings at home or at Aunt Valia's place mark May"—referring to the spring month—"and we draw closer and closer, and I think very little now of Ella"—a reference to the previously mentioned great love of his life.

Throughout this period of Lee's adventures in the Soviet Union, he and Ernst were connected by way of another interest. This one had to do with the military and with violence. There was nothing nefarious going on, mind you (or perhaps there was; later, some wondered if Titovets was a Soviet agent trying to set Oswald up). They were just boys being boys, though it is noteworthy, especially the part that involved killing people, and this is how it played out.

At the medical institute that Ernst attended, military instruction was part of the curriculum. He could become a military doctor if he wanted to (he didn't), and students were introduced to military drills, taught how to use guns, and taken to a firing range, and there was even an excursion to a bomb shelter. "It was supposed to protect people against radiation," Ernst wrote, "but not the effects of a direct hit." The same thing was going on in the United States at the same time; construction of "fallout shelters" was proceeding apace, and a frequent topic of conversation was "Would you let your neighbor in if America was bombed and you had a shelter and he didn't?" In Russia, Ernst said, "The presumed enemy number one was the imperialistic warmongering USA," and that was why students were required to take classes in military instruction. With Lee, he now had the opportunity to expand his military vocabulary. One night at Lee's apartment, they got to talking about these matters, and Ernst asked him for the names of drill commands and how they worked. Right away, Lee expounded on the topic. He gave the names of the commands and explained the mechanics: the first part indicated what drill the soldier was about to perform, and the second part gave information about how to do it. It was just like in the Soviet Union, Ernst later wrote, and Lee acted out the commands vocally. Once again, his posture came into play. "His straight bearing with his precise and dapper movements made him a model serviceman," said Titovets, "even in civilian clothes."

Soon Ernst was trying out the moves, trying to impress his "American counterpart." To his surprise, the American version of "about face" was different than the one that was used in the Soviet Union. Ernst had long believed that such a movement, along with the others, would be no different in the armies of the world—although why anyone would ponder the international aspects of "about face" is a question for another time. There was nothing new to add or subtract, he thought, but now he began to examine the matter differently. He asked Lee to demonstrate the movement once again so he could learn it. They then began to compare the Russian and American versions of "about face," and Lee decided that the American one was better. Ernst disagreed, and they began to squabble, with each man becoming patriotic, overcome by passions for their respective countries. The exercise escalated, and they added other drill movements to their demonstration. And then Lee went into the kitchen and retrieved a broomstick. Suddenly it was a pretend rifle, and the men showed each other how their respective armies handled that particular firearm. That in turn became an episode of hand-to-hand combat, and Ernst admired Lee's ability to stay cool in the heat of a fight. He was "invariably patient and benevolent," Ernst said, "a born teacher."

Both out of breath from their exertions, they finally ended the quasi-military roughhousing. Their friendship had now deepened, and Ernst wrote about the irony of how a mock fight showed him more about Lee's character than everything that had come before. Somehow, Lee had convinced Ernst that he was a highly educated person of many accomplishments—or that is how Ernst chose to interpret what he saw, and now he was just a down-to-earth guy who could take a hit, throw a punch, and, presumably, fire a rifle. It was time for tea, Lee said, and then the friends played gin rummy and listened to records. They decided to invite some girls over for the following evening, and then they called it a night.

On another occasion, Lee and Ernst engaged in playacting, mainly so that Ernst could further expand his knowledge of English, but also because it was a fun way to study. To that end, Titovets made tape recordings of his friend so he could listen to Lee's Southern accent when he wasn't around and compare his own understanding of the language with Lee's pronunciation, making adjustments accordingly. For Lee, it was a new version of "Let's Pretend," and judging from the dialogue, you can tell that he liked the game. It began with Titovets giving him pieces to read from Shakespeare's *Othello*, and then from Ernest Hemingway's writings. And then they just made stuff up:

> ERNST: Will you tell us about your last killing?
> LEE: Well, it was a young girl under a bridge. She came in carrying a loaf of bread and I just cut her throat from ear to ear.
> ERNST: What for?
> LEE: Well, I wanted the loaf of bread, of course.
> ERNST: Okay. And what do you think—what do you take to be the most—your most famous killing in your life?
> LEE: Well, the time I killed eight men on the Bowery sidewalk there. They were just standing there, loafing around. I didn't

like their faces, so I just shot them all with a machine gun. It
was very—very famous. All the newspapers carried the story.

It was certainly a curious exchange on the face of it, and it has
become kind of notorious among assassination buffs, for obvious reasons. When asked about it in the years following the killing of JFK,
Titovets said that he and Lee were just kidding around, laughing their
heads off. Aside from the violent images, the really strange part of the
dialogue was the reference to the broadcasting of the story and that it
had become known to many. Famous, just like Lee said.

At some point amid his stay, Lee began to tire of Russia. He had
been shunned by coworkers, and while he had good friends among
college students, including Ernst, he was unsatisfied. "I am starting to
reconsider my desire about staying," he wrote in his diary. "The work
is drab, the money I get has nowhere to be spent. No nightclubs or
bowling alleys, no places of recreation except the Trade Union dances.
I have had enough." It was while he made plans for departure that he
met Marina and their courtship of three months intervened. But one
day, it was time to quit the worker's paradise.

Before he left, he removed a silver ring from his finger and gave
it to Ernst. Titovets felt that the gift was unnecessary and did not accept it. But he remained a good friend from a distance, even if he and
Lee would soon fall out of touch. Already viewing Oswald as "highly
educated," he realized much later that Lee had displayed great courage
in standing up to the onslaught of American propaganda regarding
Russia. *Life* magazine was on to something, he wrote in his book,
when its special 1957 issue on education contrasted "the typical hardworking Soviet sixteen-year-old with his slovenly American counterpart. The Soviet youth, dedicated to becoming a nuclear physicist,
read Shakespeare, studied calculus, and kept in shape by playing vol-
leyball and avoiding sex. The American youth could barely read comic

books and spent his spare time listening to rock music and lusting after girls." That's not exactly where Lee was coming from, but it was certainly something Ernst sensed. Titovets may not have known about Lee's past, but the renegade whom he met was someone to be admired.

On February 15, 1962, Lee's first daughter, June Lee, was born in Minsk. He and Marina applied for exit papers, and on May 24, they picked up the documents in Moscow. On June 1, they left for America, traveling to London and boarding the *Maasdam* for Hoboken, New Jersey. They arrived on June 13 and then flew to Fort Worth on the following day. When they arrived, they were met by Lee's brother Robert. But where were the reporters? Lee wondered. The prodigal son had returned, the defector after all, and he was ready to make amends with his country. But was there no one to offer a headline? Would this moment go unrecorded? Here he was with a beautiful wife and a five-month-old daughter and he could now prove that he had accomplished something. *Look Maw, I'm married! See what I did?* Several days later, he reunited with Marguerite and introduced her to Marina and her new grandchild, June. Marguerite too had something for Lee. She had kept the parakeet that he had given her with his first paycheck from Tujuage's some time ago. Lee opened up the cage and set it free.

Lee Harvey Oswald at two years old.

The Most Dangerous Animal in the World, Bronx Zoo installation that opened on April 27, 1963, six months before the JFK assassination. Oswald often visited the zoo while living in the Bronx, 1952–54.

Restored New York City subway car from the Pelham
Expressway line, 1950s. Teenage Lee often rode the
subway while living in the Bronx at that time, and
liked the idea that you could buy one token and ride
everywhere all day long. Perhaps this was also a way
of tapping into family history; his grandfather was a
streetcar conductor in New Orleans, quite possibly on
the line called Desire.

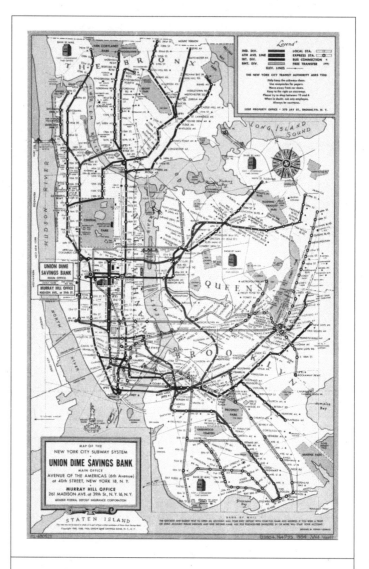

Map of the New York City subway system, early 1950s. While living in the Bronx in 1952–54, Oswald often rode the subways and kept maps such as this one in his pocket.

Lee Harvey Oswald holding rifle and wearing handgun, with copies of *The Militant* and *The Worker*. Photo taken by his wife Marina in March, 1960, in Dallas backyard.

WANTED

FOR

TREASON

THIS MAN is wanted for treasonous
THIS MAN is wanted for treasonous
THIS MAN is wanted for treasonous
activities against the United States:

1. Betraying the Constitution (which
   he swore to uphold):
   He is turning the sovereignty of
   the U. S. over to the communist
   controlled United Nations.
   He is betraying our friends (Cuba,
   Katanga, Portugal) and befriend-
   ing our enemies (Russia, Yugosla-
   via, Poland).
2. He has been WRONG on innu-
   merable issues affecting the security of the U.S. (United Nations-
   Berlin wall-Missle removal-Cuba-
   Wheat deals-Test Ban Treaty, etc.)

3. He has been lax in enforcing Communist Registration laws.
4. He has given support and encouragement to the Communist insp-
   ired racial riots.
5. He has illegally invaded a sover-
   eign State with federal troops.
6. He has consistently appointed
   Anti-Christians to Federal office:
   Upholds the Supreme Court in
   its Anti-Christian rulings.
   Aliens and known Communists
   abound in Federal offices.
7. He has been caught in fantastic
   LIES to the American people (including personal ones like his
   previous marraige and divorce).

Flyer distributed in Dallas in the days before the assassination by devotees of General Edwin A. Walker. Walker organized protests against the desegregation of the University of Mississippi in 1962, which President Kennedy championed.

President John F. Kennedy exits the Hotel Texas in Fort Worth at 8:45 a.m. on November 22, 1963 on his way to greet crowds and make a speech.

Lake Pontchartrain, popular New Orleans destination which Oswald and his wife Marina used to visit.

Lee Harvey Oswald funeral in Fort Worth, Texas: Marina Oswald holding their daughter June, Robert L. (brother), Marguerite Oswald holding Lee and Marina's daughter Rachel, and Reverend Louis Saunders.

Marguerite Oswald in room at Fort Worth home where photos of Lee hang among Kennedy memorabilia and books, 1973.

PART THREE

BACK IN THE USA, OR, THE SON MAKES HIS MARK

"Men are what their mothers made them."

—Ralph Waldo Emerson, *The Conduct of Life*

Something just spoke
Something I wish I hadn't heard

—Stephen Sondheim, "Something Just Broke," *Assassins*

The opportunity did not offer much in the way of fanfare, but still it was something. Upon his return from Russia, Lee had taken on a series of jobs; the pattern of his inability to last long at any particular place of employment persisted, and he kept running out of money. By July of 1963, Marina was pregnant with their second child and their marriage had suffered because of the financial burdens, among other things, and accordingly, they didn't even live together all of the time. She would leave after an argument, availing herself of living quarters offered by friends she had made in her new country, moving from place to place, becoming a nomad just like Lee and Marguerite, and taking her two-year-old daughter with her. Sometimes they would reunite and things would be okay for a while, and then the trouble would erupt yet again, and the pattern would start all over. It was obvious to members of his family that Lee and Marina were in dire straits, and to provide something of a lifeline, Lee's cousin Gene Murret offered a speaking appearance at Spring Hill College in Mobile, Alabama.

Gene, a son of Lillian and Dutz, was studying for the priesthood at the Jesuit center; the college was one of the oldest Jesuit institutions in the country, known in that community for its rigorous academics. Often, the school brought in experts on international affairs and politics and culture, and Gene thought that Lee might have something to say about life under Communism in Russia. Of course, Lee had much to say about his experiences, but he was hardly ever asked—at least by anyone offering the chance to expound in a public venue, let alone one that involved a dedicated program of inquiry. After having been back for a full year, Gene's request was the first time such an offer had come his way and he welcomed the opportunity. The Murrets were happy that the trip had been arranged as well. Their side of the family had been hoping that Lee might pay a visit to his cousin and the Jesuit school, perhaps to reacquaint himself with a relative who was around his age and with whom he had played as a little boy, but also to see what sort of religious life might be available to a person who often seemed lost. That latter possibility was unlikely to appeal, however, as Marina would later tell a seminarian in her broken English, Lee was "without God."

His talk was scheduled for July 27 of that year, and he embarked on a full-on family road trip from New Orleans to Mobile with Uncle Dutz, Aunt Lillian, two of their sons, their spouses and children, and Marina and two-year-old June. Uncle Dutz had offered to drive; Lee didn't know how and didn't have a car. It's just a two-hour trip from the Crescent City to Mobile, and they would have crossed the Huey

P. and then hit the interstate, driving along the Gulf Coast through Biloxi and Gulfport until they arrived in Mobile, where they registered at the Palms Motel on Government Boulevard. As FBI agents later learned, it was Dutz who picked up the tab for the lodging; evidently, the excursion was something of a treat for everyone.

That evening, a small crowd of academics, priests, and various guests assembled for Lee's talk. Lillian and Marina and presumably other female relatives were not present because only men at this Jesuit institution were allowed to attend such events. Oswald spoke of what it was like to live in Russia and work for a factory in Minsk. He also spoke of belonging to a hunting club that the factory had sponsored, providing firearms that people were otherwise not allowed to have, and the club's travels to peasant villages, where residents who appeared to be starving slept in huts. It was a sight that made him reassess his beliefs, and he became disappointed in Communism because it didn't live up to its ideals. But he disliked capitalism as well because it was based on exploiting the poor. "In returning to the US," he said, "I have done nothing more or less than select the lesser of two evils."

Although the speech was even-keeled in terms of discussion of the rival superpowers, the US and the USSR, some in the audience were upset, according to a seminarian who had attended the talk. Yes, this was a Jesuit school, but its freewheeling pursuit of serious inquiry only went so far amid the ongoing Cold War. "What struck me was that he first complained about everything he'd experienced in Russia," this fellow said. "And then he complained about everything he found in the United States. And my reaction was one of frustration and some anger, and I thought, if he is totally frustrated with what he finds here, then why should we, as a matter of fact, be subjected to listening to his complaining if he's unhappy with both the Russian world and the world of the United States."

While Lee was giving his talk, Marina was befriended by Robert

J. Fitzpatrick, a student at the school. He knew some Russian and began speaking with her in her native tongue, and from that point on, the pair made some small talk about where the Oswalds were living and how Marina was faring in this new land. She indicated that she and her husband didn't have much of an income and life was kind of a struggle. Fitzpatrick asked her if they could stay in touch via letters when she went home—the exchange could help him improve his Russian—and so shortly after the visit, he began writing to her, and she would send back his letters with corrections. Such communication was one way that Marina supplemented her family's meager income; from time to time people would ask for similar help, and she would work out various trades. Lee really didn't like the attention she received from men, or the fact that she seemed to encourage it, and at one point, he became enraged when she received a letter from an old flame in Russia. He had sent her a picture, and although Lee already knew him, he was reminded of the fact that he looked very much like John Fitzgerald Kennedy, whom Marina thought was handsome, just like millions of other women.

After Lee's talk there was a question and answer period, and someone asked for his opinion of the President. This probably came up because of the general discussion having to do with relations between America and Russia. "Oswald said that he wasn't quite sure, but Kennedy looked like a good man," a Spring Hill student said years later. "He said he was very suspicious that somebody from a wealthy family, another oligarch, was president of the United States. But he said he thinks basically that this guy's heart was in the right place."

Kennedy, in fact, was kind of a benevolent king, even in his own private view of himself. Just four days after Oswald killed him, his wife Jacqueline sat down for an interview with *Life* magazine journalist Theodore H. White, whom she had called to the White House as the country was grieving. She wanted to make sure that her husband's legacy endured, and she knew that the task must be carried out quickly. "There will be great presidents again," she said, "but there will never be another Camelot." She was referring to the mythical realm of Jack's favorite childhood book, *The Story of King Arthur and His Knights*, and she urged people to think of him as a little boy with a recurring illness who would pass the time by reading about the Knights of the Round Table. "For Jack," she said, "history was full of heroes." Jacqueline Kennedy had put forth a dream, and it had a name, and America did indeed honor its king.

So, too, had Lee and Marina Oswald, once upon a time. The *Time* magazine issue that Marguerite had sent to Lee while he was in Russia was displayed on their coffee table in Fort Worth, where the young Oswalds lived for a while after they returned, and Marina was glued to television coverage of JFK's visit to Fort Worth and Dallas when she was living with a friend during one of her separations from Lee. Amid a dark cloud of threats and menace, the king and his entourage had come to town, and his subjects thronged the streets in adoration. Lee Harvey Oswald may have resented royalty, just as he had learned from his mother, but JFK was front and center in his life, in his house, and soon right before his very eyes.

IT'S FUNNY HOW EVERYONE WANTS to be a writer. You never hear anyone saying that they'd like to weave rugs or be a sculptor. The dream of expressing yourself in a creative way generally involves pen and paper, or, nowadays, keyboard or social media platforms. We are all hardwired for narrative, when you get down to it; for some people, fame and recognition are really the attraction, and they endeavor to get their stories out there so they can stand in the spotlight and identify themselves as an author. Such identification, in their view, accords instant esteem, and their worries will cease; they'll be living on Easy Street and have lots of friends and, if they play their cards right, get on the morning shows. When Lee returned from Russia, one of the first things his mother told him at a family reunion was that she was writing a book. As it turned out, he had been working on one too—like mother, like son—and his goal was to get it published as soon as he could and cash in on his life story. Marguerite had the exact same plan!

She had been in Robert's Fort Worth home for just a few moments, having come in from Crowell, Texas, where she was working as a practical nurse, taking care of an elderly invalid. She seemed elated at seeing Lee again, Robert recalled, and she raved about Marina's beauty, and she held baby June on her lap. And then came the announcement: "You know, Lee," she said, "I am getting ready—I was getting ready to write a book on your so-called defection."

"Mother, you are not going to write any book," Lee replied.

"Lee, don't tell me what to do," she said. "I cannot write the book now, because, Honey, you are alive and back. But don't tell me what to do with you and Marina. It is my life, because of your defection."

"Mother," Lee said, "I tell you, you are not to write the book. They could kill her and her family."

You see, she did have a story about Lee's defection, to some degree. While he was in Russia, she later told investigators, she had no way of knowing if he was dead or alive (though in reality she had been sending him books at his request, reading the notes that he had sent, and it was unlikely that he was dead and someone could have been impersonating him and second-guessing his taste in reading matter). And she felt that she was responsible for bringing Lee home, having sent affidavits to the State Department guaranteeing support for Marina so that she could qualify for a visa. She had written letters to various officials in Washington seeking Lee's reinstatement as a Marine, explaining why she felt he did not deserve a dishonorable discharge. And that was why she had planned to write the book. Then she moved on to the next announcement.

She was planning to quit her job and move to Fort Worth to help Lee and Marina. Lee waved off her idea and told Marguerite that he and Marina were going to find their own place as soon as they could (they had been staying at Robert's since their arrival a few days earlier). But Marguerite headed back to Crowell, resigned, and returned a few weeks later. She rented her own apartment and Lee and Marina packed up and moved in with her. The quarreling began, and Lee continued looking for his own place. He soon got a job as a welder at Louv-R-Pak for $1.25 an hour, and he hated it. That August, he found an apartment on Mercedes Street, and the rent was $39.50 per month. He and Marina were able to pay a month's rent in advance, and Robert helped them move in the next day, packing up his car with their suitcase and boxes as the arguments with Marguerite continued. The scenario was familiar to Lee and Robert, the shouting, the yelling, but to Marina it was a strange way to become acquainted with her mother-in-law.

After they moved, Marguerite tried to make amends with her son and his wife. "She bought a high chair for June Lee," Robert wrote, "and some clothes for Marina." And her generosity continued. She would bring food and dishes and presents for the baby whenever she visited, but Lee resented it. To him, the gifts were an attempt to control the situation, to even just be near him. It had always been hard for him to accept help—"do I look like I need it?" was the idea—but with his mother, the situation was much more loaded, and he seemed to take it out on Marina. One day, Marguerite entered and found Marina in the bedroom, nursing June. "Nursing is a baby's right and the mother's pride," Marina would say to a friend much later, quoting from a childcare book in Russian. Now, her head was down, and when she looked up, Marguerite noticed that she had a black eye.

"Mama-Lee," Marina mustered, and Marguerite approached Lee in the living room where he was reading. "Lee," she said, "what do you mean by striking Marina?" "That's our affair," he said—and she actually agreed. "There may be times," she said later, "that a woman needs a black eye." But having Marguerite around, even if she did come to her son's defense sometimes, was becoming too much for Lee to bear. There was always something she wanted, she was always running some sort of hidden game, and one day he told her not to visit anymore, instructing Marina not to let her in if she returned. Marina thought it an extreme reaction and secretly permitted Marguerite to visit while Lee was at work. When he found out, he erupted, and it was around that time, Marina later said, that the deterioration of their marriage began. She had already noticed a change in his behavior upon their return to the States. He was always hot-tempered, she told investigators, and now this character trait prevented them from "living in harmony." Lee had become very irritable, "and sometimes some completely trivial thing would drive him into a rage." Marina added that she herself did not have "a particularly quiet disposition," but she had to change her character to maintain "a more or less peaceful family life."

Marina was lonely and spoke no English, and Lee liked it that way, circumventing her efforts to learn the new language whenever the opportunity seemed to arise, and he would often speak to her in Russian, heading off the possibility that she could learn English at home. But this would soon change. Through a local library, Lee had met some people known around town as the "Dallas Russians," émigrés who were doing well in Texas. They were a tight-knit circle of comrades who hated Communism and wanted no part of what was going on in their homeland, except for the culture, which they shared through language and food and a general shorthand of exchange in America. This community was a lifeline for Lee and Marina, inviting them to dinner and events, and looking out for one another in general—although it was Marina who was able to fully take in their hospitality.

One of the things that Lee had tried to do when he and Marina first returned was find work as a translator or interpreter. The Texas State Employment Commission referred him to Peter Gregory, a geologist who taught Russian at the Fort Worth Public Library and at the Carswell Air Force Base. Gregory felt that Lee was accomplished enough in Russian to use it in employment, and said so in a certificate that he gave to Lee. Gregory had a young son, Paul, who came to know Lee and Marina over the years, and much later, after Lee had become notorious, he wrote his own book called *The Oswalds*. Paul remembered visiting Lee and Marina in one of their apartments, with its "threadbare living room, baby June sleeping on a bed improvised from two open suitcases." It was one of a series of low-rent dwellings that the couple would live in throughout that period, whether in Fort Worth or Dallas or New Orleans.

Lee never did find work as a translator or interpreter and continued his tenure as a wage-slave worker, a laborer whose elevation had been promised by the Soviet Union—if only such a thing could happen somewhere. In addition to the abovementioned welding job, the jobs he had upon his return to America were machinery greaser at a coffee company, technician at a photography lab, and his last one, order filler at the Texas Book Depository, a job he applied for on October 15, 1963, and was hired for shortly thereafter. At the depository, his job was packing up books for shipping to schools, Scott Foresman books mostly, and soon enough he would be the subject of some of them, entering the slipstream of history.

While Lee was able to talk Marguerite out of trying to sell her book, if in fact she had a manuscript, he continued to try to sell his own story during the early days of his return to Fort Worth. His book was complete, it just needed to be typed up, and one of the first things he did after his reunion with Robert and his family was check the Yellow Pages for a public stenographer. This was Miss Pauline Virginia Bates, as she was evidently listed, and on the morning of

June 18, he walked into her office in dark trousers, a dark blazer, and a T-shirt, she later recalled, and asked her to do some typing. In her book *Marina and Lee*, Patricia McMillan reported that "out of a large manila envelope, he took a sheaf of notes and explained that they had been smuggled out of Russia under his clothes. 'Some are typed on a little portable,' he said, 'some of 'em are handwritten in ink, some in pencil. I'll have to sit right here and help you with 'em because some are in Russian and some are in English.'"

Over a period of three days, they spent eight hours together, as Miss Bates typed and Lee sat next to her, "deciphering his own handwriting, translating Russian phrases here and there, answering her questions about Russia. Not that Miss Bates found him talky. 'If he didn't want to answer a question,' she said, 'he'd just shut up. If you got ten words out of him at a time, you were doing good.' All in all, she found his notes 'fascinating' but 'bitter.' Every afternoon when he left, he took everything with him, including the carbon paper. At some point, he had begun pacing up and down, looking over her shoulder, and asking for a progress update. He stopped her at the tenth page, and she told him that the charge was ten dollars. That was all he had, anyway, it turned out; he gave it to her and walked out. Later, she told investigators that "he had the deadest eyes I ever saw."

It later turned out that the manuscript Miss Bates had been typing was Lee's "Historic Diary." It wasn't written in the moment after all; he had been framing his experiences all along with an eye towards posterity. But he was never able to sell it, and it's not clear what submissions were made, if any. Apart from the gig with the Jesuits in Mobile, no one had asked for his story. And over time, he realized that "his story"—what he had experienced in Russia—may have been a mirage anyway. He was probably used by the Russians, he realized; the payment from the Red Cross, and even his job and salary, was for his "denunciation of the U.S. in Moscow . . . and a clear promise that for as long as I lived in the USSR life would be very good." Yet this too could have been another lie, one more transaction that would take him from point A to point B in the endless act of treading water.

Back in the states, he was heading into a downward spiral. His abuse of Marina escalated over time; once she fell down some stairs while pregnant and she lay in their sidewalk as Oswald looked on and did nothing. Sometimes he gave her caviar and trinkets to atone and she accepted his contrition, and this pattern of abuse and fighting and making up characterized much of their marriage. At the time, she would later tell investigators, "I felt that this man is very unhappy and that he cannot love in any other way. All of this, including the quarrels, mean love in his language. I saw that if I did not go back to him, things would be very hard for him. Lee was not particularly open about his feelings, and always wore a mask. Then I felt for the first time that this person was not born to live among people, that among them he was alone. I was sorry for him and frightened. I was afraid that if I did not go back to him something might happen. I didn't have anything concrete in mind, but my intuition told me that I couldn't do this. Not because I am anything special, but I knew that he needed me. I went back to Lee."

Their make-up periods seemed intense, as they often are in such relationships. One time, after an especially momentous reconciliation, he "did the twist in the kitchen" and said, "Come dance with me"— all while holding a cup of coffee in one hand and a doughnut in the other. "Every night," Patricia McMillan wrote, "he took her walking and bought her doughnuts and coffee. He escorted her to a bowling alley down the street and suggested that he teach her to bowl"—she didn't want to because the balls were too heavy—and then he played "Moscow Evenings" on the jukebox "while they watched others bowl, and he crooned the words to her in Russian. 'No one but us here speaks Russian,'" he said, and then a few days later, just before Thanksgiving

at Robert's in Fort Worth, they squeezed into a photo booth at the
bus station and when Marina saw the photo, she said, "Anyone can see
you ran away from Russia. You look frightened to death." He laughed
and played "Exodus" on the jukebox—the popular movie theme song
about the birth of Israel and flight from bondage, into freedom. We
can imagine him singing along as the stirring chords swept across the
waiting room—

> So take my hand
> And walk this land with me
> And walk this lovely land with me

And then they boarded the bus and headed to Fort Worth, where
they were met by Robert and John Pic. Lee hadn't seen John in ten
years; the oldest of the three brothers was now a sergeant in the Air
Force with a wife and kids, and they were all staying at Robert's.
Marguerite was not invited, and according to reports, a good time
was had by all on that particular Thanksgiving, November 1962, and
it was the last one they would all have together.

One day Marina told Lee that she wanted to see the city where he
was born, so they returned to New Orleans. In Audubon Park, one
of his favorite places, they would walk through the avenues of oak
and enjoy the flowers and fragrances, just like they did in the park
in Minsk during their courtship. He showed her the French Quarter
with its hidden courtyards and lush gardens, and then they walked
along Bourbon Street, and Marina "adored the lights and the music
and the glimpses of strippers dancing," McMillan wrote. To her dis-
appointment, he refused to take her beyond the doors, saying that
Bourbon Street was "a dirty place," though Marina thought that he
secretly liked it.

"Aside from June, whom they both adored," McMillan said, "sex was again the brightest feature of their marriage . . . After intercourse, he would go into the bathroom to wash off, emerge singing one of his arias, and lie down with his back to Marina." And then he'd say, "Don't touch me, don't say a word. I'm in paradise now, and I don't want my good mood spoiled." Sometimes Lee would "pile up pillows at the head of the bed so he could watch them making love" in the mirror at the foot of their bed. Marina didn't like it, she told McMillan, turning her head away and feeling hurt because "the mirror seemed to excite Lee more than she did." Sometimes while sitting in front of the mirror and brushing her hair, "he would bend down to kiss her, looking into the mirror, and call her 'Mama' or 'my little girl.'" Marina would ask him if he was kissing her for herself, or the mirror, and Lee would say, "You mean you don't like it," and she'd say, "Of course not," and "give him a little rap on the rear end."

It was during one of their reunions that Lee and Marina visited Aunt Lillian and they all went crabbing on Lake Pontchartrain. This turned out to be a bad idea, as Lee came up empty and Marina said something in Russian that was clearly derogatory, and Lee asked Lillian if she understood what Marina was saying. She didn't and Lee translated; what Marina had said was "Here you are spending all that money on nets and bait, and you are catching nothing, and we could have gone to the French Market and bought the same thing at the same cost, so what was the point?" In the scheme of things, it seems like a trivial matter, but as always, it represented so much more. "They are all alike," Lee said to Lillian. "Russian, American, typical women." Of course, that was said for Marina, and so the excursion ended with a round of recriminations and they were back to ground zero in their relationship dead end.

As always, Lee was keeping a lot to himself. On April 10, 1963, prior to the trip to New Orleans, Lee had attempted to assassinate General Edwin Walker in Dallas. Marina knew all about it, but no one else did, including Aunt Lillian. Questioning her husband about his reason for wanting to kill Walker, he told her that Walker "was a very bad man, that he was a fascist, that he was the leader of a fascist organization." "All of that might be true," Marina had replied, but "just the same you had no right to take his life." Lee replied that "if someone had killed Hitler in time it would have saved many lives."

General Walker was a notorious white supremacist who had run for Texas governor against John Connally, the Democratic candidate who beat him and who was in the limousine next to Kennedy on the day the President was shot and killed. Connally was also hit. Walker had a terrible history. He had instigated riots at the all-white University of Mississippi after black student James Meredith had enrolled, and because of that, Attorney General Robert Fitzgerald Kennedy (John's brother) ordered that Walker be committed to a mental hospital for evaluation. (The Kennedys weren't messing around when it came to integration.) Walker was released a few days later when a large, social media–style response from the right wing erupted, and he was later acquitted on the charge of fomenting unrest at the university. It's not clear why he became a target of Oswald's. Lee may have lived in Russia and been proficient in the works of Karl Marx, but that motive—that he hated racists—fell apart after he killed Kennedy, hardly a white supremacist. What Walker and Kennedy had in common was that they were famous, but that was all. And Oswald had missed, even telling Marina about it, hiding the rifle in their house after fleeing the scene on foot and appearing to get away with the attempted hit—until JFK was killed and Marina came forward with a note and an incriminating picture.

It turned out that in March of 1963, about a month before the attempt on Walker, Oswald had posed with the rifle that he used in his backyard in Dallas and asked Marina to take a picture. That's the famous photo that we all know, the one where he stands with a hint of a smile, rifle at his side, pistol in his pocket, brandishing a copy of *The Militant*, the newspaper of the Trotskyist Socialist Workers Party; it was a souvenir of some sort, for he later signed it "Killer of fascists, Lee Harvey Oswald" for a friend. He had ordered the Mannlicher-Carcano rifle on March 12, 1963, and it arrived two weeks later on March 25. He bought it through a mail-order house in Chicago with a fake name and a coupon from *American Rifleman* magazine; with telescopic sights, the total cost was $19.95. "You lookin' at me?" he seems to be saying in the photo, years ahead of *The Joker* and Robert DeNiro as Travis Bickle in *Taxi Driver* standing before a mirror and trying out poses with a gun. "You lookin' at ME?" "Who're you lookin' at—me?"

In September of that year, Marina Oswald moved in with Ruth Paine in Irving, Texas, a comfortable middle-class suburb of Dallas that was named after Washington Irving, author of "The Legend of Sleepy Hollow," the short story about the headless horseman of the Revolutionary War. The name of the town was a typical real estate nod to some vague history that we all shared—in a state that prided itself on having been part of the Confederacy. Marina had met Ruth early the previous winter at a party thrown by the Dallas Russians. The Russian language was an interest of Ruth's; as the Cold War was heating up, Ruth wanted to learn more about Russian culture and Russians in general. She also had a corresponding interest in folklore and belonged to a group dedicated to singing madrigals from around the world, and it was through that group that she got to know the host of the Dallas party. Her wide-ranging curiosity about the world was rooted in her spiritual beliefs; she was that rare person who followed the tenets of her religion. When it came to the Oswalds, she was a Good Samaritan just like in the Bible, as the writer Jessamyn West later observed in *McCall's* magazine, pulling over on the metaphorical road and offering the beleaguered couple a ride. As a lifelong Quaker, she was committed to understanding "the other" and that night, she formed almost an instant bond with Marina because both women were mothers and Ruth too was separated from her husband. "I seek to fill the needs of those I meet," she had written in a college paper, "to give to the fullest of my ability to all who ask of me. I want to accept others, and to express this acceptance. Too many of the world's people go friendless through life, unable to share their deepest sorrows and joys with anyone. Too often we do not have the time, or the inclination, to reach out to those who need help."

Everyone in the community of the Dallas Russians knew all about the problems between the Oswalds on the night of the party when Marina met Ruth. They had witnessed the verbal abuse, the torment, the physical evidence of beatings that Marina had undergone. They had done what they could to extract Marina, but it just wasn't working. "On Saturday the 23rd of February," Thomas Mallon wrote in *Mrs. Paine's Garage*, "in the worst fit of temper he'd ever thrown—over the way she'd prepared his supper—he started to choke her. A fortuitous cry from Junie made him desist, but later the same evening he found Marina standing atop the toilet, attempting to hang herself with a length of clothesline. Oswald halted the strangulation."

Lee too was at the party on the night that Marina met Ruth. In the middle of the room, he was holding forth on his experiences in the Soviet Union, and Ruth was struck by how much he liked being the center of attention. But there was something about him that also drew her own attention. As she told me during a phone conversation while I was working on this book, "I have always been aware of the look on the face of a person who does not expect to be accepted, the look about the mouth of the person who expects defeat. Lee Oswald had this look." She and Marina exchanged addresses that night, with Ruth sensing that the young wife needed a way out, and inviting Marina to come and stay with her at her home in Irving. Marina accepted and moved in that fall with her two-year-old daughter, and Lee remained in Dallas in a rented room, although he would visit on weekends. "I didn't care for Oswald," Ruth told me. "I thought he was an inflexible, dogmatic oddball." Though, like a lot of killers, he did express occasional feelings of sympathy, and he meant it. While Ruth was going through her divorce, for example, he commiserated and told her that she "must be having a hard time."

She didn't think he was dangerous and he was very affectionate with June. When he and Marina had their own place, he frequently played with his little girl, taking baths with her and spending a fair amount of time putting her to bed. Around June, he became kind of a baby himself, McMillan wrote, competing with her for Marina's attention. Sometimes when June was finished with her bath, he'd talk in baby talk, saying, "Quick, there are drops of water on my leg!" and if Marina didn't dry him off quickly, he'd threaten to stay in the tub all day. "Stop it, Alka!" Marina would say, using her affectionate term for him. Clearly they had this familiar routine, and it was one of the things that cemented their relationship. At Ruth's, he often played with her own children; Ruth remembered the time that her young son Christopher crawled all over him while he was lying on the floor watching football. Lee didn't seem to mind it at all. Later, after Marina gave birth to a second daughter in October, a few weeks before the assassination, he seemed elated, though throughout their marriage he had said to Marina that he was hoping for a son. "Maybe he'll grow up to be president some day," he would say; finally his family would have produced a king.

Like Lee, Ruth's husband Michael was often around in spite of the estrangement. He too doted on his kids and pitched in around the house. Marina began to thrive during her time at the Paines; as she and Ruth went about their days performing the usual tasks of motherhood—doing laundry, hanging it outside to dry, preparing meals, entertaining the kids, getting them ready for bed—they gossiped (sometimes in Russian, which Ruth enjoyed) and exchanged information about methods of childcare in their respective countries. Marina even had a copy of *Baby and Child Care*—in Russian. It was the bestselling childcare book of that era, perhaps of all time, written by the famous Dr. Spock, who urged women to pay close attention to their child's needs and respond accordingly; rather than recommending a kind of tough love or hands-off ethos that characterized much child raising at the time ("don't spoil them"), he advised mothers that babies need love, that they were little people with their own emotional needs, and that they should be cherished rather than told to conform to rules that pertained to adults. Marina was mindful of Dr. Spock's teachings, and of the importance of parents in general, and later, after JFK was killed, one of the first things she expressed to Ruth was what a terrible thing had befallen Mrs. Kennedy. "How sad it is that her children will have to grow up without a father!"

All in all, even with the occasional squabbling of Ruth and Michael, the scene at the Paine residence was genteel, cordial, welcoming—something borne of generations that valued an elite education and manners embedded in upper-class codes. The Paines liked tradition, and marked all holidays, and made a big deal out of birthdays. On October 18, Lee's twenty-fourth birthday, Ruth and Marina threw him a surprise party. Lee was on an upswing at the moment, having just been hired as a packer at the Texas Book Depository, a job that Ruth had gotten for him through a friend. He had told Marina that it was "good to be working with books" and that the work was "interesting and clean." His birthday was his second day on the job, so the day was twice as special. Michael had come for the party, and Ruth had baked a cake, decorated the table, and supplied the wine. When the little group entered, carrying the cake and singing "Happy Birthday," Lee started crying and blew out the candles. After a few glasses of wine, everyone was in a jovial mood, and Lee said, "I'd like the baby to be born today, my birthday." He added that he didn't like late birthday presents and wouldn't accept them. "You won't keep your baby?" Marina said, teasing him back. "We'll see," he said. You see, Marina was now nine months pregnant, about to give birth at any moment. She was uncomfortable, with swollen ankles and aching legs. "I'm sorry," Lee told his wife. "I'll never put you through this again."

The next morning, Lee scanned secondhand ads in the paper. He was looking for cars and a washing machine, according to McMillan. For Marina, a washing machine was a big deal. Having grown up in Russia, she did not have a washing machine in her home, nor was there one accessible at a laundromat, because there were no laundromats. No one had washing machines, or at least not a family of little import like hers, and when she came to the States, she became fascinated with them and reveled in having access to such a modern miracle. She had in fact become fascinated with material goods in general, the myriad grocery items and home furnishing selections that her new country had to offer. In Dallas, or perhaps in Fort Worth, they lived across the street from a Montgomery Ward, and she loved to go shopping there; she loved its wide aisles and marveled at all of the things that you could buy. Texas had definitely rolled out the welcome wagon for one and all, and one of the things that she really wanted was her very own washing machine. There was a lot of laundry to do if you had a baby, plus there were all of the other items that needed cleaning at any given time, and being able to throw them into a machine when you felt like it was a serious luxury. For Marina, the offer suggested that Lee was really ready to commit to his marriage. But it wasn't enough to make her return with him to Dallas. The arrangement that she and Lee had seemed to be working at that moment, and she left the question of the washing machine up in the air.

Later that night, they watched two movies, both about assassinations. The first was *Suddenly*, a little-known noir classic with Frank

Sinatra as a deranged war veteran who has been hired to kill the President after he debarks from a train and then joins a motorcade that heads through a small Western town. The assassin has set up a vantage point in a house overlooking the parade route, and he's poised with a rifle. "Don't play God just because you've got a gun," a cop who has been kidnapped tells him. But there's a tip-off and the train carrying the President doesn't stop, and the sniper is killed.

The second movie was *We Were Strangers* about the assassination of a Cuban dictator, with John Garfield as an American who has come to help revolutionaries, kind of an echo of Lee's fascination with Cuba and Marxist governments, as well as his murky involvement with the Fair Play for Cuba committee a few months earlier in New Orleans where his leafletting on the streets got him arrested. (Was leafletting an idea he got from that day in New York when someone handed him a flyer about the Rosenbergs? Who knows—but the image of Lee leafletting is one of those things that became imprinted on the national consciousness, just like the "elderly woman" handing him the leaflet about Julius and Ethel became something of a turning point in his own life.) At the end of *We Were Strangers*, John Garfield is killed—and there's a revolution—and everyone is dancing in the streets.

Later that night, Marina and Lee made love and it was the last time it happened.

On October 20, the baby was born. When Marina went into labor, it was Ruth who drove her to Parkland Hospital, with Lee staying at Ruth's to take care of June. Ruth donated her own blood in case Marina had a problem, and she waited until Marina was close to delivering before returning home. It was Ruth who waited by the phone for news of the baby's delivery, and not hearing anything, called the hospital to find out what was going on. Shortly after eleven that evening, she learned that everything was fine, and Marina had delivered her second daughter. Ever the master of the grand gesture, Lee was not available. He had gone to sleep, and Ruth told him about the birth of Audrey on the following morning. Later at the hospital, he told Marina she was wonderful and had tears in his eyes. Marina apologized that she had had another girl, and Lee said they'd keep trying. Marina said there would not be another child. "I can't go through ten babies to get a boy." And then Lee asked what name she put on the birth certificate. It was Audrey Marina Rachel Oswald. "Audrey" was for Audrey Hepburn, whom Marina admired, though she had wanted Rachel as a first name. But Lee felt that it was too Jewish and it was bumped into a supporting position. Now sixty years old and a mother with children of her own, she goes by the name Rachel.

To save money, Lee and Marina continued to live apart. Strangely, as McMillan reported, on October 23, three days after the birth of Audrey, Oswald attended a meeting sponsored by a right-wing organization headlined by General Walker. As the general addressed a large crowd, what was Lee thinking while listening to the man he had tried to kill six months earlier? Perhaps he considered the fame that was almost his, if only he hadn't missed. Maybe he thought, "You lucky son of a bitch . . . one of these days, I might try again." Or maybe he thanked his lucky stars that the episode had passed and he got away scot-free, with no one except Marina the wiser.

In late October, Lee was visiting the Paines, Marina, and his new baby, and the conversation turned to politics; Lee told Michael that he had just been to a speech of General Walker's. As it happened, Michael was going to an ACLU meeting that night and invited Lee, who accepted. On their way out the door, Lee leaned in to Marina and whispered a secret. "If only Michael knew what I wanted to do to Walker!" he said. "Wouldn't he be scared!" He sounded like a little boy who was still playing "Let's Pretend." He delighted in tricking people—which is to say, he had a hidden thing that was quite possibly his true self, the center of his own personal Russian egg—and wouldn't it be amazing if he pulled off the covers and "Lee-boy" stepped forward?

If Lee felt out of place whenever he visited the Paines, he gave no indication. He spent the night before the assassination with Marina, arriving unannounced, to her surprise and to Ruth's, explaining that he was lonesome for his girls. But Marina was angry about a recent visit from an FBI agent who had gotten wind that she was living with the Paines; Oswald had come to their attention because of time he had spent in New Orleans that summer with some suspicious characters involved in anti-Castro activities (or was it pro? He appeared to be switching sides in his own version of *I Led Three Lives*, perhaps finding some kind of perverse delight in alternating between sides and hiding, even from himself—a situation that to this day people are trying to unravel). Fearing that she might be sent back to Russia, or that there was some sort of parallel KGB scenario playing out in the United States, she sent the agent away, offering no help. She had tried to alert her husband at his rooming house in Dallas, calling and being told that there was no one named "Lee Harvey Oswald" living there, and in short order, she found out that he was indeed there, under an assumed name—the one that, it later turned out, he had ordered the rifle used to shoot at Walker and the one he was about to use again.

In fact, the rifle was in Ruth's garage, wrapped up in some blankets, unbeknownst to the Paines. What on earth was going on? Marina asked him when she finally made contact. Somehow, Lee was able to talk his way out of the mess, and now he was at the Paines, seeking a reconciliation once again. He pressed his case, saying that he was lonesome, and Marina said that she'd return at Christmas. At the moment, it was for the best that she remain at Ruth's. She expressed concern over money, and Lee told her not to worry, he had some saved up, and he'd rent an apartment. And one more time, he said he'd buy Marina a washing machine. She said that he should buy a car instead, and that she didn't want a washing machine. He explained that he could continue traveling by bus, and used cars always broke down and became an expense. "I don't want my girl to do all of the laundry in the bathtub," he said, making a Hail Mary pass. Marina said she'd think about it, and then they all had dinner, and then Lee sat down with June and read her a book. Soon afterwards, he went to bed, and she took a bath and followed Lee.

"Marina still had pregnancy privileges," McMillan wrote later. "That is, she was allowed to sleep with her feet on whatever part of his anatomy they came to rest. About three in the morning, she put a foot on his leg. Suddenly, with a sort of wordless vehemence, he lifted her leg, shoved her foot hard, then pulled his leg away." She realized that he was very angry about the fact that she wasn't moving back in with him. That morning, he slept through the alarm, and she woke him up for work. He got dressed, approached her in bed, and asked about some shoes she had been planning to get. "You must get those shoes, Mama," he said, and then he told her not to get up. "I'll get breakfast myself."

And then he kissed his daughters but not Marina, headed out, stopped in the doorway, and told her that he had left some money on the bureau. It was for everything that she and the girls needed, he said. And then he made his exit, and shortly thereafter, she discovered that he had also left his wedding ring, in a cup that once belonged to her grandmother.

The fact that he had spent the night in the home of a man Thomas Mallon later described as belonging to "Ralph Waldo Emerson's great-great-grandson and also the distant scion of a man who had signed the Declaration of Independence" wouldn't have mattered; the ghost that had emerged was Robert E. Lee's and Lee Harvey Oswald was about to call out a rebel yell. But what we know of his last night is that he did try to quell this voice—and all of the other things in his life that had now contrived to end it—and the president's.

On September 25, 1963, two months earlier, John Fitzgerald Kennedy was in Billings, Montana. He was on a swing through the West to shore up support for the election coming in the following year and to press his campaign for "the new frontier," space exploration, which one day would take people to the moon. At the Yellowstone County Fairgrounds, he addressed a large crowd, which included noted members of the Blackfeet tribe such as Walter "Blackie" Wetzel, Dick Spanish, and Earl Old Person, federal and state officials, and a range of residents from various quarters, with many decked out in the regalia of their circles, from Stetsons to war bonnets. It was the kind of gathering—Native Americans and white people—generally only seen at frontier battle memorials; while Montana had voted for the Republican Richard M. Nixon in the 1960 Presidential election, a broad swath of citizens turned out in droves to see the youthful and handsome President. With soaring rhetoric, he ended his speech by quoting Henry David Thoreau: "Eastward I go, only by force. Westward I go free." It was a line he used in other speeches across the West, and in November, two months after Billings, he was entering the heart of the Wild West, the place where it all began—at least in the mind of PR-minded boosters—and the myth was so entrenched by the time he arrived that many could not distinguish between the fable and reality, including Lee Harvey Oswald, lying in wait for an ambush far above the President's motorcade route, just like an old-time outlaw up in the cliffs. It was almost 12:30 p.m., a little after high noon. And somewhere a song was playing, and its melody was all around him. *"I do not know what fate awaits me / I only know I must be brave."*

Like all of us, JFK had his demons. Something he wrestled with all his life was the specter of death and his own mortality. From the time that he had scarlet fever as a child and nearly died through his

heroic rescue of fellow sailors who were plunged into the Pacific when
their boat, the PT 109, sank during World War II, right up through
his appointment in Dallas, he seemed to be aware of a lurking shadow.
Even on the second night of his honeymoon, he recited a poem to
Jackie as they lay in bed. It was called "I Have a Rendezvous with
Death" and its opening lines were "I have a rendezvous with Death /
At some disputed barricade," and it alternates images of springtime
and rebirth with the inevitable engagement, "on some scarred slope of
battered hill," when spring and meadow flowers first appear.

Was it his Irish sense of fate? A sense that really and truly, he
did not have all that much time on this Earth? Whatever the source,
the shadow was very much with him as he approached Dallas on
November 22. The city was filled with the President's enemies; he
knew that he was entering an inferno of rage, and even some of his
own aides had advised him against heading to the Big D. The anger
had been playing out across the country, fueled by hatred of liber-
als, what they were doing, and most of all, Kennedy himself. Just a
week before while he was in Miami, someone had sent a death threat
to the Miami Chief of Police: "The Cuban Commandos have the
BOMBS ready for killing JFK and Mayor KING HIGH either at the
AIRPORT or at the Convention Hall," it said. "A Catholic PADRE
is going to give instruction at Cuban Womens Broadcast at [illeg-
ible time] tonight by [illegible RADIO] and then all are invited to
Bayfront Park Auditorium and take along a BOTTLE of wine."

In Fort Worth at the Hotel Texas, he and Jackie had just returned
to their suite at 10:00 a.m. following breakfast on his second last
day. The hotel had a seedy history, not one that was generally known
beyond certain longtime locals, or readers of the crime novelist Jim
Thompson, who worked there in the 1920s as a bellboy. His experiences informed much of his writing, including an early blueprint
called *What the Bellman Saw* in which a porter furnishes call girls,

booze, you name it for guests at an outwardly fancy hotel. At the end of the day, Thompson would come home from work and recount the bleak and shabby stories for his family. He was in bad shape, his sister later told a biographer, and they "were all kind of scared to death." When President Kennedy stayed at the Hotel Texas, there was nothing that would have indicated any such past—or present even. In fact, the usual hotel art in the Kennedys' room, probably generic though respectable Western landscapes, had been seriously upgraded. Looking around their suite that morning, Jackie realized that priceless paintings were on display, something she hadn't noticed when they arrived. There was a Monet, a Picasso, a Van Gogh, and other notable works, borrowed from a local museum in honor of the President and First Lady, Jackie mainly, known for her devotion to fine art. There was even a catalogue just for the occasion and it included the name of the woman who arranged the exhibit. They immediately called her and offered their thanks. A moment later, an aide entered with a copy of *The Dallas Morning News*. On page 14, there was a full-page ad. It was a menacing announcement, surrounded by a funereal black border, with the headline "WELCOME MR. KENNEDY TO DALLAS." It contained twelve questions, including one that asked, "WHY Gus Hall, head of the U.S. Communist Party, has promised his support for the 1964 election" and then "WHY has the Foreign Policy of the United States degenerated to the point that the CIA is arranging coups and having staunch Anti-Communist Allies of the U.S. bloodily exterminated?" The ad had been placed by "The American Fact-Finding Committee," chaired by a prominent local businessman, and his sentiments were shared by other wealthy Texans, oilmen, ranchers, and the paper's owner Ted Dealey, and on November 22, they swirled through the atmosphere like a poison.

"Can you imagine a paper doing a thing like that?" Kennedy said to his aide, and then turning to Jackie, he said, "Oh, you know, we're heading into nut country today," and then, continuing the thought, he said, "You know, last night would have been a hell of a night to assassinate a President." He was referring to the scene outside the hotel. "There was the rain, and the night, and we were all getting jostled. Suppose a man had a pistol in a briefcase." And then he pointed at a wall with his finger and pretended to shoot. "Then he could have dropped the gun and the briefcase and melted away in the crowd." A few weeks earlier, Kennedy had had a White House meeting with Jim Bishop, the author of *The Day Lincoln Was Shot*. In the meeting, Kennedy had learned that he and Lincoln shared a view about assassination: "Any man who is willing to exchange his life for mine can do so," he told his aide. And then he walked over to a window and looked outside.

"It would not be a very difficult job to shoot the president of the United States," he said. "All you'd have to do is get up in a high building with a high-powered rifle with a telescopic sight, and there's nothing anybody could do." It wasn't the first time he had such a vision. Once, outside his family's compound in Hyannisport, Massachusetts, he was messing around with his Secret Service agents on the docks. He pretended to have been shot and fell to the ground, with "blood" oozing from his body. It turned out to be ketchup; the whole thing was some kind of prank that he had been planning for a while, to the dismay of his Secret Service agents. Now there were no games afoot and it was time to go.

At 10:30 a.m. he and Jackie joined a motorcade from the hotel to Carswell Air Force Base, and at 11:25 they departed. Fifteen minutes later, when the First Couple stepped off Air Force One on the tarmac in Dallas, they were greeted by a throng of admirers, yelling and screaming so loudly that reporters couldn't hear each other speak. This was contrary to expectations, although there were also some in the crowd who were brandishing menacing signs: YANKEE GO HOME

AND TAKE YOUR EQUALS WITH YOU, said one, and then there was HELP
JFK STAMP OUT DEMOCRACY. And then another: LET'S BARRY KING
JOHN, a distant echo of Huey Long and his anti-American royalty
speeches referencing Senator Barry Goldwater, who had announced
a run for President on a platform of small government. No such rally
is complete without misspelled signs, and in that regard, there was a
cardboard placard that read YOUR A TRAITOR. Standing high above
everyone else, someone was waving a giant Confederate flag.

"THE MOTORCADE IS LEAVING LOVE Field," an announcer says on television
as millions of viewers watch across the country. In the uncovered limousine, the First Couple is in the rear seat and Texas Governor John
Connally and his wife Nellie are in the seat in front of them.

THE PROCESSION HEADED THROUGH DOWNTOWN Dallas, taking Cedar
Springs to Harwood, turning right on Main, and turning on Houston
Street to Elm, and then heading on to the Trade Mart for a luncheon
where he was scheduled to give a speech. "We in this country, in this
generation, are—by destiny rather than choice—the watchmen on
the walls of world freedom," he was about to say. "We ask, therefore,
that we may be worthy of our power and responsibility, that we may
exercise our strength with wisdom and restraint, and that we may
achieve in our time and for all time the ancient vision of 'peace on
earth, good will toward men.' That must always be our goal, and the
righteousness of our cause must always underlie our strength. For as
was written long ago: 'except the Lord keep the city, the watchman
waketh but in vain.'"

Up on the sixth floor, Lee Harvey Oswald was about to make his
move. The motorcade route had just been published the day before,
and once he learned of it, he retrieved his rifle from the Paines' garage. In fact that was the real reason for his unannounced visit with

Marina on the eve of the big event; the rifle was hidden in that garage and on the following morning, this day, November 22, he smuggled it out, still in the blankets, and he got into the car of his friend who had been driving him to work every day since he had started at the book depository, and he headed up to the sixth floor, package in hand. Through the rifle sight he could see the motorcade approaching and the limo with its occupants. The moment was nearly at hand, and he may have heard more voices, had some second thoughts. The ghosts of Presidential assassins past began to appear; there was John Wilkes Booth (Lincoln) and Charles Julius Guiteau (Garfield) and then Leon Czolgosz (McKinley), and they urged him not to waver, to join them (or at least that was the vision of Stephen Sondheim in his dark musical *Assassins*), and Oswald cocked his rifle and was ready to fire. Down below, the crowds were so exuberant that Nellie Connally, the First Lady of Texas, turned around and said, "You can't say that Dallas doesn't love you."

"No, you certainly can't," the President replied, and then the shots rang out, and Kennedy's head was blown open and the blood spilled all over Jackie as she cradled him.

And the streetcar is heading for Elysian Fields and Cemeteries— and another stop that is even beyond, Fame, and then Life Everlasting. The bell clangs; Lee Harvey Oswald steps on board. *Look Maw! Do you love me now? Are you lookin' at ME?*

PART FOUR

AFTERMATH
OF AN EXECUTION

"Here comes his mother."
—William Shakespeare, Junius Brutus in *Coriolanus*

"Leaving New Orleans also frightened me considerably. Outside of the city limits the heart of darkness, the true wasteland begins."
—John Kennedy Toole, *A Confederacy of Dunces*

And that was the beginning of a wave of conspiracy theories without end, and they started with Lee Harvey Oswald.

It was 7:55 p.m. in Texas, and Oswald was in the custody of the Dallas Police Department. Recall that he had fled the scene of the crime—and his flight was not glamorous at all, as in other famous fugitives, such as Bonnie and Clyde or John Dillinger or predecessors such as Jesse James or Billy the Kid; it did not involve a getaway car or any other cowboy thing like a gang who helped him. He ran away on foot and then by bus and then by cab; recall that he had been caught at the Texas Theatre after killing Officer J. D. Tippit and trying to kill another cop in the process. Reporters had invaded the city jailhouse, and they were now peppering him with questions.

"Did you kill the President?" someone shouted.

"I'm just a patsy," he said, and then he was whisked away.

Two days later, on November 24 at 11:21 a.m., Oswald was shot in the stomach by Jack Ruby, owner of the Carousel Club, a strip joint in Dallas. That shocking incident was televised, just like the JFK assassination—with the fleeing limousine and Jacqueline Kennedy trying to clamber her way out of it until she was shoved back in by a Secret Service agent and the bloody vehicle headed towards Parkland Hospital where the President would soon be pronounced dead. Oswald's murder became the second homicide within a period of two days that millions of American watched in real time, up close and personal, and a week later, on November 29, *Life* magazine published thirty frames from what became known as the Zapruder film, a cinematic recording of the JFK assassination made by Abraham Zapruder, a local manufacturer of dresses who had brought his movie camera to the parade to capture the event.

To his endless shock and sadness, his eighteen-second film had captured the murder of the President. "I heard the first shot, and I saw the president lean over and grab himself," he later told the Warren Commission. "For a moment I thought it was, you know, like you say, 'Oh, he got me,' when you hear a shot . . . but before I had a chance to organize my mind, I heard a second shot, and then I saw his head opened up and the blood and everything came out . . . then I started yelling, 'They killed him, they killed him . . .'" That moment—forever known as frame 313—has also fueled the obsession with conspiracy theories among students of the assassination, provoking never-ending discussions of shooting angles and bullet trajectories and how many people may have been involved in the act and from what point in the area they may have carried it out, (the Grassy Knoll? the roof of the book depository?), and what if the film itself was edited to show one thing when something else entirely may have happened?

Over the years, four-time Pulitzer nominee Hugh Aynsworth has tried to tamp down this conspiracy fever. He is regarded by many reporters as the go-to guy when it comes to this affliction, having been there through that terrible three-day sequence from November 22, 1963, through November 24, and witnessing all of its major events—the Kennedy assassination, the arrest of Oswald after the murder of Officer Tippit, and then Oswald's own murder in Dallas lockup, which made it impossible for there to be a trial—and cranked up many in the early days of the investigation who already thought that there must have been a plot to take down the President. Aynsworth wrote about all of those events for *The Dallas Morning News, Newsweek* and other publications. Along with a partner, he maintains a vast archive of source material, and it's all housed in what he calls the "Assassination Room" at his apartment in Dallas. Thirteen years after Kennedy's murder, he gave a tour to a reporter from *Texas Monthly*, gesturing towards what the visitor described as "overflowing file drawers, boxes of tape recordings with loose tape dangling out, stacks of photographs, piles of books."

"Have you ever seen such junk?" Aynsworth asked his visitor. "I ought to give it to a university, to some place where they could make sense of it, where somebody besides a tired old reporter could make use of it." Yet regardless of his and other research into the events of that moment, many Americans still believe that Oswald was probably a patsy, like he himself had said, set up by a you-name-the-entity or group or individuals with hidden motives.

A litany of names runs throughout conversations about that awful day, and it's like some weird roll call of those who dwell in various depths of America's shadows, including some who are front and center but because of their prominence have done as they please, and others who really are like rockfish hidden in murky hollows. Those who populate this roster may or may not be connected in one way or another, but in some cases actually are, though to what end it is not clear and probably never will be. There's Guy Bannister and Carlos Bringuier; there's David Ferrie and the Miami Cubans; there's Sylvia Odio and Clay Shaw and Mark Lane, Carlos Marcello and Santo Trafficante, George de Mohrenschildt and assorted Dallas Russians, the Dulles Brothers (John Foster, Secretary of State, and Allen, director of the CIA), James Jesus Angleton (chief of CIA counterintelligence), Yuri Nosenko (defector of the KGB to the United States), and even Lyndon Baines Johnson (Vice President under JFK, successor to the Presidency upon his assassination). It has long been said that a monster resides in Lake Pontchartrain and bayous of New Orleans, some kind of shape-shifting creature that surfaces at times as a werewolf, passing on a curse to its victims. The cloud of obsession and madness that has manifested over the years around the demolition of the President has surely taken on the contours of such a monster. The thing grows and grows, in different shapes and forms, a boogeyman that never leaves and deflects attention from the source of what happened that day in Dallas. Can we drive the monster back into the lake? Let us name it and give it a try.

ON NOVEMBER 25, PRESIDENT KENNEDY, Officer J. D. Tippit, and Lee Harvey Oswald were laid to rest. What a peculiar triple header of funerals this was, though it was difficult to take in the convergence at that time because everything was happening so fast, and of course— and rightly so—the President's funeral took precedence. Those who watched television coverage of this event will never forget the funeral cortege moving through the nation's capital that morning. Over a million people lined the streets, and the pomp and circumstance was stunning, the kind of thing not witnessed in this country since the assassination of President Abraham Lincoln when a train carrying his casket moved across the country, making whistle stops en route from his birthplace to the capital, and throngs lined the tracks.

The caisson bearing Kennedy's casket left the US Capitol followed by Black Jack, a riderless horse with a Cavalry saddle, sword, and riding boots placed backwards in the stirrups, marking the end of JFK's Presidency. At 11:35 a.m., Jacqueline Kennedy and her children Caroline and John Jr. (known to the world as "John John," JFK's affectionate nickname for him) joined the procession on foot, along with other family members, followed by prime ministers and dignitaries from many a country, and throughout it all there was the rhythmic drumming of the military bands that joined the procession on foot. They walked for over three quarters of a mile, and then at 12:14 p.m. the President's casket was taken into St. Matthew's Cathedral for a private funeral, and when the mass concluded, the coffin was returned to the caisson as the Army band played "Hail to the Chief." The procession moved on, followed by its lengthy motorcade, and then traveled for three miles to Arlington National Cemetery, where the President was laid to rest as fifty military jets flew overhead in three formations, followed by Air Force One. At 3:15 that afternoon, his wife Jacqueline and brothers Robert F. Kennedy, attorney general of the United States, and Edward M. Kennedy, senator from Massachusetts, lit the eternal flame.

The funeral for Officer J. D. Tippit was held at the Beckley Hills Baptist Church in Dallas. It too was a ceremony for a man who had been killed in service to his country, with all of the attendant flourishes. In addition to his wife and three children, two thousand people had assembled, including eight hundred members of the police force. On the night of the assassination, Robert Kennedy and newly sworn-in President Johnson had called Tippit's widow, offering condolences, and Jacqueline Kennedy wrote a letter about the bond of sorrow that the two women shared. There was an outpouring of sympathy from people across the country, including many donations for Tippit's family, among them a large contribution from Abraham Zapruder after he had sold his film to *Life* magazine. While not often remembered as a hero of November 22, Tippit is commemorated in Dallas with a plaque at the corner of 10th and Patton where he was killed by Oswald after he had been alerted to a description of the suspect in Kennedy's murder, saw him on foot, engaged him in conversation, and then was shot to death as Oswald tried to flee. He was buried at Laurel Land Memorial Park in Dallas in the Memorial Court of Honor.

Oswald's funeral was remarkable not for public fanfare or notice but for the opposite—a howling emptiness attended by few. Marguerite Oswald, ever the media savant, had already been in touch with Bob Schieffer, then a reporter on the police beat, nightshift, at the *Fort Worth Star-Telegram*. It was a job for rookies, and mainly it involved answering the phone.

"Is there anybody there who can give me a ride to Dallas?" came the voice when Schieffer picked up.

"Lady," he said, "we're not running a taxi service here. And besides, the president's been shot."

"Yes," said the voice, "I heard it on the radio. I think my son is the one they've arrested."

Thinking he had the scoop of the century, he immediately drove to Fort Worth and picked up Marguerite Oswald. "She was a very peculiar person," he told CBS News, where he's been a reporter for years, "and she began to talk about how nobody would feel sorry for her, they'd feel sympathy for his wife and they would give her money. She was completely obsessed with money. She expressed no remorse about the president being killed." At the police station, Schieffer asked a detective if someone would arrange for Marguerite to visit with her son, who was inside lockup. "The cop said, 'Are you a reporter?' And

I said, 'Well, yes.' And he said 'Get outta here. I never want to see you again.' And he looked like he could kill me. And so the story for me on this particular day ended right there." In those early days following Kennedy's assassination, Schieffer went on to become something of a media star: "The Reporter who Drove Marguerite Oswald to the Police Station Following her Son's Arrest." It was not the kind of thing that could happen today—someone, anyone, calling a city desk and asking for a ride—but in that era, there were few barriers between the press and the public, and Marguerite Oswald was ever attuned to working the crowd.

When she visited Lee, she asked about the bruises on his face, which he had incurred during his fight with cops in the Texas Theatre, following his murder of Officer Tippit. Although he had tried to kill one of the policemen at the theater, prompting that fight, he downplayed the altercation as a "scuffle" and told his mother not to worry and not to interfere. He was planning to get an attorney, he said, and then added that time-honored mantra, "I know my rights," which of course he did; like many a guy who had run-ins with law enforcement, he was well versed in the code of personal freedoms, more so than other fellow citizens who were hardly ever in trouble, and it was a line that he had deployed for years and now he had one more chance to assert himself in that regard. From then on, Marguerite too would often raise the subject of rights—and their violation—whenever she was talking about what happened to Lee. It was a family tradition, and mother and son lived under the umbrella of defiance.

At the jailhouse, Marguerite had another reunion, this one with Marina, whom she hadn't seen in months, and certainly, seeing family members this way—because the President had just been assassinated and her own son was implicated—made communications among the estranged parties all the more fraught. But pleasantries tend to prevail when they are most needed, and the conversation proceeded accordingly. Marina had brought June and her new baby Rachel, and this was the first time that Marguerite learned that she had a new granddaughter, and she expressed wonderment and delight, and also questioned why Lee hadn't yet told her about the birth of Audrey Rachel. During the visit, Lee noticed that June's tennis shoes were threadbare and said that he'd arrange for a new pair. Later Robert arrived; the brothers hadn't seen each other since the previous Thanksgiving, and now the same holiday was around the corner. There would be no talk of who was bringing what dish and what time everyone was supposed to arrive. Nevertheless, the brothers exchanged chitchat and then Robert got to the matter at hand.

"Lee," he said, "what the Sam Hill's going on?"

"I don't know what you're talking about," Lee replied.

"Now, wait a minute," Robert said. "They've got you charged with the death of a police officer and the death of the president. They've got your pistol. They've got your rifle. And you tell me you don't know what's going on." And then he searched Lee's eyes, looking for a sign of something, some emotion, and finding nothing. Finally, Lee responded.

"Brother," he said, "you won't find anything there."

The next day, Jack Ruby entered the jail and killed Oswald. It was a vigilante-style hit, *The New York Times* said; a stranger had taken matters into his own hands and meted out revenge, just like gunslingers in the Old West. Twenty-four hours later, reporters were once again pressed into service, although not in the way anyone might have expected. On November 25, Mike Cochran of the *Star-Telegram* was assigned to cover Oswald's funeral at Rose Hill Cemetery in Fort Worth. The flag was at half-staff, and as Marguerite drove through the entrance, she took note; while she knew it was flying low because the President had died, she felt that it was also an acknowledgment of her son. He too had done a lot for his country, she began to tell everyone, he too was a hero. And it was shortly thereafter that she began a campaign to get Lee Harvey Oswald buried at Arlington National Cemetery.

"When I arrived at Rose Hill," Cochran wrote years later, "I discovered dozens of police, federal agents, writers and photographers but no mourners. In time, officers delivered the family members: mother Marguerite, Lee's brother Robert, the widow Marina and her two daughters, June Lee, 2, and the infant Rachel. Before their arrival, a rumor had spread among the reporters that the Oswald casket was actually empty or, if not, contained a body other than Oswald's. Finally, to curb the controversy, former Police Chief Cato Hightower ordered the casket opened and confirmed that it contained the body of Oswald."

But there were no other mourners in attendance, and no one to carry the coffin. "Even the minister selected to conduct the service had failed to show," Cochran wrote. "Shaking his head ever so slightly, Jerry Flemmons, the *Star-Telegram*'s ace reporter, turned to me and said solemnly, 'Cochran, if we're gonna write a story about the burial of Lee Harvey Oswald, we're gonna have to bury the son-of-a-bitch ourselves.'"

When officials—cops and FBI agents—asked gathered reporters if they'd carry the assassin to his grave, Cochran said, "Hell no." He had voted for Kennedy, and there was no way that he would perform that task. Then another reporter, a competitor, agreed to pitch in, and Cochran, worried about losing an "I was Oswald's pallbearer" story, changed his mind. A local reverend either volunteered or agreed to officiate. "We are not here to judge, only to commit for burial Lee Harvey Oswald," he said, and to that, no one—not Marguerite, Marina, or Robert—added a word. The ceremony was punctuated by muffled sobs, and when it was over, Marina, "her eyes red and swollen, stepped beside her husband's body and whispered a message of love." At 4:28 p.m. on that gloomy November day, Oswald's body, in its modest wooden casket, was lowered into a grave on a slight rise with sparsely growing grass. For many years afterwards, Marguerite tended the site, watering a tree that she had planted—one that to her dismay was photographed in a shriveled state and then the image was disseminated to newspapers.

After the funeral, Marguerite Oswald embarked on a new career. She was now a celebrity and, in today's parlance, tried to "monetize" the situation. She sold access to herself to reporters, sold off a number of items belonging to Lee (letters and documents or articles of clothing), and started hanging out at Dealey Plaza where Kennedy was killed, selling autographed business cards to tourists for five dollars bearing the inscription of *Marguerite Oswald, Mother of Lee Harvey Oswald.* "It is no crime to sell the pictures," she told the Warren Commission, before she had even gotten into full saleswoman mode. "I have no job or income. If I want to sell a picture to a magazine or a newspaper and protect myself financially, I am going to continue to do that." She also hit the lecture circuit with attorney Mark Lane, both charging fees and proclaiming Lee's innocence, pressing the case that he was framed, a patsy, just as he had stated in jail—a statement that his brother Robert later described as a ploy to take control— "Look! I'm running the show again!"—and deflect attention from what he had done.

All of Marguerite's behavior served to advance conspiracy theories, and then in 1965, she wrote and published—finally, an author!—a booklet called *Aftermath of an Execution.* It was released by Challenge Press, a small house in Dallas, although exactly where it was sold or advertised is not known. The cover features Lee's tombstone—a tasteful affair with a border of roses and a simple inscription bearing his name, his birth and death dates in the middle—along with a cross and her picture just below it. Then there is the subtitle, *The Burial and*

Final Rites of Lee Harvey Oswald as Told by His Mother. The book itself includes photographs of the service, and it talks about such things as Marguerite's attempts to keep the gravesite well tended following reports of the scrawny-looking tree next to the tombstone.

"There has been over eighty thousand people by to see the boy's grave," Marguerite wrote. "They take pictures, and I want the grave neat for the benefit of people who do take the pictures for history's sake. I mow the lawn myself and I get down on my knees and weed the weeds out of the grave, I plant flowers around. So when I saw pictures stating the assassin's grave was unkempt and even had a dead tree, this upset me terribly. I was determined that by the next Sunday my son's grave would be the nicest-looking in that particular section of Rose Hill Cemetery." She pauses to note that Lee "is buried in the middle-class section of the cemetery."

She also makes it known that she traveled thirty-five miles from the cemetery to Dallas so that she could visit a florist who sold grass that they use for golf courses. "I went to him and he recognized me," she says, "and I told him what I wanted. He had one of his workers dig the grass up." Then she asked the cemetery men to help her roll the new grass over the grave. When she offered to pay the florist, she writes, he said, "No, Mrs. Oswald, I would not accept payment from you. I'm a sympathizer. It won't cost you a cent." Marguerite noted that the grass was very beautiful and stayed green in the wintertime, and she made it known that she had pruned the tree with ordinary scissors because she didn't have pruning shears. The cemetery man told her not to bother because the tree was dead and offered to dig it up. "Oh, no," she said. "Let the tree alone. Let me see what I can do." Convinced that there was some life in the roots, she went to the cemetery twice a day, every day, and she watered the tree. This account may well be true, at least in part; the writer Jean Stafford took note of Marguerite's way with plants and flowers in *A Mother in*

History, which was published in 1966 around the time that *Aftermath of an Execution* hit the market. On the cover of Stafford's book there's a picture of Marguerite standing at her son's tombstone, in front of a robust-looking tree with overhanging fronds and a plant with flowers in front of it. Inside Marguerite's house near the television set, there was a jardiniere filled with plants "whose patterns were picked out in assertive shades of purple and red and leonine yellow," Stafford observed. "The health of these plants was so obviously robust that they testified to a green thumb." Most lives have moments of grace, intimations of a love of beauty, a need for it—Lee placing his wedding ring in a teacup—and gardening, however erratic, may have expressed this for Marguerite, taking her out of her personal prison, if only briefly, here and there.

Americans are quick to spot an opportunity, especially those for whom everything is transactional. And so, a parade of items associated with Oswald and the assassination have hit the auction block over the years, including an autographed typescript of Marguerite's booklet that was sold off in 2013—at what price, it is not known—and it joined other objects of interest, such as Oswald's life insurance claim ($79,436), his Marine Corps rifle score book ($75,000), his final uncashed paycheck from the Texas Book Depository (auction price not known, paycheck amount $43.37), his coffin (for $87,469, after his body was exhumed because of a dispute between Marina and Robert regarding an accusation from someone that an Oswald double had been buried; that turned out not to be the case, and Lee was reinterred in a new casket), his original mug shot ($1,523.85), his baby crib (assembly required, minimum bid $1,500), his original tombstone (stolen and then shuttled around between those who claimed ownership or asked for ransom money, now in the possession of the man who bought Marguerite's old house, where she had it stored in the basement, lest someone steal it again), Marina Oswald's wedding ring ($90,000), Jack Ruby's fingerprints on a signed card from his arrest following Oswald's murder (asking price $77,400), and even Jack Ruby's can opener ($1; this author knows the fellow who bought it. It was the late writer Tom Miller, who actually wanted Jack Ruby's kitchen sink, up for grabs at the same auction, but had arrived too late to place a bid).

The Texas Book Depository has itself become a shrine—a respectful and tasteful one—with the Sixth Floor Museum dedicated to memorializing the assassination of John Fitzgerald Kennedy. It has a deep archive of documents and newspapers and books related to the event, photos and magazines and oral histories of those who knew Oswald or Kennedy or were at Dealey Plaza when the event transpired, and it has preserved the sniper's nest and replicas of the boxes packed with schoolbooks that were there on that terrible day. "If we choose to believe in the Camelot legend as it relates to the Kennedy administration," museum curator Stephen Fagin writes in *Assassination and Commemoration*, "then Dealey Plaza perhaps serves as a kind of Avalon—the place where Arthur went to die but may have actually lived on in some form, haunting the hallowed ground." About a million people visit the plaza every year, he notes, all for different reasons: reflection, continuing investigation, social activism, and memorial services. Every year on the date of the assassination, the place becomes a kind of altar, with wreaths and flowers placed there in honor of President Kennedy and in memory of the blow that the country suffered. Dealey Plaza is a powerful presence, a center of historical and spiritual energy that brings people into its orbit like other sites of magnetism where warfare has been waged, whether it involves armies or individuals; twenty years ago, one man actually chose to check out there, killing himself on the spot marked with a giant X, which indicates the place on Elm Street where the President's journey came to an end. The man who took his own life was wearing a camouflage jacket, clutching a gun on his chest, and lying in the middle of the street. I find myself returning to the idea that maybe he was a warrior, a veteran of one of our wars; perhaps he was terminally ill or he just couldn't take it anymore, and he wanted to go out in proximity to the death site for a man he served and admired—the king—and thus join him in glory in the afterlife.

As for the city of Dallas itself, it has long tried to purge itself of the stain of the assassination. "Terrible history has been made in Dallas," the *Dallas Times Herald* said just after the incident, "and the magnitude of our city's sorrow can only be measured against the enormity of the deed . . . We do not know, we may never know, why it happened in Dallas. And it is no comfort to our grief that an insane chance, operating with blind destiny, brought our President's death to us . . . The bullet that felled our President was molded in an unstable world. But to our great sorrow, it found its mark here." Years later there came the TV show *Dallas*, one of the most popular shows in television history. Writer Lawrence Wright spoke of the nighttime soap opera and its connection to his hometown in a *Texas Monthly* article about the assassination called "When Will They Stop Hating Us?"

"I stood amazed when the television show *Dallas* appeared, with a right-wing millionaire villain as its protagonist. Smug and cruel, J.R. Ewing personifies the evil that people associate with the city— and yet people all over the world love him. He represents their own grasping ambitions; he has become a hero of the id. When Dallas laughed at *Dallas* it was a sign that the city was ready to forgive itself, to lay its burden down." Wright went on to note the perpetual boomtown nature of the Big D, the endless construction, cranes everywhere, the constant tearing down of things and replacing them with glass towers, new, new, new—all rendering it a world-class metropolis stripped of authenticity.

"The only time I put on my cowboy hat," *Fort Worth Star-Telegram* reporter Bud Kennedy told me, "is when I go into Dallas." It's a popular joke in the city "where the West begins," an acknowledgment that Dallas may have the symbols and the frontier bling, but the main contender is really Fort Worth.

"There is a price to pay for living in a city that is continually being born," Wright continued, invoking President Kennedy as a sentinel of the future.

> It can be measured in the lost feeling of rootedness that old hardware stores provide. To love Dallas is to be able to live without the consolation of the past, without the feeling of history underfoot. To love Dallas is to celebrate the thrill of the new, to smile at the cranes always on the horizon and the bulldozers clearing the pasture beyond the last development. Dallas does not build itself incrementally but exponentially, and it takes a kind of courage to live in a city that never pauses. And yet I have come to respect Dallas, in a way that I respect very few cities. In the melodrama that we made of Kennedy's death it seemed that the promise of America had been extinguished in Dallas. But as I see that city now, I see the new world that Kennedy promised fulfilled in the place of his death. It is a human city, flawed and ambitious but with a self-knowledge that many another bustling town will never learn. It is both the burden and the nobility of Dallas that they shouldn't have to.

Today, there's a plan afoot to refashion Dealey Plaza. Called "Reimagine Dealey Plaza and the Triple Underpass," it was commissioned by *The Dallas Morning News*, the paper that had published the full-page mock obituary for the President on the morning of the assassination. It's no longer owned by George Dealey or his family, transformed like much of the city. The plan seeks to make the banal and infamous site with its nondescript buildings and crisscrossing railroad lines into something beautiful. "Dallas has long had a vexed relationship with Dealey Plaza," a reporter on Texas Public Radio said recently, "for obvious reasons." The relationship is detailed in *Assassination and Commemoration*. "For many years," the book notes, "the city wished that the Texas School Book Depository would go away, get bought up and bulldozed"—like so much else in Dallas. "Or maybe just forgotten."

"In its defense," the public radio reporter said, "no city before Dallas had ever created a museum about an assassination. In the early '60s, Ford's Theatre in Washington, D. C., where Abraham Lincoln was shot, was more or less deteriorating. In Buffalo, where President William McKinley was murdered in 1906, there's just a plaque on a rock." The new plan for Dealey Plaza would perform some sort of alchemy, rendering an off-putting location that the *LA Times* once described as "part high-traffic intersection, part gateway to the city, part flood-control project, and part accidental historical monument," into a public commons with bicycle paths and upgraded walkways along the adjacent Trinity River. What would remain intact is the Texas Book Depository and the Sixth Floor Museum, a location that is the centerpiece of the plaza and that nothing—short of being razed and obliterated, as per Dallas tradition—could ever change.

Regardless of a proposed beautification, what happened at that plaza nearly sixty years ago resonates in a troubling manner all over America, in malls, schools, and places of work. I speak of the plague of gun violence and mass shootings that has befallen the country. The bullets fired by Lee Harvey Oswald are still ricocheting across the land and even abroad, and this is not hyperbole. In 1988, Don DeLillo's novel *Libra* was published, and it was a masterful conjuring of the life of Lee Harvey Oswald and the forces that coalesced around him in those final November days. "After Oswald," DeLillo said in an interview following the book's publication, "men in America are no longer required to lead lives of quiet desperation. You apply for a credit card, buy a handgun, travel through cities, suburbs and shopping malls, anonymous, anonymous, looking for a chance to take a shot at the first puffy empty famous face, just to let people know there is someone out there who reads the papers."

On June 13, 1981, Queen Elizabeth was riding her horse on her way to the annual Trooping the Color ceremony. A teenager along the parade route fired six shots. The Queen was unharmed, though her horse was momentarily spooked, but they regrouped and continued along. "Security rushed into the crowd to find the would-be assassin wearing a 'Charles and Di' pin," according to a report, "and they were surprised to discover that he had fired six blank shots." It turned out that the seventeen-year-old was obsessed with the assassination attempts on Ronald Reagan and Pope John Paul II, and he idolized Mark David Chapman, who had killed John Lennon, and Lee Harvey Oswald. After the attempt on Reagan earlier that year, he had said that he wanted to be the first one to take a shot at the Queen. And he was hoping to become as famous as his violent forebears, writing about his plans to "stun and mystify the world with nothing more than a gun" and sending photos of himself posing with his father's revolver to various media outlets prior to the pretend hit on the Queen. These photos were surely an echo of the image of Oswald posing with his rifle and pistol, the shot that was pictured around the world, in effect the first selfie of a killer in the modern era—though taken by Oswald's wife Marina at Lee's request in the couple's backyard.

Let us also recall John Hinckley, Jr., who tried to assassinate President Ronald Reagan with the peculiar goal of impressing actress Jodie Foster, the object of his desire. When they searched his room, detectives found newspaper articles about assassinations and a photo of Oswald holding a gun (it was not reported which gun, or whether this was the *Life* magazine image, although it probably was, considering that there are no other photos of an armed Oswald out there in the public ether). The forensic psychologist Park Dietz testified at Hinckley's trial that he "did not want to be an accountant or salesman" and he "liked the idea of fame without following rules."

As recently as last year, twenty-two-year-old Robert Crimo III joined the lineup of Oswald fans, shooting up a parade in Highland Park, Illinois, on July 4, wounding forty-eight participants and killing eight. When police searched his house, they found a music video called "Are You Awake?" inside, drawings of a man aiming his rifle, and newspaper clippings about Lee Harvey Oswald. And then there was Kyle Rittenhouse, seeking attention in another manner; he's the fellow who shot three men, two fatally, amid a protest related to the police shooting of a black man in Kenosha, Wisconsin, in 2020. His weapon of choice was an AR-15, the automatic rifle deployed in dozens of mass shootings, the one that has become a focal point of America's culture wars, with Republicans recently attempting to certify the rifle as "America's national gun"—although we already have one, the Winchester, "the gun that won the West." Or maybe it's the Remington, a revered weapon in the history of the American West. Sharpshooter Annie Oakley used a Remington as a headliner in Buffalo Bill's Wild West show, and Buffalo Bill Cody owned several and used them in life and in his wildly popular spectacle. His favorite was the Remington 1858 New Model Army Revolver, recently reissued by a heritage house called America Remembers. "It never failed me," Cody would often say of his preferred weapon.

One of the photos in Robert Oswald's memoir is of Lee at nine years old on the porch of the family home in Benbrook, Texas. He's wearing Robert's beret from military school and brandishing a toy pistol. Then there's another one of Lee on a pony in the front yard of one of their homes in Dallas, about six years old, all dressed up Western-style. The images are barely remarked upon in the Lee Harvey Oswald annals. Yet we can say that in a way, he never did grow up and out of the "shoot 'em up" stage of a young boy's life, especially common during that time. Killing Kennedy at the age of twenty-four, he was only two years older than Billy the Kid, who died in a shoot-out at the age of twenty-two. In that regard, and others, they were not so different than the mass shooters of today. I think it's safe to say that Billy the Kid ran through Oswald's blood—as he does through the veins of all Americans, taking over when roused by the fates. That's why Oswald became a man of action, buying a gun and pulling the trigger, all by himself, trailed by the whisperings of his mother as he walked his solitary path.

"I thought it looked cool," Kyle Rittenhouse said of the AR during his trial—and that had been the idea all along. (Rittenhouse claimed self-defense; a jury acquitted him of all charges.) According to its own manufacturers, the AR had been rolled out with a marketing campaign that presented it like a Corvette. Oswald may not have been brandishing an AR-15 in his famous photo, but in posing with his rifle, he had joined the long line of American gunslingers on the road to high noon. It's not likely that he would have called it "cool," a word that was probably not in his repertoire—he was not a "cool cat" of his era and he knew it. But to some latter-day seekers of fame and fortune, he has entered the national memory bank and become what is now known as "an influencer."

A common element of the stories regarding killers and mass shooters is that they have grown up in what was once called "a broken home," now known as a "single-parent household," or they have been raised by grandparents or other relatives who have stepped up when the father and mother are not present in the lives of their children. Of course, many who were raised by a single parent have fared well—President Barack Obama comes to mind—but in general, a thread running through many of these stories is "Where's Dad?" Even Oswald's brothers spoke of the fact that Lee was damaged by not having grown up with a father, and Robert in particular, whose father was also Lee's, said in his memoir (as recounted earlier in this book) and in various interviews that his younger brother suffered from never having known his father, and thrived for a time when he gained the attention of a father figure via his mother's marriage to Ed Ekdahl. At least two of the abovementioned violent events involve an intense bond that the killers had with their mothers, forged by way of a love of guns. Add to those the case of Adam Lanza, killer in the 2012 Sandy Hook Elementary School shooting in which twenty students lost their lives along with six adult teachers. His mother Nancy—whom he also killed—"collected powerful weapons," her ex-husband said in a divorce filing. She would bring her increasingly troubled son to "multiple shooting ranges," according to a statement from the Bureau of Alcohol, Tobacco, Firearms and Explosives, and there mother and son would practice using those weapons.

A similar scenario characterizes the life of Christopher Harper-Mercer, who shot up his classroom at Umpqua Community College in Roseburg, Oregon, in 2015, wounding eight classmates and killing eight others as well as an assistant professor with four semiautomatic weapons. He had become proficient at shooting at local rifle ranges, which he had frequented with his mother, who had also given him guns. One of the things that she liked to do before he was born was read to him, and strangely, one of the books that she read was *The Art of the Deal* by Donald Trump. It was a kind of fairy tale, conjuring a magic world of high finance and international empires and if you played your cards right, you too could live in a skyscraper; all you had to do was think positive and make a lot of money. She hoped that her son would grow up to become an investor, a real estate baron, just like

Trump, and he bought and sold a few things, evidently, for a while, and then things didn't work out. In a note found after the incident, he had spoken of having no job, no girlfriend—a life of no prospects or hope. "Keep your options open," the book urged; or as John Fitzgerald Kennedy said more eloquently, "A man does what he must—in spite of personal consequences, in spite of obstacles and dangers and pressures—and that is the basis of all human morality." That statement is from Kennedy's book, *Profiles in Courage*, which Lee Harvey Oswald was reading in the months before the President's assassination (along with a book about the murder of Huey Long, as well as James Bond novels by Ian Fleming; coincidentally, both he and JFK were fans of the spy novels—but Kennedy actually knew Fleming). We can imagine how an unhinged person such as Harper-Mercer might have taken Trump's bromide. At some point, when it became unlikely that he would ever own a 747 or be able to purchase "air rights," he had reached the end of the line, run out of options, and there was only one more fallback position. Just as his predecessors had done on that selfsame trail, he would go out in a blaze of glory.

We can also picture Oswald reading in the library on a rainy night, finding sanctuary there amid the noise of his life and his heart, or in the dark on his porch, where neighbors would often spot him under a solitary bulb in the relentless heat of a summer night in the Crescent City. At some point, he had come to a guidance, that line about doing what you must—*as a man*—and it must have percolated over the days and weeks, and combined with the other dictates that had swarmed his thoughts, that's what he finally did: heed that final call.

There is a lineage of American mothers who have come forward to defend their violent sons. In 1864, Zerelda James, mother of Frank and Jesse, slaveholder and Confederate, stepped up on their behalf after they took part in the infamous massacre of thirty-four unarmed Union soldiers at Centralia, Missouri, led by "Bloody Bill" Anderson during the Civil War. She was proud of Frank and Jesse, she said, and she asked God to protect them. Later, when the boys became fugitives following bank and stagecoach robberies, she proclaimed their innocence and told newspaper reporters that "no mother ever had better sons." During the 1920s, Ma Barker, matriarch of a crime gang, encouraged her sons' rampages across the Great Plains, and to those in her own Missouri town who objected to their behavior she would say, "If the good people of this town don't like my boys, then the good people know what to do." She was later memorialized in *White Heat*, the classic film noir starring Jimmy Cagney as one of her wayward sons. At the end of the movie, he dies above it all, almost like they always planned—at the top of a clock tower in prison in a shoot-out with guards, yelling, "Top of the world, Ma." In real life, Ma Barker herself went out in a hail of gunfire, along with one of her sons and other members of her gang, surrounded by federal agents in a cottage in Ocklawaha, Florida.

In 1965, Jean Stafford visited Marguerite Oswald over a three-day period, and a historic conversation unfolded. The meetings took place in Marguerite's modest apartment, one of two in a white stucco bungalow, in the living and dining room area. "The armchair I sat in was hard and soft enough," Stafford wrote, "and there was an adequate table to the right of it on which stood an ashtray, a small vase of artificial violets, and a copy of *The Wounded Land*, Hans Habe's high-strung book on the American state of mind following the assassination." It was part of Marguerite's extensive library of books about the Kennedy assassination, including all twenty-six volumes of *The Warren Report*. Above the couch was a print of *Whistler's Mother*. Marguerite poured hot water over instant coffee, and Stafford turned on her tape recorder. Stafford began by asking her about her early life in New Orleans, but Marguerite went right to the heart of the matter. "Now maybe Lee Harvey Oswald was the assassin," she said, stirring the coffee. "But does that make him a louse? No, no! Killing does not necessarily mean badness. You find killing in some very fine homes for one reason or another. And as we all know, President Kennedy was a dying man. So I say it is possible that my son was chosen to shoot him in a mercy killing for the security of the country. And if this is true, it was a fine thing to do and my son is a hero."

Marguerite went on to talk about her sacrifices as a mother (some of which was true) and her expertise in stretching a dollar to pay for food. "Oh, yes, we didn't have steak, but we never even thought about steak—I didn't anyway, I was always grateful to eat. And the children never really and truly complained. I know of one or two occasions when the boys said, 'Mother, why don't you have a platter of chops? I was at such and such house yesterday and they served seconds,' and I said, 'Well now, honey, this is all Mother can do.'" And then she described cooking up a pot of rice and beans and cornbread or a big pot of spaghetti and meatballs and making it last, whereas some women would take that dollar and buy hamburgers and Coke. "There's your difference," she said. "I have always done what I thought was right, and I always did it in a true Christian way . . . Now I'm patting myself on the back as a mother only so that the people will understand. Why am I so concerned that the people will understand? It is natural because I am a mother in history. I am in twenty-six volumes of the Warren Report, which is all over the world, so I must defend myself and defend my son Lee."

In addition to insisting on the heroic nature of what her son may have done, Marguerite also talked about some of his qualities. "Lee was this type person, he had wisdom," she said. "A formal education he did not have. He had the know-how." And he knew Russian, she pointed out, which was a very hard language. And then the conversation turned towards herself. "I myself don't have a high school education and I know I speak very bad English, but a ten thousand

dollar year engineering man begged me to marry him . . . I've been
on television with the highest caliber of people and held my own, so
I don't think I do so bad in that department. I'm uneducated, but
very versatile . . . it's just doing things that come naturally, and Lee
had it. Believe me, Lee Harvey Oswald had natural wisdom. Some
people with a formal education are so dull that really and truly I find
them stupid."

At the end of each session, Stafford would return to her hotel
room, stunned by Marguerite's self-centered nature and her demeanor
in general. She was cordial enough, but exhausting, a vortex of self-
pity and manipulation, with inadvertent insight into her son thrown
in, but the subject would return sooner or later to her own martyrdom:
"And let me tell you this, if you research the life of Jesus Christ, you
find that you never did hear anything more about the mother of Jesus
after He was crucified. And really nobody cares about my welfare . . . "

Fortuitously for Stafford, her machine had run out of tape at
that point. She turned it off, and Marguerite suggested that they
head to the cemetery for a visit to Lee's gravesite. They drove over in
Marguerite's brand-new Buick Skylark, the one she had gotten with
her money from *Esquire*, she said, and once they passed through the
cemetery gates, Marguerite immediately adopted the voice of a tour
guide. "Like everything else in life," she said. "this is divided up into
classes. There is the section for the rich people, and some very fine
people are buried there, and there is one for the poor people, and
then there is one for the middle class. Lee Harvey Oswald is buried
in the middle-class section, as it should be according to his station in
life." When they approached the grave, there were five teenage boys
emerging from a black vehicle that looked like it had once been used
as a getaway car, and Marguerite whispered that they were heading
straight for Lee. "Now that's the age I want to reach with my books,"
she said, but the boys took off upon being noticed. The women paused

for a moment at the grave, and then Marguerite engaged in some grave tending. She "plucked a weed from among the pansies" that were growing around the tombstone and "bent the plastic freesias" that had been arranged around the cross "into a more becoming embrace." And then she extended a hand to Stafford, offering a shake. The day was done, and it was time to go. "It turned out to be a right nice Mother's Day after all," Marguerite said. "But on some Mother's Day, it would be wonderful if they would come out in behalf of his family and his mother and say he died in service of his country . . . Let's have a little defense of Lee Harvey Oswald! On Mother's Day, let's come out and say that he died in the service of his country."

The conversation seemed to have reached its natural conclusion, but Marguerite wasn't finished. As they were leaving, she told Stafford to think about her offer to spend the summer in Fort Worth. "I'll be happy to cooperate with you," she said, referring to the proposed collaboration on her life story. "It would be a big deal." The title that she had in mind was "One and One Don't Make Two." Either that or "This and That." But Stafford never returned, and actually came to feel uneasy about the three-day enterprise about midway through it and especially on that final day; she was worn out by then, having listened to Marguerite's vociferous and lengthy proclamations about her own martyrdom and festering resentments. Some of Marguerite's remarks didn't even make it into Stafford's final draft, as they were superfluously bizarre (at one point, Mrs. Oswald says that the owners of Nieman Marcus, the high-end department store with headquarters in Dallas, were behind the President's assassination), and these outtakes are archived with Stafford's papers at the University of Colorado in Boulder. Several years ago, a reporter for *This American Life* on NPR was granted access to the tapes. It was the first time that anyone but Stafford or Marguerite Oswald had heard these recordings. "Jean," Marguerite admonishes in one of the tapes, "you left the tape recorders yesterday afternoon in my home, which was Saturday, so that we could work again about an hour today. Upon waking up this morning, and it being Mother's Day, I've decided that in defense of myself and my son, Lee Harvey Oswald, I would put a little something on the tape. I sincerely hope that you will find it newsworthy and print it." And then she proceeded to read page 378 of *The Warren Report* and explain why it wasn't true, blasting it on the recorder before Stafford had even entered her house.

In 1977, on her seventieth birthday, Marguerite told a reporter that she had conducted her own investigation of the assassination and it confirmed her belief that Lee was innocent. He was undoubtedly a US intelligence agent who had been framed, she said, and she was going to defend him until she died. On January 17, 1981, at the age of seventy-three, she succumbed to cancer. Funeral arrangements were made by her son Robert, who had flown in from Wichita, Kansas, and was the only person to view her body. Information about the ceremony was never released. At her request, she was buried next to Lee.

And now let us return for a moment to November of 1963, a few days after President Kennedy had been assassinated. A reporter from *The New York Times* had been sent to Fort Worth to interview Marguerite Oswald. He drove from the airport to her house, and at the curb, FBI agents checked his credentials and waved him on. Marguerite greeted him warmly at her front door, and after they got comfortable inside and began conversing, she started to open her mail. Checks spilled out of envelopes, reporter A. J. Langguth recalled fifty years later in an essay for the *LA Times*. Out of sympathy, people had been sending checks to Marina and Officer J. D. Tippit's widow, and, it turned out, to Marguerite as well (although she would continue to say for months and years afterwards that no one was sending her any money). Before the year's end, she had received $6,000. (Marina had evidently been receiving more. Young and beautiful and a stranger in a strange land, she was easier than Marguerite to sympathize with; moreover, she had a number of suitors, and would soon remarry and have another child.)

As the reporter and Marguerite chatted, Marguerite told him that she was estranged from her sons; they never speak to me, she said, and the reporter tried to cheer her up by assuring her that they would call before Christmas, which was about a month away. They won't call, she said, but thanks anyway. Soon enough, Langguth began to realize why they never called. "The portrait that was emerging from our interviews was of an angry woman," he wrote, "aggrieved at being cheated out of what life had owed her." Shortly before the holidays, he called Marguerite to see if she had heard from her boys. She hadn't, she declared triumphantly, and Langguth arranged to pick her up at 1:00 p.m. on Christmas day. She directed him to a modest steakhouse nearby, he wrote. During their meal, she gave him a gift: two bars of guest-room hand soap decorated with sequins. They must have been left over from when she sold notions from the front room of one of her houses, and we must consider the nature of this offering. It was Amanda Wingfield from *The Glass Menagerie* all over again, only this time she was giving away a free subscription—and it sparkled—it was Christmas!—and there were no strings attached.

In the restaurant, there were families laughing and exchanging gifts, Langguth recalled. Marguerite thought that they were eavesdropping and became concerned. "When we leave," she whispered, "walk a little behind me and hear if people say, 'That's Lee Harvey Oswald's mother.'" He caught up with her at the cash register and said, "You were right, Mrs. Oswald. Everybody recognized you." That lie was all that he had to give her, he said. It was Christmas, after all, and it would seem that a strange and tender moment had just played out in this Fort Worth steakhouse, four weeks after John Fitzgerald Kennedy had been assassinated and Jack Ruby had whacked Marguerite's son.

Perhaps she thought of the time that Lee sang "Silent Night" in that church in Covington so long ago. He was seven years old and he sang it all by himself, and all around them were those healing vapors from the pines of Ozonia.

IT TOOK ME A FEW days to track down Ruth Paine, subject of Thomas Mallon's *Mrs. Paine's Garage.* My mother had given the book to me shortly after it was published in 2002; it was one of the first accounts to shed light on a little-known aspect of Lee's life, beyond what was in *The Warren Report* and a few other explorations. It's a fascinating account of the time that Marina Oswald came to live with Ruth and her husband Michael, then going through a divorce that paralleled the separation of Lee and Marina. Ruth had invited Marina to move in with her as she and Lee tried to sort things out during one of several periods of alienation and separation. Marina brought two-year-old June with her, and they joined Ruth and her two kids in the aforementioned suburban home in Irving, Texas. I've read the book several times over the years, each time finding a new facet to examine. In the beginning it was the sheer bizarreness of the whole story—the fact that the future killer of the President of the United States would visit from time to time, making nice with Ruth's kids and his own daughter, conversing with Ruth and Michael about the news of the day, sports, the weather, whatever, and, unbeknownst to them, also storing his rifle in their garage. I think maybe it was the second or fourth or fifth read that I began to realize the story was also about men and women and mothers and their children; about how couples who were separating could do so in a respectful way and why they might be unable to achieve that state, and how Ruth had tried to provide the Oswalds with a sanctuary, a time-out, if only they could make the most of it. Or perhaps the idea was really to open up an escape hatch for Marina, who was clearly trapped in an unhappy marriage in a land she barely knew, raising an infant with another one on the way.

Mrs. Paine is now in her nineties and makes her home at an assisted living community in Northern California. I left a message for her with the community manager, and she got back to me right away. She might have been concerned that all I wanted to talk with her about was whether or not Lee had been framed or was part of some conspiracy, perhaps even involving her was a suspicion I'm sure, as she and her husband are sometimes mentioned as participants in one of the countless plots that supposedly went into operation on November 22, 1963, believed to have befriended the Oswalds only to keep tabs on the unsuspecting couple, and in Ruth's case, even gotten Lee the job at the Texas Book Depository not to help him out but to provide the vantage point—or cover story, depending on which theory is being talked about at any given time—for the assassination. I assured her that my interest had to do with other matters; there were, of course, many other writings that people could read on the subject of conspiracies, and I wanted to learn more about what life was like with Marina and get her thoughts about the fact that her garage had been the hiding place for Lee's weapon. Of course, that was the subject of Mallon's book, but now it was twenty years later, and I wanted to speak with her directly and hear things for myself. To give her an idea of my work, I sent her a copy of a previous book, and when she received it, we arranged a time to talk. Here are some of the things that she told me.

On the day after Oswald killed the President, Ruth drove Marina to the Dallas jailhouse, which is where she first met Marguerite. She already knew that Lee wanted nothing to do with her and that Marina shared his disdain. Marina did not want her to be around her grandchildren, and had it not been for the assassination, Marguerite may not have met the new baby at all. That night, November 23,

Ruth and Marina returned to Ruth's home in Irving, and Marguerite joined them for the evening. Ruth felt that she couldn't turn her down when she asked if she could spend the night there; although she knew that Marina didn't want Marguerite to be near June and the newborn Rachel, Ruth was a Quaker, after all, and there was never a time that she did not follow her life's calling, which was be kind to others and always extend a hand. What would it say about her, to herself, that suddenly she turned someone down in their moment of greatest need?

When they arrived at the Paine home, they were met by a team from *Life* magazine. Marguerite immediately began a negotiation, and a deal was struck; photographs were taken, and thus began the media extravaganza. Sometime that evening, Marina told Marguerite that there was something she wanted to show her. She had been keeping two photos in June's baby book since they lived in Dallas earlier that year; they were not images of June, Mallon wrote, but of Lee, "in back of the Neely Street apartment, brandishing a rifle, a pistol, and two rival Communist newspapers, *The Militant* and *The Worker*." She had taken the photos herself, Marina told her mother-in-law, at Lee's insistence. "Marguerite now implored her to keep the photos away from Ruth," wrote Mallon. "Tomorrow, while visiting Lee, Marina would hide them in her shoe. Later, she would burn them, not knowing that Oswald had been sufficiently proud of the pose to make numerous prints at the graphic arts firm where he worked. The police would have a set that had been with his things in the garage." Soon, one of the photos would make its way to the cover of *Life* magazine—and into the lives of future killers. Ruth told me in our phone conversation that her worst moment—ever—was seeing the empty roll in the garage. That was where Lee said he was storing curtain rods, and it was then that Ruth knew the rifle had been there all along, and that was why he had come to see Marina the night before. Knowing that the man who killed the President had been in such close proximity to her children, playing with them, even, was a source of great distress for Ruth—how could she have let this happen?—and a burden that she has never stopped carrying. At the same time that she learned this terrible truth, she was undergoing a divorce, and the loss of President Kennedy and the dream he had put forward—one of world peace and a call to our better angels, which, after all, was her own personal calling. So she found herself in sadness and turmoil without end for some time.

"No one I cared about so much had ever died before," she told me. "I felt it personally, not just as a citizen. Then my sorrow was offended, was soiled, by this association with the assassin, with anger and horror that the man who killed the president had left my house to fire that shot." And yet, after a while, she found comfort in her beliefs, the ones that had taken her through life's devastations and joys, and they still do. Taking care of others is what she does, and as Jessamyn West would soon write, "It is entirely possible, on the weekend when we all watched the assassination of John Fitzgerald Kennedy and the shooting of Lee Harvey Oswald, that hundreds or even thousands of women were doing exactly what Ruth Paine was doing: offering food, shelter and friendship to a family in need of it. These women will never be known to us. They did not befriend the family of a man accused of assassinating the president . . . Some of us on occasion may be capable, as Mrs. Paine was, of doing unto others as we would be done by."

So the Golden Rule prevailed even after the terrible events of November had unfolded. Ruth tried to keep in touch with Marina, but at some point, they fell out of touch. When the FBI confiscated all of the Oswalds' possessions in the Paine house, including the garage, for some reason, they left Marina's childcare books behind, the ones that were in Russian. Ruth tried to get them to Marina and sent them via the police station in Dallas, but she does not know if they were given to her friend. It's telling that baby books were what remained of Marina's belongings; in the end, after all, this is a story of how we raise children, and how they break when love is deprived, of how even grown-ups cannot survive without it.

Sometime after Marguerite had passed away, after the waters of Hurricane Katrina began to recede, a letter surfaced in New Orleans. She had kept up a correspondence with various people over the years, and one of them was a woman in Jefferson Parish, Louisiana, the wife of a lawyer she had contacted when she was looking for representation in one of her legal campaigns in defense of her son. Marguerite was living in Fort Worth at the time, and although the lawyer wanted to represent her, he would have had to partner up with a lawyer in Texas to do so, but no one he knew of wanted to represent the mother of Kennedy's assassin. Meanwhile, Marguerite and the lawyer's wife, Lora Lee Meyer, had struck up a long-distance friendship. One of the things that drew them together was a belief that Lee did not act alone, and she was hoping that her husband could help Marguerite advance her case. At the time, Lora Lee was pregnant, and they got to talking about children; at some point, she even asked Marguerite to be the godmother of her baby. It was shortly after Katrina that Lora Lee was visiting her son Byron in Chalmette, a town in St. Bernard Parish near New Orleans. On the second floor of his house, they started going through a box filled with newspaper clippings, old Christmas cards, and various photos and letters to see if there was anything that had survived the flood without too much damage. There they retrieved a note dated February 1969; it was addressed to Lora Lee Meyer when she was six months pregnant, and it said, "I would be so honored to act as 'Godmother' for the new baby." The child would turn out to be Byron Meyer, and the sender was Marguerite Oswald. For some reason the women fell out of touch, and that never happened. "It's weird, it's bizarre, it's freaky," Byron Meyer said to a reporter a few days after the letter came to his attention. "She was going to be my godmother—the mother of the assassin of one of the best presidents in the history of America. It was so close." It was clear to Lora Lee that Marguerite was lonely. "I do have my moments of sadness, frustration, and tears," Marguerite confided to Lora Lee. She would cry over the phone, and Lora Lee would cry back. As Ruth Paine told me in our conversation, "that's what women do."

In 1964, Marguerite made a recording called *The Oswald Case: Mrs. Marguerite Oswald Reads Lee Harvey Oswald's Letters from Russia*. There are sixteen letters and you can listen to her read them on YouTube. Her voice is lilting, with a slight New Orleans accent; she sounds youthful, even girlish, here and there (she was fifty-seven at the time), and while the letters aren't especially eloquent or noteworthy in terms of personal style, they are typical letters to a parent from a child who doesn't want to or doesn't know how to get beyond small talk, filled with weather reports ("it's cold here") and other news of the day. Yet they are clearly an attempt to maintain a connection with his mother, his family, and his country, offering certain intimacies and expressing a desire to return. "Dear Mother," says letter number 5. "We received your postcard and it was very interesting for Marina. Well, at the end of February or beginning of March, we should have a baby. We want a boy. There is very little information about the visas. We still have not received them and until we do cannot leave the Soviet Union. You can send me a few pennies if you like. A lot of my friends are interested in collecting coins from America. If you have any photos, old photos, of you and myself, please send them. Do you ever hear anything from Aunt Lillian and how about John? Marina asks do you want to be a grandmother again? Are you still working for these people. You have changed addresses quite often. Well that's about it for now. Write soon. Love, Lee. Enclosed is some pictures of Leningrad where Marina was born. This is not Minsk."

It is said that conspiracies can unfold with a nod and a wink; no one has to say that you should go out and rob a bank or make life miserable for someone or kill so-and-so. If there's any conspiracy in the case of the murder of John Fitzgerald Kennedy, it was that of mother and son in a silent pact—two souls allied against going through life as nobodies, a pair determined to let everyone know that they mattered. When Lee returned to the United States with Marina, the luster of being the new kid in town wore off quickly. In fact, it was almost as if his arduous and dramatic journey never happened. Things returned to normal and the old ways set right back in. But the subterranean thing that joined him to Marguerite—their own particular mother-and-son bond—kicked in, and it wasn't long before Lee made his final statement.

About a week before he was assassinated, President Kennedy had talked to Nikita Khrushchev about his idea for a joint USA-USSR mission to the moon, as Khrushchev's son Sergei noted in one of his books about the Cold War. The elder Khrushchev had gone against the wishes of his rocket scientists and felt that the Soviet Union should accept the President's invitation to go to the moon with America in a joint expedition. Together, they would blaze a trail in the New Frontier, up there in the new Wild West. It was a big step towards cooperation between the two superpowers, and behind the scenes, the men had developed an interesting friendship. They wrote to each other and exchanged presents regularly. In an interview with the BBC in 2014, Kennedy's daughter Caroline, then ambassador to Japan, spoke of a story her mother had told about the unique nature of their bond. Mrs. Kennedy, the story goes, was sitting next to Khrushchev at a state dinner in Vienna. "She ran out of things to talk about," Caroline said, "so she asked about the dog, Strelka, that the Russians had shot into space. During the conversation, my mother asked about Strelka's puppies. A few months later, a puppy arrived, and my father had no idea where the dog came from and couldn't believe my mother had done that. The puppy was Strelka's daughter, Pushinka, and she was cute and fluffy. In fact, the name translates as Fluffy."

But it seems that Jack was quite taken with the puppy—or at least the effort to send her. "Dear Chairman," he wrote in a thank-you note to his Russian counterpart. "Mrs. Kennedy and I were particularly pleased to receive 'Pushinka.' Her flight from the Soviet Union to the United States was not as dramatic as the flight of her mother, nevertheless, it was a long voyage and she stood it well. We both appreciate your remembering these matters in your busy life. We send to you, your wife, and your family our very best wishes. Sincerely yours, John F. Kennedy."

Today, JFK's dream of a shared mission to outer space endures. Although trouble abounds on planet Earth, just like during the Cold War, America and Russia are up there somewhere on the international space station, along with a rotating crew of astronauts from around the world. The project receives scant coverage or fanfare in this time of scary headlines and stories of war and mass shootings and other horrors among the land-bound. But judging from the daily reports that are sent back, the ongoing studies involving botany, heart ailments, and physics and the camaraderie in general, people are cooperating regardless of their differences, collaborating, even, and not cutting the other guy or gal loose when they are outside the station on space walks. "I believe it is a providential fact that the anniversary of President Kennedy's assassination always falls around Thanksgiving," wrote James Douglass in *JFK and the Unspeakable*. "Thanksgiving is a beautiful time of year, with autumn leaves falling to create new life. Creation is alive, as the season turns. The earth is alive . . . the fact that the human family is still alive with a fighting chance for survival, and for much more than that, is reason for gratitude to a peacemaking president, and to the unlikely alliance he forged with his enemy."

In 1960, *Camelot* the musical opened on Broadway. It told the story of King Arthur, his knights, and their golden world. It featured Richard Burton as Arthur, and one could not have cast a more charismatic figure as Arthur. "In Camelot, Camelot," he sings in his magnificent baritone voice, "That's how conditions are." The rain never falls till after sundown, and by eight the morning fog must vanish. "In short," he goes on, there's not a better spot "for happily-ever-aftering than here in Camelot." The Oswalds may have had a coat of arms, but they would be forever consigned to the wrong zip codes, the wrong dwellings, the wrong way of speaking, wrong, wrong, wrong, never to gain entry to Camelot, no matter what they did. "Look into my eyes, brother," Lee told Robert in their last conversation. "There's nothing there." The man who had taken down our youthful king was an empty vessel, older than want and desperation, now forever famous, the caboose at the end of the American parade. "Forgive your enemies," JFK once said, "but never forget their names."

ACKNOWLEDGMENTS

First of all, I must extend a heartfelt thank you to my editor, Carl Bromley, who acquired this book and encouraged me every step of the way, from the beginning to the end, meaning our initial conversations after he read my proposal, his comments as I delivered the manuscript in sections as I was proceeding, and his extreme patience as I missed several deadlines en route to completion. In the past I've also missed deadlines with previous books ("time is not your field," as my mother used to tell me), but this time around, there was a pandemic (lockdown meant no trips to the library, among other locations, where I love to write) and the matter of being laid off by an MFA writing program which I had helped found, after teaching in it for thirteen years—both of which contrived to make for a double whammy which sent me reeling. Moreover, for the first time in my life, this book had a hard deadline, meaning it had to come out in time for a particular moment—specifically, the sixtieth anniversary of the JFK assassination—and none of my earlier books had such writing constraints. So Carl's patience in this regard—and that of the entire team at Melville House—has meant the world to me.

I should also add that Carl acquired a previous book of mine, *Desert Reckoning*, when he was an editor at Nation Books. Any writer who seeks to have a book published well knows how important it is to have an editor who gets what you're doing and can help you bring it to fruition. I am grateful that I have a publishing partner with whom I can speak a shorthand.

This brings me to my literary agent, Michael Signorelli, at Aevitas Creative Management. Michael helped me through several drafts of this proposal and his insights into areas that merited amplification enabled me to advance my ideas to the best of my ability. So I offer many thanks to him, and for his patience as well, and to Allison Warren and her team in the film/TV department at Aevitas, for ongoing support for this project as it now moves beyond the virtual and conceptual world and into the real.

For help in telling this story of Lee Harvey Oswald and his mother Marguerite, I would also like to thank Maryann Sasaki and her husband Andrew, who loaned me a library card so I could retrieve records that were only available in a certain library (for more on all libraries and archives that were helpful to me in writing *American Confidential*, see the "Author's Note" section following this one). And I'd like to thank reporter Bud Kennedy of the *Fort Worth Star-Telegram* for his work and for conversations regarding Fort Worth and Dallas and Oswald and related matters. For research regarding Oswald family genealogy, many thanks to Siobhan "Ruby" McConnell, herself a writer of note. And for her willingness to talk about those terrible days in Texas, I am most grateful to Ruth Paine, who provided Marina Oswald, her daughter June, her newborn Rachel, and sometimes Lee, with a literal room at the inn; this was because her Quaker religion required her to offer sanctuary or a helping hand to those in need, which probably accounted for a quick yes to my request for a conversation.

Finally—and I know this is going to sound weird—I would like to offer a shout-out, say hey, or yeah, baby, you're the best to the Bill of Rights. To put it quite simply, I would not have been able to write this book—or any of my books or other works—without the First Amendment and I am keenly aware of its reach and meaning. With previous books, I've had encounters that are up close and personal regarding this very first of constitutional amendments. For instance, with *Twentynine Palms*, my book about two girls who were killed by a Marine after the Gulf War in Twentynine Palms, California, the killer's lawyer subpoenaed my notes. Actually, I hadn't even finished my book yet; this request had to do with an article I had written on the same subject for *Los Angeles Magazine*, which was then owned by Cap Cities/ABC, a large corporation which urged me to turn over my notes rather than mount an expensive legal battle. I had no intention of relinquishing years of confidential material and contacted the head of the Cap Cities legal department, threatening to alert the media. Yes, I actually said that—and it worked, which was weird because they were the media. Meanwhile, another branch of the media came to my rescue in the form of *LA Times* reporter Bill Boyarsky, who devoted a column to my situation and enlisted the aid of Reporters Committee for Freedom of the Press. In fairness, it must be noted that the lawyer who sought my notes was making a legitimate argument involving due process vs the First Amendment. After a lengthy courtroom battle I prevailed, thanks not only to free press guarantees accorded by the constitution but because of the related California Shield Law as well. But what if I had been forced by a court order to turn over my notes? I talked a good game, but I'm not sure that I would have had the fortitude to withhold them and thus go to jail; I'm seriously claustro-phobic—which is probably why I am often drawn to stories of "don't fence me in." Moreover, some of the people who had entrusted me to tell their stories—a process that took ten years in this case—lived on the edge and were wary of reporters, or anything that had the word "media" or "press" attached to it, so it was a big deal that they permit-ted me into their lives and their world. What would have happened if I were forced to turn over my notes? Thanks to my guardian angels and the First Amendment, I didn't have to.

With *Blood Brothers*, my book about Sitting Bull, Buffalo Bill, and Annie Oakley in the Wild West show, I was reminded of another kind of suppression that takes place, an unspoken one that involves a way of looking at things that sometimes overrides the truth. This occurred after my book was published, during my tour. I was speaking at a library in Cody, Wyoming (the town named after Buffalo Bill). Following my talk, after everyone else had left, I was approached by a woman in a duster and scarves and other wrappings; there was a blizzard outside and she had come to my talk in spite of the weather, along with maybe about twenty or thirty others who had shown up on that winter's night. She had a secret to tell and leaned in as she spoke, although no one else was around or even listening. "I didn't know that Sitting Bull didn't kill Custer," she said, referring to a theme of my talk, and book, which was that the great Lakota patriot, Sitting Bull, had been "blamed" for killing Lt. Col. George Armstrong Custer at the Battle of the Little Bighorn, and thus became public enemy number one. This framing ultimately led to his assassination—though it was cloaked in his refusal to surrender for his alleged involvement in the Ghost Dances of the late nineteenth century, the frenzied Lakota dancing that sought to invoke the apocalypse and the resurrection of the buffalo and the old ways. "That's what they told us in school," she continued. "I just never knew." And then she thanked me and headed out into the drifts. She certainly wasn't alone in her beliefs, I knew from my travels across the country, but she was alone in wanting to tell me that she stood corrected. In this case, official censorship of the truth about the Little Bighorn wasn't needed, which is to say that there had been no banning of books; the view that Sitting Bull had himself killed Custer dominated the ethers, and we see this playing out over and over again today, meaning that the official record is often ignored or hidden away, and it's only because of the First Amendment that we are able to discover or have the right to come forward with corrections to the official record.

I am of course aware of the fact that many believe the story of Lee Harvey Oswald and the assassination of John F. Kennedy has been suppressed by all manner of entities and agencies and powerful individuals (and for conspiracy meisters out there, I suggest following up on the alleged mafia plot; just a vibe—but even that trail seems to lead nowhere—or to a million others). If a First Amendment case can bring forth concealed information that answers riddles in this case once and for all, I for one would love to see it. For now, and for as long as I have been working on this book, I remain grateful for the right that I have to tell this story in the way that I see it, in spite of strong headwinds, a kind of suppression in the form of a cultural ban, which have mostly eliminated a discussion of the human element, and a most basic one at that. It was my instinct that pointed the way, but to really recount this tale, to add flesh to its bones, I needed access to libraries and archives and all manner of books and records, a liberty which some would like to shut down, and in some cases, have already obliterated. So yes, thank you, Bill of Rights and the First Amendment—number one, in other words, and that says a lot. I must also say that behind it all, or maybe because of it, my work has often reached individuals who seek to tell me their secrets in one way or another—whether it's for five minutes at a library or over a period of years in remote outposts—and I am ever mindful of the task that I have been assigned and ever thankful to those who have helped me carry it along.

AUTHOR'S NOTE

Years ago I was working at a shop called Queen of Diamonds on St. Marks Place in New York City. It sold exquisite hippie clothing, necklaces and bracelets from India and Afghanistan, and all manner of items hinting at an alt-lifestyle, from incense to books such as *Siddartha*, *The Whole Earth Catalog*, and *The Tibetan Book of the Dead*. The owner's boyfriend was Charles Mingus and one day Jack Nicholson walked in and examined the wares. The store was kind of a scene in the way that the counterculture itself was: all paths and pathways were crossing, as if someone had shaken up the world's snow globe and everything and everyone was settling in new patterns and a soundtrack was involved and the music was everywhere.

Across the street there was a vendor selling records mostly and after work I would browse through the bins. There was always a new reggae album from Jamaica and of course there were the must-haves of the day—"In A Gadda da Vida" by Iron Butterfly ("Did you know the name of that song means 'In the Garden of Eden' but they were stoned?"), *Disraeli Gears* by Cream ("Did you know that Ginger Baker played the drums so hard that he passed out during a solo?"), and then, one day I came across a record I had never seen before. It was *Oswald: Self-Portrait in Red*. While Oswald needed no introduction, the package itself was strange; it was not exactly the kind of thing that said "Buy me," but it had a certain appeal. The album cover was indeed red, but the reference was really to Oswald presenting himself as a Communist, aka he was part of the "red menace," meaning the Russian threat to the world. I wasn't particularly interested in who Oswald was as a person at that time but realizing that there was a recording, I remember thinking, "This guy has a voice?" The only time I had heard him speak was when he was in jail in Dallas following the JFK assassination and he had said "I'm a patsy" in front of a bank of microphones as he was being led away—and we would never hear from him again. That statement fueled a zillion conspiracy theories but what did he sound like beyond that short clip? I wondered. I mean, the man who killed the President and brought the world to a halt— how did he present himself and in what tone? Was he a wiseguy or just some schmoe? Did he have a deep voice or one that was soft and maybe even self-effacing?

I was also intrigued by the record's red cover—yes, red sells! — and the weird portrait, a badly drawn look-alike with a blank expression, anatomically outlandish high forehead, and eyebrows in some sort of weird what-the-hell rendition, as if he himself were surprised by what was before him. All in all, it looked like a collector's item, and evidently it became one; it's now selling on eBay for $500. I bought it for a couple of bucks, took it home, and stored it away. Every now and then I'd listen, searching along with millions of others lost in archives, autopsy reports, maps of bullet trajectories and conspiracy forums, for some sort of skeleton key to the secret of Lee Harvey Oswald. The recording was made for a radio show in New Orleans a few months before he killed President Kennedy. He had come to the attention of local media because he had been arrested during an altercation with anti-Castro Cuban exiles while passing out flyers from the "Fair Play for Cuba" Committee, a pro-Castro group which was protesting America's involvement with the failed Bay of Pigs invasion, an operation Kennedy had signed off on in order to take down Castro. (Oswald was nothing if not impressionable; proffering pamphlets in the streets was something he seems to have picked up on since the day in New York when someone handed him the flyer about the Rosenbergs. Today he might be diagnosed as having Attention Deficit Disorder, Asperger's Syndrome, or some combo platter of modern afflictions in which a free-floating and all-encompassing anxiety latches on to whatever action or possibility presents itself, even including the arrival of JFK in his rifle scope.) Questioned by an interviewer on the radio show, he provides his thoughts on Cuba and Marxism as they relate to America—elements of the red or Communist menace that was fueling hysteria of the time—and what he was saying was not all that interesting. The recording itself is a stop-time revelation of a guy who was caught in a loop, and more importantly, at least as far as I was concerned, he sounded flat, with a hint of a New Orleans accent; there seemed to be no affect, no modulation except for one laugh as I recall . . . so that's the guy who whacked the President, I remember thinking, and even his own interviewer had described the revelations as kind of a "piano roll" of Oswald's thoughts. Listening to it again now after considering the assassination for such a long time, my thoughts turned to deeper matters. What was the sound of the voice that blasted through America and the comfort of status quo, America and its false front and its longings and its dreams, America and its physical beauty—the Grand Canyon, Yosemite, Yellowstone— and made us think of the opposite? Only one thing comes to mind: there's no there there, to use the popular quote from Gertrude Stein regarding her childhood home, no longer in existence upon her return to Oakland, California, long ago. Oswald, the man of many moves and addresses, really belonged nowhere. But regardless of his tone or affect, Marguerite Oswald was always right there with him, up to the very end.

For a long time I knew nothing of this "mother in history" as she called herself. In the years immediately following my purchase of *Portrait in Red*, I was writing for the underground and alternative press, and through those endeavors, I did come to know various people who were wrapped up in lesser or greater degrees in conspiracy investigations, some of whom had studied every aspect of the JFK assassination and Oswald's life. They were not unlike people obsessed with anything, from the details of breaking waves to the placement of cereal boxes on supermarket shelves—math and tidal charts and bar codes and all manner of calibrations were involved—but of course in this case, there was something much greater at stake: Who or what sent Planet America off its course and why did it happen? And so it was through them, and the paranoia-tilted ethers in general, that I absorbed a working knowledge of the theories and plots around the cataclysmic event. Over time, I found myself thinking more and more about this great puzzle of our era, and after writing several books about the modern and frontier West and the origins of American violence, it was a natural progression for me to zero in on the assassination of JFK, one of the most devastating manifestations of our great disconnect, and as much as I tried to shake it, I just couldn't, and therefore it was time to write.

To write means to read, or to have read, and over the years, there have been several books which are foundational to this one. They are: *Oswald's Tale: An American Mystery* by Norman Mailer, *Libra* by Don DeLillo, and *Marina and Lee: The Tormented Love and Fatal Obsession Behind Lee Harvey Oswald's Assassination of John F. Kennedy* by Patricia McMillan. *Oswald's Tale* and *Libra* are masterpieces of writing and I've read both books several times. Both have opened up lines of thinking in *American Confidential*, and Mailer's work in particular has pointed the way in my own writing in general, and this is something that I've tried to pass on to my students over the years.

As well, *Marina and Lee* is an astonishing work, combining a massive amount of research with personal knowledge of the lives of key players. About a year after Oswald was killed, McMillan made an arrangement with Oswald's wife; Marina and her two children would move in and live with McMillan and Marina would recount the story of her life with Lee on an exclusive basis, for however long it took. Two things appealed to Marina Oswald in making this arrangement with the author: McMillan spoke Russian and she had interviewed Lee after he had defected to Russia. A reporter for the North American News Alliance at the time, she was stationed in Moscow and sat down with Lee for a conversation in his new home.

It should be noted that there is some controversy surrounding *Marina and Lee*. After the book was published, it came to light that McMillan also knew Kennedy, the only reporter to have interviewed both men. She had worked for JFK as an intern when he was a senator—a situation that has given rise to the theory that you shouldn't trust anything McMillan says or writes; she probably had an affair with Kennedy and/or is/was working for the State Department which had infiltrated or set up news organizations such as the one that McMillan was working for in Moscow (and CIA penetration of media at that time was indeed a thing; even the late and truly great writer Peter Matthiessen was an intelligence operative while publishing the *Paris Review*). Much of her testimony for the House Select Committee on Assassinations in 1976 has been redacted, which has further fueled speculation about her possible involvement with the US intelligence community.

After *Marina and Lee* was published, McMillan translated Stalin's daughter's memoir into English, which added yet more heat to the fire. Her book is so good and so palpably authentic that I'm giving her a pass, or more specifically, I'll say that any alleged romantic involvement with Kennedy is beside the point and any connection with the intelligence community, while worth noting in and of itself, is prob-ably not relevant; short of a massive payout, there's just no reason that someone would cook up a 688-page book designed for commercial release filled with scenes such as Oswald singing the theme song from "Exodus" in a bus station for his wife as a smokescreen for a covert operation, and one that was published fourteen years after the fact at that. *Marina and Lee* bears so much gravitas that it speaks for itself. The intimate details that McMillan elicited from Marina about her life with Lee could only have come from a place of trust between the two women (and yes, I realize that people can be tricked)—and good timing for McMillan; Marina was clearly ready to talk. On the fiftieth anniversary of the JFK assassination, *Marina and Lee* was reis-sued, at which point McMillan spoke of Oswald's "unfitness for any conspiracy outside his own head." There was no need to advance that idea by way of untold labor devoted to writing this book unless she really believed it.

And yet, when it comes to assassination literature, *Marina and Lee* has often been overlooked (even though it influenced the much more widely admired *Oswald's Tale*), and so has *A Mother in History* by Jean Stafford, another well-written work that reveals much but bespeaks a certain class condescension. I think that this is mostly because these books are written by women, though lots of writers, women and men alike, have been forced to take a backseat when it comes to Mailer, often for good reason. (And on a curious side note, if you were mak-ing a list of famous people who admired Fidel Castro, it would include Mailer and Oswald, who both wanted fair play for Cuba, and whom Mailer once compared to Muhammad Ali and Charlie Chaplin.)

Another book that has informed this one is *Mrs. Paine's Garage* by Thomas Mallon. It sheds light from a different angle on Marina and Lee's life, this time from the point of view of the woman who gave Marina a home during her estrangement from Lee shortly before the assassination of President Kennedy. Nomenclatural destiny is something that I've long observed in a range of people; for instance, everyone who is named after Jesse James has run into one problem or another, and sometimes had a life of violence. When I say everyone, I refer to those people named in honor of the outlaw who have come to the public's attention. And why is it that they have attracted such attention? I suggest that it is their name that has led them to a certain place in life which in turn has made them notorious, just like their namesake. Consider "Jesse James Hollywood," the infamous Los Angeles teenager who kidnapped and ordered the murder of a classmate over a drug deal gone bad. This name was perhaps the mother of all nomenclatural curses; there was no escape from the strange burden of that verbal cloak. Was it Mrs. Paine's destiny to live a life of pain? That might sound facile, and it's her married name, not the one that she was born with. Yet still, I wonder. (On a side note, Ruth has speculated that there's really no mystery when it comes to answering why Oswald once used "Alek J. Hidell" as a pseudonym, contrary to what many of the conspiracy-minded may think. This was the name he deployed to order the gun that he stored in her garage, unbeknownst to Ruth—the rifle that he used to kill JFK. Her maiden name is "Hyde," as she has pointed out, and "Hidell" rhymes with "Fidel," so it was easy enough to combine the two names and come up with the fake one. Strangely, there is yet one more nomenclatural tell—"Hyde"— which is exactly what happened when it came to this gun.)

When it comes to mothers and sons, I should also mention *The Gunman and His Mother: Lee Harvey Oswald, Marguerite Oswald, and the Making of an Assassin* by Steven Beschloss. While this is largely a synthesis of previously published material, especially *The Warren Commission Report*, the multi-volume government report put together by the Warren Commission, the group that came together under the orders of President Lyndon B. Johnson following JFK's assassination, it does serve as a primer devoted to Lee and his mother, and Beschloss encourages other writers to pick up where he has left off. I was well into research on this book when I came across this one, and I hope that in writing my own, I have fulfilled Steven's suggestion.

Other books that have played a part in this book are mentioned in the narrative itself and/or in the bibliography. Two that are important are *Reclaiming History* by Vincent Bugliosi and *Case Closed* by Gerald Posner. I encourage those interested in learning more about the assassination of JFK to read both of those books, including the footnotes; well beyond the murder itself, there is a wealth of information having to do with Oswald and his family.

Finally, when it comes to voluminous material, *The Warren Report* is a must-read. I haven't read all twenty-seven volumes, but I've read many passages therein, and I refer to and quote several in this book. Don't be put off by its length. It's filled with fascinating testimony from a parade of people associated with this story, from members of Oswald's family including his mother to those who had direct contact with him in one way or another—all in all a cast of hundreds. It has an index that is quite comprehensive and it's accessible through government archives listed below in this bibliography. For my purposes, I found what I needed through the extensive resources at the Mary Ferrell Foundation. You could say that Ferrell was the ultimate civil servant. While working as a legal secretary in downtown Dallas when JFK was assassinated, she heard the news of Oswald's arrest and embarked on what became a lifelong campaign of assembling any and all information about the case. Over the years, with the help of her sons, she put together what is viewed by writers including Anthony Summers and Gaeton Fonzi (themselves authors of significant works on the JFK case) as the go-to library about all things related to this story from all angles, including official reports, newspaper articles, essays, photos, and all manner of ancillary documents. In becoming a citizen historian and researcher, Ferrell has performed a great service for the country and I could not have written this book without her library. Other libraries and archives were helpful to me as well, and they are listed following my bibliography.

I should also mention that one of the great pleasures of my work is that it involves travel and all of it to fascinating places. Certainly place is an underpinning of my work and I think if a place held no appeal for me, I would not be able to write about anything that happened there. Writing this book took me to New Orleans, Fort Worth, Dallas, and even the Bronx Zoo. Visiting that zoo was not a chore by any means; although based in Los Angeles I visit New York City periodically and it was while writing a previous book, *Blood Brothers*, about Sitting Bull and Buffalo Bill in the Wild West show, that I began visiting that zoo, at first to check out its historic bison herd, descendants of the country's few remaining bison which had been taken there in the early twentieth century to save the species. Some of them have been shipped over the years back to the Great Plains where they have been reintroduced in certain Native American preserves. It was in this zoo that Oswald found solace as a teenager and I tried to retrace his steps there, imagining his path through the exhibits and thinking about what animals whose company he sought. Later, when I visited the other cities in which he lived, I thought about what parts of each city he may have traversed, and my thinking about all of this was drawn from references in the annals to certain locations he favored such as libraries and subways, trips he had made to Lake Pontchartrain and Audubon Park in New Orleans, descriptions and photographs and addresses of his various homes, commentaries about them in his brother Robert's memoir *Lee: A Portrait of Lee Harvey Oswald*, the testimony of Marguerite and others before the Warren Commission, and maps and guidebooks to each city at the time he was living there.

Finally, I must acknowledge the various actors I've worked with over the years, in my plays, on television shows, and in recordings of my books. Quite possibly they have informed my work even more than my travels or extensive readings and research, for it is through them that I've learned to think about why a certain character may do certain things, how a certain scene or exchange between characters may unfold, and how those characters may engage with his or her surroundings, whether exterior or interior. Sometimes, I actually ask the characters a question: "What happened here?" or "What do you want me to know?" I don't always get an answer, but when I do, portals that I couldn't have imagined tend to emerge and they always go to the heart of things. "All the world's a stage," Shakespeare wrote in *As You Like It*. "And all the men and women merely players." That might be a cliché, but it's all too true—and in my work, the stories I tell play out on a scape where I see the characters making entrances and exits, some by their own choice, others by a hand unseen.

BIBLIOGRAPHY & CREDITS

BOOKS AND PLAYS

Algren, Nelson. *Walk on the Wild Side*. New York: Farrar, Straus and Cudahy, 1956.

Aynesworth, Hugh. With Stephen G. Michaud. *JFK: Breaking the News*. Richardson, TX: International Focus Press, 2003.

———. *Witness to History*. Dallas, TX: Brown Books Publishing Group, 2013.

Baker, Judyth Vary. *Me & Lee: How I Came To Know, Love, and Lose Lee Harvey Oswald*. Walterville, OR: Trine Day. 2010.

Beschloss, Steven. *The Gunman and His Mother: Lee Harvey Oswald, Marguerite Oswald, and the Making of an Assassin*. Independently published, 2013.

Boulard, Garry. *Huey Long Invades New Orleans: The Siege of a City, 1934-36*. Gretna, LA: Gretna Publishing Company, 1998.

Bugliosi, Vincent. *Reclaiming History: The Assassination of President John F. Kennedy*. New York: W. W. Norton and Company, 2007.

Busse, Ryan. *Gunfight: My Battle Against the Industry that Radicalized America*. New York: Public Affairs, 2021.

Cain, James M. *Mildred Pierce*. New York: Knopf, 1941.

Christopherson, Edmund. *"Westward I Go Free": The Story of J.F.K. in Montana*. Missoula, MT: Earthquake Press, 1964.

Davison, Joan. *Oswald's Game*. New York: Norton, 1983.

DeCuir, Randy. *Cousin Lee: The Roots of Lee Harvey Oswald*. Las Vegas, NV: Indepdently published, 2013.

DeLillo,, Don. *Libra*. New York: Viking, 2008.

de Mohrenschildt, George. *Lee Harvey Oswald as I Knew Him*. Lawrence: University Press of Kansas, 2014.

Didion, Joan. *South and West: From a Notebook*. New York: Knopf Doubelday Publishing Group, 2018.

Douglass, James W. *JFK and the Unspeakable: Why He Died and Why It Matters*. New York: Touchstone, 2008.

Epstein, Edward Jay. *The Secret World of Lee Harvey Oswald*. New York: McGraw-Hill, 1978.

Fagin, Stephen. *Assassination and Commemoration: JFK, Dallas, and the Sixth Floor Museum at Dealey Plaza*. Norman: The University of Oklahoma Press, 2013.

Federal Writers' Project of the Works Progress Administration for the City of New Orleans. *New Orleans City Guide*. Boston: Houghton Mifflin Company, 1938.

Fleming, Ian. *Live and Let Die*. London: Jonathan Cape, 1954.

Fonzi, Gaeton. *The Last Investigation*. New York: Skyhorse, 2018.

Ford, Gerald, and John R. Stiles.. *Portrait of the Assassin*. New York: Simon and Schuster, 1965.

Fowler, Karen Joy. *Booth*. New York: G. P. Putnam's Sons, 2022.

Fuhrman, Mark. *A Simple Act of Murder: November 22, 1963*. New York: William Morros, 2006.

Goodwin, Doris Kearns. *The Kennedys and the Fitzgeralds: An American Saga*. New York: Simon and Schuster, 1987.

Gregory, Paul R. *The Oswalds*. New York: Diversion Books, 2022.

Groden, Robert J. *The Search for Lee Harvey Oswald*. New York: Penguin Books Inc., 1995.

Guelzo, Allen C. *Robert E. Lee: A Life*. New York: Knopf, 2021.

Habe, Hans. *The Wounded Land: Journey Through a Divided America*. Munich:

Verlag Kurt Desch, 1964.

Hamilton, Nigel. *JFK: Reckless Youth*. New York: Random House, 2012.

Hastings, Michael. *Lee Harvey Oswald: A Far Mean Streak of Independence Brought On by Negleck*. Middlesex, UK: Penguin Books Ltd., 1966.

Hepburn, James. *Farewell America*. Voduz, LI: Frontiers Publishing Company, 1968.

Holloway, Diane. *The Mind of Oswald: Accused Assassin of President John F. Kennedy*. Victoria, BC: Trafford Publishing, 2000.

Janney, Peter. *Mary's Mosaic: The CIA Conspiracy to Murder John F. Kennedy, Mary Pinchot Meyer, and Their Vision for World Peace*. New York: Skyhorse, 2012.

Kennedy, John F. *Profiles in Courage*. New York: Harper and Brothers, 1955.

King, Stephen. *11/22/63*. New York: Scribner, 2011.

Klebold, Sue. *A Mother's Reckoning: Living in the Aftermath of the Columbine Tragedy*. New York: Crown Publishers, 2016.

Korda, Michael. *Clouds of Glory: The Life and Legends of Robert E. Lee*. New York: Harper, 2014.

Lane, Mark. *Rush to Judgment*. New York: Holt, Rinehart, and Winston, 1966.

Long, Huey P. *Every Man a King: The Autobiography of Huey P. Long*. Cambridge, MA: Da Capo Press, 1996.

Mailer, Norman. *Oswald's Tale*. New York: Random House, 1995.

Mallon, Thomas. *Mrs. Paine's Garage and the Murder of John F. Kennedy*. New York: Pantheon Books, 2002.

Manchester, William. *The Death of a President: November 20—25, 1963*. New York: Back Bay Books, 2013.

McMillan, Priscilla Johnson. *Marina and Lee: The Tormented Love and Fatal Obsession Behind Lee Harvey Oswald's Assassination of John F. Kennedy*. New York: Harper and Row, 1977.

Miller, Tom. *The Assassination Please Almanac*. New York: Henry Regnery Company, 1977.

Minutaglio, Bill, and Steven L. Davis. Dallas, *1963*. New York: Twelve, October 8, 2012.

Moore, Jim. *Conspiracy of One*. Fort Worth, TX: The Summit Group, 1990.

Morley, Jefferson. *The Ghost: The Secret Life of CIA Spymaster James Jesus Angleton*. New York: St. Martin's Press, 2017.

Myers, Dale K. *With Malice: Lee Harvey Oswald and the Murder of Officer J. D. Tippit*. New York: Open Road Media, November 12, 2013.

Nechiporenko, Col. Oleg Maximovich. *Passport to Assassination*. New York: Birch Lane Press, 1993.

Oswald, Marguerite. *Aftermath of an Execution—The Burial and Final Rites of Lee Harvey Oswald as Told by His Mother*. Dallas: Challenge Press, 1964.

Oswald, Robert. *Lee: A Portrait of Lee Harvey Oswald*. With Myrick and Barbara Land. New York: Coward-McCann, Inc., 1967

Peterson, Jillian, and James Densley. *The Violence Project: How To Stop a Mass Shooting Epidemic*. New York: Harry N. Abrams, 2021.

Piazza, Tom. *Why New Orleans Matters*. New York: HarperCollins Publishers Inc., 2005.

Posner, Gerald. *Case Closed: Lee Harvey Oswald and the Assassination of JFK*. New York: Random House, 1993.

Robbins, Tom. *Jitterbug Perfume*. New York: Bantam, 1984.

Savodnik, Peter. *The Interloper*. New York: Basic Books, 2013.

Schmelzer, Janet L. *Where the West Begins: Fort Worth and Tarrant County*. Glenmont, NY: Windsor Publications, Inc., 1985

Shaw, Mark. *The Reporter Who Knew Too Much: The Mysterious Death of What's My Line TV Star and Media Icon Dorothy Kilgallen*. Brentwood, TN: Post Hill Press, 2016.

Shenk, Joshua Wolf. *Lincoln's Melancholy: How Depression Challenged a President and Fueled His Greatness*. Boston: Houghton Mifflin Harcourt, 2005.

Shenon, Phillip. *A Cruel and Shocking Act: The Secret History of the Kennedy Assassination*. New York: Henry Holt and Co., 2013.

Shriver, Lionel. *We Need To Talk About Kevin*. New York: Harper Perennial, 2011.

Sites, Paul. *Lee Harvey Oswald and the American Dream*. New York: Pageant Press, Inc., 1967.

Solnit, Rebecca, and Rebecca Snedeker. *Unfathomable City: A New Orleans Atlas*. Berkeley: University of California Press, 2013.

Sondheim, Steven, and John Weidman. *Assassins*. New York: Theatre Communications Group, January 1, 1993.

Stafford, Jean. *A Mother in History*. New York: Farrar, Straus and Giroux, 1966.

Stone, Robert. *A Hall of Mirrors*. Boston: Houghton Mifflin: 1997.

Summers, Anthony. *Not in Your Lifetime: The Defining Book on the JFK Assassination*. New York: Open Road Integrated Media, 2013.

Talbot, David. *The Devil's Chessboard: Allen Dulles, the CIA, and the Rise of America's Secret Government*. New York: Harper's, 2015.

Titovets, Ernst. *Oswald: Russian Episode*. Washington, DC: Eagle View Books, 2020.

Toole, John Kennedy. *A Confederacy of Dunces*. New York: Grove Weidenfeld, 1987.

United Press International and American Heritage Magazine. *Four Days*. Rockville, MD: American Heritage Publishing Co., Inc., 1964.

Wecht, Cyril, and Dauna Kaufmann. *The JFK Assassination Dissected: An Analysis by Forensic Pathologist Cyril Wecht*. Jefferson, NC: Exposit Books, 2021.

Williams, Tennessee. "A Streetcar Named Desire," New Directions, 1947.

Williams, Tennessee. "The Glass Menagerie," New Directions, January, 1949.

Wilson, Robert Clifton. *Guilty Until Proven Innocent*. 2013.

Wylie, Philip. *Generation of Vipers*. New York: Rinehard and Company, Inc., 1942.

Zapruder, Alexandra. *Twenty-Six Seconds: A Personal History of the Zapruder Film*. New York: Twelve, 2016.

ARTICLES AND ESSAYS

Associated Press. "Oswald's Brother Feels for Families of the Infamous." *LA Times*, December 7, 1997.

Babb, Christina Hughes. "Lee Harvey Oswald Slept Here, the Rooming House that Made Oak Cliff Famous." *Advocate Magazine*, May 16, 2022.

Bailey, Sam. "Oswald: Myth, Mystery and Meaning." *Frontline*, November 19, 2013.

Barry, Dan. "Bronx Tale of a BB Gun and Infamy in the Making." *New York Times*, November 20, 2013.

Blackwell, Sam. "Officer Who Nabbed Oswald Relates Ordeal." *Southeast Missourian*, November 22, 1993. Reposted from archive November 24, 2020.

Bruno, R. Stephanie. "Once Home to JFK Killer Lee Harvey Oswald, Magazine Street House to Get New Look and Purpose as Law Offices." *Advocate Magazine*, March 7, 2019.

Burton, Susan. "One and One Don't Make Two." thisamericanlife.org, September 8, 2000.

Byrne, Jeb. "The Hours Before Dallas." *Prologue Magazine* 2000, Volume 32, no. 2 (Summer 2000).

Carlson, Peter. "Nikita Khruschev Goes to Hollywood." *Smithsonian Magazine*, July 2009.

Carlson, Peter. "Nikita Khruschev Ogles Marilyn Monroe." Historynet.com, June 12, 2017.

Capote, Truman, "Notes on N.O." *Harper's Bazaar*, October 1946.

Cochran, Mike. "Living, Working Through Four Days that Changed the World Forever." *Fort Worth Star-Telegram*, November 12, 2014.

Cockburn, Alexander. "Mother of the Decade." *Texas Monthly*, November, 1973.

Colloff, Pamela, and Michael Hall. "Married to the Mob." *Texas Monthly*, November 1998.

Cox, Jimmie R. "Lee Oswald: His Mother's Story." *Christianity Today*, December 20, 1963.

DeLillo, Don. "American Blood." *Rolling Stone*, December 8, 1983.

Feldman, Harold. "The Unsinkable Marguerite Oswald." *Realist*, September 1964.

Govea, Michael. "How Fort Worth Became 'Where the West Begins.'" fwtx.com, June 21, 2021.

Grier, Peter. "Marina Oswald Sells Wedding Ring, Powerful Symbol of JFK Assassination." *Christian Science Monitor*, October 24, 2013.

Hardy, Arthur. "A Mardi Gras Style Parade Was Staged in 1953 for President Eisenhower." Nola.com, February 20, 2020.

Holmes, John Clellon. "The Silence of Oswald." *Playboy Magazine*, November 1965.

Jackson, Donald. "The Evolution of an Assassin." *Life Magazine*, February 21, 1964.

Kachkick, Keith. "Lee Harvey Oswald's Legacy." *Texas Monthly*, March 1995.

Kelley, Kevin. "An Encounter with Lee Harvey Oswald." Westlifenews.com, December 7, 2014.

Kennedy, Bud. "Lee Harvey Oswald in Fort Worth: A Legacy of Brawls, Bitterness and a Lost Gravestone." *Fort Worth Star-Telegram*, November 21, 2017.

Kennedy, Bud. "In 1963, Reporters Became Pall Bearers for Lee Harvey Oswald—but Two Remain a Mystery." *Fort Worth Star-Telegram*, November 15, 2019. Updated November 22, 2022.

Kirby, Brendan, "The Spring Hill College Link to Lee Harvey Oswald." Fox10news.com, November 19, 2019.

Kraft, Dina. "How Oswald's Childhood Friend Found Himself in Israel and Ended Up 'Helping the Mossad.'" *Haaretz*, October 30, 2017.

Langguth, A. J. "Christmas with Oswald's Mother." *LA Times*, November 22, 2013.

Lardner, George, Jr. "Following the Footsteps of an Assassin." *Washington Post*, October 30, 1983.

———. "Zapruder Film Likely to Restart Debate." *Washington Post*, June 26, 1998.

McFadyen, Chris. "Lee Harvey Oswald Visits Spring Hill." *Mobile Bay Magazine*, January 23, 2014.

New York Times. "Oswald's Mother Tells Her Story." February 11, 1964.

North, Steve. "Oswald's Mother Was a Thoroughly Disagreeable Piece of Work," *Daily Beast*, April 17, 2017.

Pope, John. "Notes from Mother of JFK Assassin Lee Harvey Oswald Found." Nola.com, December 12, 2013. Updated June 25, 2019.

Porter, June Oswald. "The Assassination Has Shadowed—but Not Defeated—the Family of Lee Harvey Oswald." *People Magazine*, November 28, 1983.

Quinlan, Adriane. "50 Years after JFK Assassination, New Orleans Remains Hotbed of Conspiracy Theories." Nola.com, November 13, 2013, updated February 19, 2021.

Rockwood, Bill. "Interview: G. Robert Blakey." *Frontline*, November 19, 2013.

Rockwood, Bill. "Glimpses of a Life." *Frontline*, November 19, 2013.

Reston, James, Jr. "Oswald's Little Green Book Shows JFK Wasn't the Real Target." *LA Times*, November 22, 2016.

Rosenbaum, Ron. "Still on the Case," *Texas Monthly*, November 1983.

Saldana, Hector. "Oswald's Brother Was in S.A. in '63." *San Antonio Express-News*, November 21, 2013.

Salerno, Steve. "Lee Harvey Oswald's Oldest: June Oswald." *New York Times Magazine*, April 30, 1995.

Slocum, Elizabeth. "A Friend Through Tragedy," *Swarthmore Bulletin*, Summer 2018.

Smith, Chris. "To This Day, Ruth Paine Lives with the Murder of JFK." *Press Democrat*, September 20, 2019.

Spiegel, Alix. "Fame Through Assassination." npr.org, January 14, 2011.

Swenson, Dan. "Map of Lee Harvey Oswald's Childhood Homes," Nola.com, November 20, 2013.

Weeks, Jerome. "Can Dealey Plaza in Texas Really Be Improved?," tpr.org, November 11, 2022.

West, Jessamyn. "Prelude to Tragedy: The Woman Who Sheltered Lee Oswald's Family Tells Her Story." *Redbook Magazine*, July, 1964.

Wright, Lawrence. "Why Do They Hate Us So Much?" *Texas Monthly*, November 1983.

LIBRARIES, ARCHIVES, AND WEBSITES

Assassination Archives and Research Center (aarclibrary.org).

Historic Covington (gocovington.org)—about Covington, Louisiana.

History Matters (history-matters.com)—assassination site.

Jean Stafford papers, University Libraries, University of Colorado Boulder.

JFK-assassination.net.

Jefferson Morley from JFK Facts (jfkfacts@substack.com)—former *Washington Post* editor and reporter who maintains assassination blog and has advanced the case for releasing all classified JFK records, along with the Mary Ferrell Foundation.

John F. Kennedy Presidential Library and Museum (jfklibrary.org)—wide and deep JFK and it's official.

John McAdams Kennedy Assassination website (http://mcadams.posc.mu.edu/home.htm).

Marguerite Oswald papers, Texas Christian University.

Mary Ferrell Foundation (maryferrell.org)—deep and always updating archives; extensive linkage to official assassination records; reports and essays from all points of view.

The National Archives and Records Administration (www.archi ves.gov/research/jfk)—includes extensive JFK assassination records such as *The Warren Commission Report* (1964) and the House Select Committee on Assassinations (1976).

Ruth Hyde Paine Papers on Marina Oswald, Friends Historical Library, TriCollege Libraries Archives and Manuscripts.

The Sixth Floor Museum at Dealey Plaza (www.jfk.org)—site of JFK assassination with Oswald's "sniper's perch" preserved on the sixth floor; oral histories of various friends, associates, and acquaintances of Lee Harvey Oswald as well as those who attended the November 22, 1963, parade for JFK in Dallas; photos, news accounts, videos related to JFK and Oswald.

Spartacus Educational (spartacus-educational.com)—biographies of Lee and Marina Oswald.

TELEVISION AND FILM

"11.22.63," mini-series produced by Joseph Boccia and James Franco, based on novel by Stephen King, 2016.

"Executive Action," film directed by David Miller, screenplay by Dalton Trumbo, based on novel by Donald Freed and Mark Lane, 1973.

"Four Days in November," documentary produced by David Wolper Productions, 1964.

"JFK," film directed by Oliver Stone, produced by Oliver Stone, screenplay by Oliver Stone and Zachary Sklar, 1991.

"JFK Assassination: The Definitive Guide," documentary produced by the History Channel, 2013

"JFK Revisited," documentary directed by Oliver Stone, produced by Oliver Stone, 2021.

"JFK: The Lost Assassination Tapes," documentary produced by National Geographic, 2018.

"Marina Oswald Porter Talks to Oprah Winfrey," interview with Oprah, November 22, 1996—(transcript: https://novemberdays1963.tumblr.com/post/37177099041/marina-oswald-porter-on-oprah-1996)

"Oswald's Ghost," documentary directed by Robert Stone, produced by Robert Stone for PBS, 2007.

"Rush to Judgment," documentary directed by Emile de Antonio, produced by Emile de Antonio and Mark Lane, 1967.

"Who Was Lee Harvey Oswald?," *Frontline*, November 19, 2013.

Youtube—enter the name of almost any of the players in this book and you will find links to a wide range of interviews and media appearances.

The Zapruder Film, filmed by Abraham Zapruder, November 22, 1963; now available on amazon with an interview with Zapruder shortly after the shot this film.

RECORDS

Note: There are many songs about JFK and Lee Harvey Oswald and the assassination, including offerings from Phil Ochs "(Crucifixion"), Lou Reed ("The Day John Kennedy Died"), and Pearl Jam ("Brain of J"). Here is what I was listening to while writing this book, other than the jazz, rock, and blues that infuses much of my work. Of these recordings, although he seems to be advancing a conspiracy, Dylan's "Murder Most Foul" has been the most impactful and resounding in terms of its sweeping look at America and what converged on that terrible day in Dallas.

Can't Keep from Crying: Topical Blues on the Death of President Kennedy, Otis Spann, Big Joe Williams and others, Testament Records, 1974.

Dylan, Bob. "Murder Most Foul," Columbia Records, a division of Sony Entertainment, 2020.

The Oswald Case: Mrs. Marguerite Oswald Reads Lee Harvey's Letters from Russia, Folkways Records, 1964.

Tragic Songs from the Grassy Knoll: JFK 50th Anniversary, Norton 2013.

PHOTO CREDITS

Oswald with rifle: PictureLux / The Hollywood Archive / Alamy Stock Photo. Subway: Ellen McKnight / Alamy Stock Photo. JFK at Hotel Texas: AP Images. Two-year-old Oswald: Corbis Historical via Getty Images. Oswald Funeral photo courtesy CSU Archives/Everett Collection. Marguerite Oswald with books: AP Images. Bronx Zoo / World's Most Dangerous Animal: © Wildlife Conservation Society. Reproduced by permission of the WCS Archives. Flyer distributed in Dallas in the days before the assassination courtesy National Archives.